A VI

OF THE
COVENANT OF GRACE
FROM THE
SACRED RECORDS

WHEREIN

THE PARTIES IN THAT COVENANT, THE MAKING OF IT,
ITS PARTS, CONDITIONARY AND PROMISSORY,
AND THE ADMINISTRATION THEREOF ARE
DISTINCTLY CONSIDERED

TOGETHER WITH

THE TRIAL OF A SAVING PERSONAL INBEING IN IT,
AND THE WAY OF INSTATING SINNERS THEREIN,
UNTO THEIR ETERNAL SALVATION

Published by

FOCUS CHRISTIAN MINISTRIES TRUST
6 Orchard Road
Lewes
East Sussex
BN7 2HB

December 1990

ISBN 1 870223 21 7

The front cover picture
shows the pulpit in Ettrick Parish Church,
where Thomas Boston laboured
from 1707 to 1732

Printed by

The Craven Herald & Pioneer
Skipton, North Yorkshire

INTRODUCTION

THOMAS BOSTON was born in 1676 at Duns, Berwickshire, where his father, a God-fearing Presbyterian, had suffered severely on account of Nonconformist principles. At the age of twelve, Thomas was taken to hear Henry Erskine (father of Ebenezer and Ralph), under whose gracious ministry he was brought to see his "lost state by nature" and his "absolute need of Christ". He became a student of Edinburgh University in 1691 and, after completing the Arts Course there, he began in 1695 to study theology under the professorial care of Dr. George Campbell. In order to support himself financially, he became a schoolmaster in Glencairn and then a private tutor to a young man in Kennet, Clackmannanshire.

Licensed to preach the gospel in 1697, he was eventually ordained in 1699 as Minister of Simprin, a small parish about five miles east of Duns. "With joy," he says, "I saw myself in Simprin as in my nest, under the shadow of Christ's wings."

It was there, in 1700, that he married Catherine Brown, "a woman of great worth, whom I therefore passionately loved, and inwardly honoured". There, too, he was providentially introduced to that great work by Herman Witsius, *The Economy of the Covenants between God and Man* and also to Edward Fisher's famous book *The Marrow of Modern Divinity*. Concerning the latter, Boston said, "I rejoiced in it, as a light which the Lord had seasonably struck up to me in my darkness".

In 1707, he was called to Ettrick, in the south-west of Selkirkshire. He ministered there for over 25 years to the spiritual blessing of many people. Ettrick, like Simprin, was a rather secluded place, but Boston soon began to emerge as a more public figure. He prepared some of his own works for publication and induced a friend, James Hog, Minister of Carnock, to publish a new edition of the *"Marrow"*. When, in 1720, this book was condemned by the General Assembly, Boston, along with eleven other brethren, urged the repeal of the Act. He took an active and prominent part in the controversy which followed. He was also involved in what became known as the Professor Simson's "affair". John Simson, Professor of Divinity at Glasgow, was first charged with Arminianism and later with Arianism. Ever valiant for the truth, Boston publicly opposed him; and when, in 1729, the General Assembly agreed to a mere suspension, he rose in the Assembly and uttered a solemn protest.

Boston died in 1732, at the age of 56. "A truly great divine" was the way Jonathan Edwards described him; and as for this book, one of the many which he wrote, let James Hervey's recommendation suffice: "Boston on the Covenant of Grace is an excellent treatise."

FEDERAL THEOLOGY (so called from "foedus", a covenant) is the scheme of revealed truth which represents God's dealings with men by covenants. In this context, the word covenant is understood to mean an arrangement whereby God sovereignly promises to receive men into a relationship with Himself and to bestow upon them the blessing of everlasting life.

Covenant theologians generally recognize two covenants relating to the everlasting happiness of mankind: a pre-Fall covenant of works, established with Adam, Head and Representative of humanity, and conditioned upon his perfect obedience (Gen. 2:16-17); Hos. 6:7 mg); and a covenant of grace, revealed to Adam as soon as he fell (Gen. 3:15), but actually made in the counsels of eternity with the Son of God, who undertook to do whatever was necessary for the salvation of God's elect (Ps. 89:3; Isa. 42:6; Lk. 22:29 — the verb here intimates a "covenant" appointment; Gal. 3:19; Heb. 12:24).

This *pactum salutis,* or counsel of peace, perfectly provides for the needs of sinners. It was implemented when the Son of God assumed our human nature and, taking His people's place under the Law, fulfilled all righteousness on their behalf (Jn. 6:38; 17:4; Gal. 4:4-5; Heb. 10:5-10). He secured the covenant's promise, as it pertains to grace here and glory hereafter (Gal. 3:29; Eph. 3:6; 2 Tim. 1:1; Heb. 9:15). And as a result, the covenant has assumed a "testamentary" form: its promise is fulfilled and its benefits are dispensed graciously and freely, without any condition (Heb. 9:15-16; cf. Ps. 68:18; Isa. 55:1; Rom. 8:32).

It is true that God is said to make a covenant with His people, but that covenant is expressly declared to be "the sure mercies of David": that is, all the blessings purchased and bequeathed by Christ (Isa. 55:3; Acts 13:34). So when God makes a covenant with men, He simply communicates its blessings (2 Sam. 23:5; Heb. 8:10-12).

It remains only to be said that, under the Old Testament, God's covenant was exhibited by means of "types" (i.e. appointed models or patterns) (Gal. 3:19; Heb. 10:1-18). It was specially revealed by means of typical covenants, such as were made with Noah, Abraham, Moses, Phinehas and David (Gen. 9:8-17, 15:18-21; Exo. 14:6-8; cf. Deut. 5:5; Num. 25:11-13; Ps. 89:3-4). But, under the New Testament, it is set forth more clearly and more fully in the Gospel, and it is now being preached as God's salvation to all the nations of the world (Lk. 24:44-48; 2 Cor. 3:6-12; Heb. 13:20-21).

This is Federalism, or Covenant Theology, in its most developed form. As a system of doctrine, it is peculiarly Reformed, emerging from the teachings and writings of the early Calvinistic Reformers; but the covenant concept, along with many of its precious truths, was well understood in pre-Reformation times, and even in the earlier centuries of our Christian era.

In the first part of the second century (but possibly even earlier, between AD 70-79), Barnabas carefully distinguished the covenant of works from the covenant of grace. He wrote: "Moses understood (the meaning of God), and cast the two tables out of his hands; and their covenant was broken, in order that the covenant of the beloved Jesus might be sealed upon our heart, in the hope which flows from believing in him." (*The Epistle of Barnabas,* chapter IV).

A few years later, soon after the middle of the second century, Justin Martyr wrote a major work with a view to proving that Christ was the Messiah of the Old Testament. In the course of his exposition, he noted the differences between the two great covenants: the condition of the covenant of works being perfect and personal obedience to the Law, and the condition of the covenant of grace being Christ in His surety-righteousness. According to Justin, "we do not trust through Moses or through the law; for then we would do the same as yourselves (i.e. the Jews). . . . Law placed against law has abrogated that which is before it, and a covenant which comes after in like manner has put an end to the previous one; and an eternal and final law — namely, Christ — has been given to us, and the covenant is trustworthy, after which there shall be no law, no commandment, no ordinance. . . . He is the new law, and the new covenant, and the expectation of those who out of every people wait for the good things of God" (*Dialogue with Trypho,* chapter XI).

Between AD 182-188, Irenaeus, another of the Apostolic Fathers, wrote a book to refute the various heresies which were then plaguing the Christian Church. Arguing against Marcion's extravagant and pernicious errors, Irenaeus showed that the prophets had envisaged a new covenant, typified by successive historical covenants, but actually sealed and ratified by Jesus Christ who procured salvation for us. "The new covenant having been known and preached by the prophets, he who was to carry it out according to the good pleasure of the Father was also preached, having been revealed to men as God pleased; that they might always make progress through believing in him, and by means of the successive covenants, should gradually attain to perfect salvation" (*Irenaeus Against Heresies,* Book IV, chapter 9).

Augustine (AD 354-430), "the greatest of all the Fathers, and the worthiest divine the Church of God ever had since the apostles' time", taught the doctrine of the covenant in several of his works (e.g. *On Baptism,* and *On the Spirit and the Letter*). When expounding the Psalms, his Messianic interpretation led him to see Christ in the eighty-ninth, and he therefore wrote of God's covenant with His Son. On verse 28 — "My mercy will I keep with him for ever, and my covenant shall stand fast with him" — Augustine comments as follows: "On his account, the Testament is faithful: in him the Testament is mediated: he is the Sealer, the Mediator of the Testament, the Surety of the Testament, the Witness of the Testament, the Heritage of the Testament, the Coheir of the Testament."

At the time of the Reformation, covenant doctrine was rediscovered. It was also developed into covenant theology, a system of truth in which God's covenant becomes the central and organizing principle. The exact origin of Reformed covenant theology is not easy to determine. Some scholars believe that John Calvin (1509-64) should be recognized as its father; and it is certainly true that he refers to "a covenant of free grace" and "a covenant founded on Christ" (*Commentary on Isaiah 55:3 and Galatians 3:17*). A section of the *Institutes* is devoted to this doctrine. Emphasizing the similarity of Old and New Testaments, Calvin teaches concerning the Jews that "the covenant by which they were bound to the Lord was supported, not by their own merits, but solely by the mercy of the God who called them". He adds that "they had and knew Christ as Mediator, through whom they were joined to God and were to share in his promises", and concludes that God made with them the same covenant as He made with us, "the covenant of the gospel, the sole foundation of which is Christ" (*Institutes,* II, x, 2 and 4).

Ulrich Zwingli (1484-1531) is also sometimes associated with the beginnings of covenant theology. In a document read to the Zurich Council in 1523, Zwingli said: "With his (Christ's) shed blood he reconciled us again with his heavenly Father and made an everlasting covenant by which we come to God through him." Later, in his *Refutation of the Tricks of the Anabaptists* (1527), he declared that there was only one covenant and therefore only one people of God in the Old and New Testaments: "Since therefore there is one immutable God and one testament only, we who trust in Christ are under the same testament, consequently God is as much our God as he was Abraham's, and we are as much his people as was Israel."

Zwingli's disciple and successor, Heinrich Bullinger (1504-75) was the first to write a Reformed treatise on the subject which he entitled *Of the One and Eternal Testament or Covenent of God* (1534). This was followed by his famous *Decades,* a series of sermons published between 1549 and 1551, set within the framework of God's covenant of grace. In one of these sermons, Bullinger said: "When God's mind was to declare the favour and good-will that he bare to mankind, and to make us men partakers wholly of himself and his goodness, by pouring himself out upon us, to our great good and profit, it pleased him to make a league or covenant with mankind." This covenant, according to Bullinger, was first made with Adam ("silly wretch") to whom God promised "his only-begotten Son" as the one "in whom he would be reconciled to the world, and through whom he would wholly bestow himself upon us" (*The Third Decade,* Sermon VI). If not Zwingli, then certainly Zwingli and Bullinger together are strong contenders for the honour of being called "originators" of covenant theology.

Influenced by both Geneva and Zurich were Zacharias Ursinus and Caspar Olevianus, the Heidelberg theologians of Germany. These men are said to be the first to thoroughly elaborate and structure the covenant scheme. In his *Major Catechism,* Ursinus (1534-83) taught a pre-Fall covenant of works; while Olevianus (1536-87) in *The Nature of the Covenant of Grace* (1585), taught an eternal and inter-Trinitarian covenant for the salvation of men. He wrote: "The Son of God, having been appointed by God as Mediator of the covenant, becomes the guarantor"; and, for Olevianus, this means Christ had to "satisfy for the sins of all those whom the Father has given him".

Traditionally, of course, Johannes Cocceius (1603-69), professor at Leyden, in Holland, was regarded as the earliest and greatest exponent of covenant theology. Modern scholarship has challenged his right to that distinction but it is nevertheless true that the divine covenant so dominated his thinking that he arranged an original and entire scheme of doctrine on covenant lines. His great work, *Summary of Doctrine concerning the Covenant and Testament of God* (1648), is a remarkably rich statement of classical federalism. "As with the first Adam God made a covenant of works concerned among other things with the inheritance of the image of God which was to be transmitted to his successors, should he maintain his stand (it actually fell out the opposite way), so he made one with the Son as the man to be concerned with the inheritance of righteousness and life for his seed through obedience to the law."

Even our British Reformers have been considered responsible for this system, and there is some evidence to support that view. They certainly made free use of the idea; and although at times they stated it rather legalistically, the more they pressed after gospel light, the more they pointed the way to covenant theology. William Tyndale (1484-1536), for example, who understood "covenant" or "testament" to mean "an appointment made between God and man, and God's promises", wrote as early as 1534 of "an everlasting covenant made unto the children of God, through faith in Christ, upon the deservings of Christ; where eternal life is promised to all that believe" (*Prologue upon the Gospel of St. Matthew*). Similarly, John Bradford (1510-1555), in a letter of comfort dated 1554, referred to "the promises and covenant of God in Christ's blood; namely, that God is 'our God' with all that ever he hath". Bradford was at pains to point out to his correspondent the gracious nature of this covenant. In doing so, he anticipated the views promoted by later, more advanced, federalists. "(God's) covenant dependeth and hangeth upon God's own goodness, mercy, and truth only, and not on our obedience or worthiness in any point, for then should we never be certain". Obedience is indeed required, but not as a condition "that thereby we might be his children and he our Father", more as a covenant obligation, "because he is our Father and we his children, through his own goodness in Christ, *therefore* requireth he faith and obedience". If it were otherwise, Bradford concludes "that were to make our obedience and worthiness the cause, and so to put Christ out of place" ("Letter to Mistress Mary Honywood", Bradford's *Works,* Volume 2, page 153).

In the British connection, Robert Rollock (1555-98), first Principal of Edinburgh University, should also be mentioned, since, in 1590, he published *A Treatise of God's Effectual Calling,* the second and third chapters of which dealt with "the Covenant of Works" and "the Covenant of Grace" respectively. Rollock began with a definition: "The covenant of God generally is a promise under some one condition". He then observed how Scripture (Gal. 4:24) distinguishes "two covenants"; and on the covenant of works he wrote as follows: "After that God had created man after his own image, pure and holy, and had written his law in his mind, he made a covenant with man, wherein he promised him eternal life, under the condition of holy and good works . . ." (Rollock's *Works,* Volume 1, page 34). His treatment of the covenant of grace is characterized by like clarity and precision: "In the free covenant of grace, or of the gospel, the first ground is our Mediator Jesus Christ, crucified also and dead; or, which is the same in effect, the blood of the Mediator" (page 38). For Rollock, this was not to deny faith as the God-appointed means by which sinners receive covenant blessing, "for faith embraces God's mercy in Christ, and makes Christ effectual in us unto righteousness and life" (page 40). But, Rollock insisted, "it is not so much our faith apprehending Christ, as Christ himself, and God's mercy apprehended in him, that is the cause wherefore God performeth the promise of his covenant unto us, to our justification and salvation" (page 40). This is undisguised federalism as early as 1590.

Who then was responsible for federalism, or Reformed covenant theology? The answer can only be no theologian in particular. The Calvinistic Reformers generally, when they returned to the Word of God, rediscovered the rich vein of truth which led them into the glorious scheme of God's covenants.

The Puritans were covenant theologians almost to a man, and they wrote extensively upon this theme. Some concentrated on the doctrine of the covenant, like John Preston (*The New Covenant or Saints' Portion,* 1629), Obadiah Sedgwick (*The Bowels of Tender Mercy Sealed in the Everlasting Covenant,* 1661), Samuel Petto (*The Great Mystery of the Covenant of Grace,* 1673), and William Strong (*A Discourse of the Two Covenants,* 1678). Others took up disputed points and treated the subject more polemically, like Thomas Blake (*A Treatise about God's Covenant made with Man,* 1633), Anthony Burgess (*A Vindication of the Moral Law and the Covenants,* 1646), and John Barret (*Good Will towards Men, or a Treatise of the Covenants,* 1675). Some traced the covenant's historical development, like John Ball (*A Treatise of the Covenant of Grace,* 1645) and Francis Roberts (*The Mysterie and Marrow of the Bible viz. God's Covenants with Man,* 1657). And other still expounded the truth in an experimental way with a view to warming the heart, like Robert Bidwell (*The Copy of the Covenant of Grace,* 1657) and Oliver Heywood (*The Sure Mercies of David,* 1672). The temptation to subject these and other Puritan works to more detailed examination must be resisted: limitations of space do not allow for that. Sufficient to say that in the seventeenth century covenant theology and Puritan theology were virtually synonymous. As Thomas Carlyle once said, " 'the Covenants' . . . (became) the grand axis of all in that Puritan Universe".

Reformed covenant theology received credal status in the Irish Articles of Religion. These articles, prepared under the superintendence of Archbishop Ussher, were adopted by the Archbishops, Bishops and Clergy of the Irish Episcopal Church in 1615. In a chapter which deals with creation, they state: "Man being at the beginning created according to the image of God . . . , had the covenant of the law ingrafted in his heart, whereby God did promise unto him everlasting life upon condition that he performed entire and perfect obedience unto his commandments. . . . " A subsequent chapter, headed "Of Christ, the Mediator of the Second Covenant" declares: "He (Christ) fulfilled the law for us perfectly: For our sakes he endured most grevious torments immediately in his soul, and most painful sufferings in his body. He was crucified and died to reconcile his Father unto us, and to be a sacrifice not only for original guilt, but also for all our actual transgressions."

The Westminster Confession of Faith (1646) drew heavily upon the Irish Articles but, in its statement, the Confession was more explicit and it gave greater prominence to the covenant concept. An introductory paragraph teaches that a divine covenant is an effect of favour, because creatures can do nothing intrinsically meritorious and the Creator is under no obligation to confer happiness. It therefore follows that "they could never have any fruition of him as their blessedness and reward, but by some voluntary condescension on God's part, which he hath been pleased to express by way of covenant" (chapter VII, i).

God could have demanded from Adam unqualified submission to His will, without making any promise of reward; but it pleased Him to make an arrangement by which Adam could secure, for himself and the whole human race, unending life and happiness. This first arrangement was "a covenant of works, wherein life was promised to Adam, and in him to his posterity, upon condition of perfect and personal obedience". On account of the Fall, God made another arrangement, "the Covenant of Grace: whereby he freely offereth unto sinners life and salvation by Jesus Christ, requiring of them faith in him, that they may be saved" (chapter VII, sections ii and iii).

The Westminster divines, with their usual accuracy, observe that properly speaking, "the covenant of grace was made with Christ, as the second Adam, and in him, with all the elect, as his seed" (*The Larger Catechism,* question 31).

Reformers and Puritans alike, then, developed their theological systems according to the covenant scheme. But what is so appealing about the covenant?

First of all, *it is the underlying theme of the entire Scripture.* This written Word throughout is the self-disclosure of a covenant God and the record of His covenant dealings with men (Exod. 24:3-8; Jer. 31:31-34; Matt. 26:26-28; 2 Cor. 3:1-11).

Secondly, *covenant doctrine is strongly Trinitarian,* since it maintains that in the Unity of the Godhead there is a Trinity of Persons working out redemption. Herein lies its excellence. It presents God redeeming fallen man to Himself, by Himself, and through Himself (Isa. 48:16; Gal. 4:4-6; Eph. 1:3-14).

Thirdly, *it emphasizes the sovereignty of God.* Conceived in the divine mind and agreed by the undivided Three, the covenant became the remedial part of God's eternal purpose. His purpose before time is made known by His power in time, and the covenant is thus effectively administered to the elect who are put into possession of all its blessings (Ps. 2:7-8; Eph. 3:8-11; 2 Tim. 1:9; Heb. 13:20).

Fourthly, *the covenant preserves the truth of human responsibility.* Faith is shown to be the God-appointed means whereby sinners are united to Christ and brought into the bond of the covenant (Isa. 55:3; Acts 16:31; Rom 4:16); and once sinners are in a covenant state, they are required to fulfil covenant obligations (Deut. 10:12; Lk. 1:68-75; 2 Cor. 6:16-18).

Fifthly, *God's covenant affords the possibility of true experimental religion* because, through it, God establishes a spiritual, direct and vital relationship wih His people (Ps. 25:14; Ezek. 16:8; Heb. 8:10-12):

Sixthly, *covenanted promises guarantee the believer's perseverance in grace and his eternal security.* This provides a sphere for the doctrine of assurance (2 Sam. 23:5; Ps. 89:28-34; Jn. 17:4, 5, 24).

Seventhly, and lastly, *the covenant of grace being the same in every age* (though progressively revealed and differing in outward administration), *God's way of salvation has always been the same and His people have always been essentially the same.* It is the covenant which establishes the unity and continuity of God's Church (Isa. 56:3-8; Gal. 3:8-9; Eph. 2:11-22; Heb. 4:2, 9:15).

Scotland produced some truly great covenant theologians. Their published works still excel, affording most able statements of the truth, unfolded with richness and fullness. Among these theologians was David Dickson (1589-1662), co-author with James Durham of that precious (but, sadly, rather neglected) treatise, *The Sum of Saving Knowledge,* 1650.

Another was Samuel Rutherford (1600-61) whose learned work, *The Covenant of Life Opened,* 1655, convincingly shows that there is "a covenant of Suretyship or Redemption between Jehovah and the Son of God". At times, Rutherford is so moved by his subject that he can hardly contain himself. "What speaketh stronger consolation, that the Father gave me to the Son Christ to be saved, and the Son undertook for me, hath given a written band under his hand to keep me? O what happiness! that I am not mine own keeper, but that Christ hath given it under his hand, and the Father and the Son hath covenant-wise closed and stricken hands, the one having given and the other received me a-keeping'' (page 294).

Patrick Gillespie (1617-75), Principal of Glasgow University, wrote two quite masterly books on the subject: one entitled, *The Ark of the Testament Opened, or, The secret of the Lord's covenant unsealed in a Treatise of the Covenant of Grace,* 1661; and the other, published posthumously, *The Ark of the Covenant Opened; or, A Treatise of the Covenant of Redemption,* 1677. Observing in the former work that ''the Doctrine of the Covenant of Grace . . . is the very sum and substance, and marrow of the knowledge of the Scriptures'', Gillespie incites his readers to ''the study of this subject'' reminding them, as he does so, of certain ''excitements and encouragements'' such as the following: ''This knowledge was long kept as a great secret betwixt God and Christ, before the world began, and after that it was included in the eternal councel of God; but (it) is now revealed, and the knowledge of these great mysteries is made possible and practicable, so that the study of the depths of this knowledge is neither desperate, nor a labyrinth that no man can pass through'' (pages 38 and 39). ''We live,'' says Gillespie, ''under the last and best expressure and administration of the Covenant of Grace'' and ''God hath promised to reveal this secret to his people, Psalm 25:14'' especially perhaps ''towards the latter end of the world . . . 'at the time of the end, when knowledge shall be increased', Daniel 12:4, 9.'' We should therefore inquire into this mystery, always remembering however that ''the Ark of the Covenant shall not perfectly be opened till we see it, nor this mystery of the Covenant be throughly understood till we be in heaven'' (pages 41-43).

Also worthy of mention is John Nevay (?-1672), the Covenanter. He preached forty-nine sermons on 2 Samuel 23:1-5 which, after his death, were published in a volume entitled *The Nature, Properties, Blessings, and Saving Graces of the Covenant of Grace* (1748). Even though the book is said to contain only his ''notes'', it exhibits Scripture's teaching on this subject in a most comprehensive, thorough and accurate way. In his fourth sermon, Nevay shows that ''the first party engaging with God, and engaged unto him in this covenant, is Christ the eternal Son of God''. Applying this truth to the comfort of believers, he writes: ''The bargain transacted betwixt the Father and the Son, it is not of Yesterday, but an Eternal Business: So, the Changes of Time will make no alteration in it: And further, however Matters stand betwixt the Believer and God, to his Apprehension; if he plead Right and Interest in Christ; all will be well; for the Covenant betwixt the Father and Christ cannot be broken; and Christ taketh in all his Party with him.''

Thomas Boston began preaching on the Covenant of Grace on July 1st, 1722, and it was nearly two years before he concluded that series of sermons. In general, Boston followed the covenantal teaching of his Scottish forbears but his doctrine does have some distinctive features. Unlike the older theologians, Boston refuses to recognize a two-fold covenant of God relating to salvation: viz., a covenant of redemption, made within the Godhead between the Father and the Son, and a covenant of grace, made with elect sinners. According to Boston, these are but ''two names of one and the same second covenant, under different considerations''. It is to Christ ''a covenant of redemption'', ''a bargain of buying and selling'', because ''he alone engaged to pay the price of our redemption''; but it is to us ''a covenant of grace'', in which ''all is to be had freely'', and ''without respect to any work of ours, as the ground of our right thereto''. Support for this view is found in the fact that Scripture mentions ''two (not three) covenants'' (Gal. 4:24) and, since one of these is the covenant of works, a single covenant of grace must be the other. Furthermore, repeated reference to the ''blood of the covenant (not covenants)'' (e.g. Heb. 10:29) clearly shows that our salvation depends upon only one covenant, the covenant of grace. For Boston, then, not only is man's ruin by one covenant, his recovery is also by one covenant.

It follows that the condition of the covenant of grace, properly so called, is ''Christ's fulfilling all righteousness'' and not, as some have maintained, ''faith in Christ'' (Isa. 53:10-11; Matt. 3:15, 20:28; Rom. 5:19; 2 Cor. 5:21). Since faith must precede the enjoyment of promised benefits (Jn. 3:16; Eph. 2:8), Boston allows that it could be called ''a condition of connection or order'' but only in the sense that ''one thing necessarily goes before another in the order of the covenant''. He illustrates as follows: ''the buyer's receiving of the commodity, and the hireling's receiving of the reward, covenanted or bargained for, must needs go before their profession or enjoyment of them; but it is evident that that receiving is not the thing upon which the buyer's right and title to the commodity, or the hireling's right and title to the reward, is founded.'' The point is well made. But is it so important? Most certainly it is; for if faith is made the proper condition, the free covenant of grace turns into a conditional covenant of works. This destroys the Gospel.

In his book, *A View of the Covenant of Grace,* published in 1734, Boston laid the groundwork for a more biblical scheme and system. Others soon committed themselves to it, among them Adam Gib (*Sacred Contemplations,* 1786), John Colquhoun (*The Covenant of Grace,* 1812) and Thomas Bell (*A View of the Covenants of Works and Grace,* 1814). Under the influence of Ralph and Ebenezer Erskine, it became the distinctive doctrine of the Secession Church and the popular evangelical theology of Scotland. The systematic theologies of men like Dr. John Brown (*A Compendious View of Natural and Revealed Religion,* 1782) and Dr. John Dick (*Lectures on Theology,* 1833) preserve this precious legacy of truth which belongs, of course, not only to our fathers but also to us.

Boston's volume will be a most valuable acquisition to the libraries of Ministers and Christians generally. Its doctrine is thoroughly scriptural; its argument is compelling; and the reading of it will certainly prove an enriching experience. It ranks among the best works ever written on the Covenant and deserves the widest possible readership.

One cannot read this book without entertaining the hope that the biblical doctrine of God's Covenant of Grace will once again be restored to our churches and, above all, to the hearts of the Lord's people.

In the last century, George Macaulay wrote words which perfectly express my own convictions: ''So important, indeed, is the place of the grace of God as dispensed to men in covenant form, in, by, and through Christ Jesus, that so long as a sound and scriptural theology prevails, the doctrine of grace in covenant will have a conspicuous and commanding place in the teaching of true theologians.''

Malcolm H. Watts — Salisbury, November 1990

A VIEW

OF

THE COVENANT OF GRACE.

PSALM lxxxix. 3,

I have made a covenant with my chosen.

1 COR. xv. 45,

The last Adam was made a quickening spirit.

As man's ruin was originally owing to the breaking of the covenant of works, so his recovery, from the first to the last step thereof, is owing purely to the fulfilling of the covenant of grace; which covenant, being that wherein the whole mystery of our salvation lies, I am to essay the opening of, as the Lord shall be pleased to assist. And there is the more need of humble dependence on the Father of lights, through Jesus Christ his Son, for the manifestation of his Spirit in this matter, that whereas the first covenant is known, in part, by the light of nature, the knowledge of this second is owing entirely to revelation.

It was from this covenant the psalmist, in the verse immediately preceding the first text, took a comfortable view of a glorious building, infallibly going up in the midst of ruins; even a building of mercy: "For I have said, Mercy shall be built up for ever;" the ground of which confident assertion is, in our text, pointed out to be God's covenant with his chosen. From the type of the covenant of grace, namely, the covenant of royalty made unto David, he saw a building up of mercy for the royal family of Judah, when they were brought exceeding low. From the substance of it, he saw a building of mercy for sinners of mankind, who were laid in ruins by the breach of the first covenant. This is that new building free grace set on foot for us; into which they that believe are instantly thereupon received, and where once received, they shall dwell for ever; a building of mercy, in which every stone, from the bottom to the top, from the foundation stone to the cope-stone, is pure mercy, rich and free mercy to us.

Of this building of mercy I shall drop a few words.

And, 1. The plan of it was drawn from all eternity, in the council of the Trinity: for it is according to the eternal purpose purposed in Jesus Christ, Eph. iii. 11. The objects of mercy, the time and place, the way and means, of conferring it on them, were designed particularly, before man was miserable, yea, before he was at all. 2. The builder is God himself, the Father, Son, and Holy Ghost, 1 Cor. iii. 9, "Ye are God's building." All hands of the glorious Trinity are at work in this building. The Father chose the objects of mercy, and gave them to the Son to be redeemed; the Son purchased redemption for them; and the Holy Ghost applies the purchased redemption unto them. But it is specially attributed to the Son, on the account of his singular agency in the work: Zech. vi. 12, "Behold the man whose name is the Branch—He shall build the temple of the Lord:" ver. 13, "Even He shall build the temple of the Lord, and He shall bear the glory." 3. The foundation was laid deep in the eternal counsel; beyond the reach of the eyes of men or angels. Paul considering it, cries out, "O the depth!" Rom. xi. 33. "For who hath known the mind of the Lord or who hath been his counsellor?" ver. 34. 4. It is more than five thousand years since this building rose above ground. And the first stone of it that appeared, was a promise, a promise of a Saviour, made in paradise after the fall, Gen. iii. 15, namely, that the seed of the woman should bruise the head of the serpent. Here was mercy. And mercy was laid upon mercy. Upon promising mercy was laid quickening mercy, whereby our lost first parents were enabled to believe the promise; and upon quickening mercy was laid pardoning mercy to them; and upon that again sanctifying and establishing mercy; and at length glorifying mercy. 5. The cement is blood; the blood of Jesus Christ the Mediator, which is the blood of God, Acts xx. 28. No saving mercy for sinners could consist, nor could one mercy lie firm upon another in the building, without being cemented with that precious blood; but by it the whole building consists, and stands firm for ever, Heb. ix. 22, 23, and vii. 24, 25. 6. Ever since the time it appeared above ground, it has been going on. And many hands have been employed, to serve in carrying on the work. In the first ages of the world, patriarchs were employed in it, such as Adam, Enoch, and Noah; in the middle ages, prophets, priests, and Levites; in these the last ages, the apostles, and other extraordinary officers, and ordinary ministers of the gospel. Great has been the opposition made to the building from the beginning, by Satan and his agents, both in the way of violence and deceit; yet has it all along been going on still. And now it is come far above mid-height; it is drawing towards the top, and the time when the last stone shall be laid thereon; for it is evident, we are far advanced in the days of the voice of the seventh angel, wherein the mystery of God is to be finished, Rev. x. 7. 7. The cope-stone will be laid on it at the last day: at what time the promise will receive its full accomplishment, in the complete salvation of all the objects of mercy, then to be advanced unto the measure of the stature of the fulness of Christ," Eph. iv. 13. In that day our Lord Jesus Christ, the great builder, "shall bring forth the head-stone thereof with shoutings," even the last and crowning mercy, saying, "Come, ye blessed of my Father, inherit the kingdom prepared for you from the foundation of the world." And then shall they dwell in the building of mercy perfected, and sing of mercies for ever and ever. 8. *Lastly*, The foundation on which it stands, is a firm one. It is necessary that it be so: for a building of mercy to sinners, from a holy just God, is a building of huge weight, more weighty than the whole fabric of heaven and earth: and if it should fall, all is ruined a second time, without any more hope of relief. But it is a sure foundation, being God's everlasting covenant: "I have made a covenant with my chosen."

In which words, together with the second text, there are four things to be considered. 1. The foundation on which the building of mercy stands; to wit, A covenant. 2. The parties-contractors in that covenant. 3. The making of it. And, 4, The nature of it.

I. The foundation on which the building of mercy stands, is a covenant, a divine covenant, a sure one. The first building for man's happiness was a building of bounty and goodness, but not of mercy; for man was not in misery when it was a-rearing up. And it was founded on a covenant too; namely, on the covenant of works, made with the first Adam: but he broke the covenant, and the whole building tumbled down in an instant. But this is another covenant, and of another nature. In the type indeed, and shadow, it is the covenant of royalty with David, 2 Sam. vii. 11—17; which was a foundation of mercy to his family, securing the continuance of it, and that as a royal family. Howbeit, in the antitype and truth, it is the covenant of grace, the covenant of eternal life and salvation to sinners, the spiritual seed of the head thereof, to be given them in the way of free grace and mercy, Psalm lxxxix. 2, 4, 29, 36; and in which they are freed from the curse, so that it cannot reach them, notwithstanding of their failures; but the Lord deals with them as his children still, though offending children, ver. 30—33; and all by the means of Jesus Christ the Saviour, the mighty One, ver. 19. This is the foundation of the whole building of mercy to sinners in their low estate, into which they were brought by Adam's fall. The revelation, promulgation, and offer made unto the sons of men, of this covenant which lay hid in the depths of the eternal counsel, is called the gospel; the glad tidings of a new covenant for life and salvation to sinners.

II. The parties-contractors in this covenant are, God, and his chosen, the last Adam: for it is evident from the nature of the things here spoken of, ver. 3, 4, and from 2 Sam. vii. 8, that these words, "I have made a covenant with my chosen," are the Lord's own words. Both heaven and earth were concerned in this covenant; for it was a covenant of peace between them: and accordingly the interests of both are seen to by the parties-contractors. 1. On Heaven's side is God himself, the party-proposer of the covenant, "I have made a covenant with my chosen." He was the offended party, yet the motion for a covenant of peace comes from him; a certain indication of the good-will of the whole glorious Trinity towards the recovery of lost sinners. The God and Father of our Lord Jesus Christ, the Father of mercies, beholding a lost world, his mercy seeks a vent, that it may be shown to the miserable; but justice stands in the way of the egress and building of mercy, without there be a covenant whereby it may be satisfied. Then saith the Father, "The first covenant will not serve the purpose of mercy; there must be a new bargain: but the lost creatures have nothing left, to contract for themselves; unless another take the burden upon him for them, there is no remedy in the case: they cannot choose such an one for themselves; I will make a choice for them, and make the covenant with my chosen." 2. On man's side, then, is God's chosen, or chosen one; for the world is singular. This chosen one, in the type, the covenant of royalty, is David; but in the antytipe, the covenant of grace, it is the Son of God, the last Adam, even Christ the chosen of God, Luke xxiii. 35. The truth is, such great things are said of the party with whom this covenant was made, of his seed, and of the efficacy of this covenant, as can fully agree to none but Christ and his spiritual seed, vers. 4, 27, 29, 36, 37. The royal family of Judah, the house of David, never recovered their ancient splendour, after the Babylonish captivity; with a view to which time, this psalm seems to have been penned. Their kingdom is extinct many ages ago; and the grandeur of that family, according to the flesh, is quite sunk. But the promise made to David in the covenant of royalty, still flourisheth, and will flourish for ever in Jesus Christ, the top-branch of the family of David. How then can it be, but that, in the perpetual building of mercy, mentioned ver. 2, and the establishing of David's seed, and building up his throne to all generations, ver. 4, Christ himself is chiefly aimed at? And indeed he only was the mighty One, fit for the vast undertaking in this covenant, ver. 19: and him the Father points out to us, as his elect, or chosen One, Isa. xlii. 1.

III. As to the making of this covenant between the contracting parties: the Father made it with his own Son, I have made a covenant with my chosen, and that before the world began, Tit. i. 2. By their mutual agreement thereto, this covenant was completely made from eternity; even as the covenant of works with the first Adam was, before we were in being. The original text calls it cutting off a covenant; which phrase is taken from that ancient usage of cutting off a beast, by cutting it asunder, at the making of a covenant, Jer. xxxiv. 17. It intimates this covenant to be a covenant by sacrifice: wherein the party-contractor on man's side was the sacrifice, and divine justice the sword that cut it asunder, according to Zech. xiii. 7, "Awake, O sword, against my shepherd, and against the man that is my fellow, saith the Lord of hosts: smite the shepherd." And withal it imports the inviolableness and pepetuity of the covenant made; no more for ever to be dissolved, than the parts of the beast cut off one from the other, to be joined again as formerly.

IV. For the nature of this covenant; there are five things belonging thereto which appear from the texts; namely, 1. The being of a representation in it. 2. The design for which it was set on foot. 3. That there are in it a condition; and 4. A promise; and 5. Into whose hands the administration of it is put.

1. There is a representation taking place in this covenant. As it was in the first covenant, so it was likewise in the second; the party-contractor and undertaker on man's side, was a representative, representing and sustaining the persons of others. This appears, in that the chosen One with whom the covenant was made, is called the last Adam: for it is plain, he is so called in relation to the first Adam, who was the figure (or type) of him, Rom. v. 14. namely, in that like as the first Adam representing his seed in the covenant of works, brought sin and death on them; so he representing his, brings righteousness and life to them; as the apostle teacheth at large in that chapter.

2. The design of this covenant was life, the most valuable interest of mankind. "The last Adam was made a quickening spirit,"

to wit, to give life to his seed. So it is a covenant of life, as the covenant of Levi, a type thereof, is expressly called, Mal. ii. 5. The first covenant was a covenant of life too; but there is this difference, to wit, that the first was for life in perfection to upright man having life before; the second, for life in perfection to sinful man legally and morally dead. The parties contracted for in this second covenant, were considered as under the bands of death, absolutely void of life; and therefore utterly incapable to act for helping themselves. They lay like dry bones scattered about the grave's mouth, before the parties-contractors; justice forbidding to give them life, but upon terms consistent with, and becoming its honour.

3. The condition of the covenant, the terms of that life, agreed to by the representative, is implied in that he was the last Adam, namely, to go through with what the first Adam had stuck in. Adam, in the covenant of works, stumbled in the course of his obedience, and fell; and by his fall was quite disabled to begin it anew: he thereby came under the penalty of that covenant also, but was utterly unable to discharge it. So the last Adam comes in the room of the first, not as the first Adam stood in his integrity; for in that case there was no place for a second Adam; but as he lay a broken man under the first bargain. And coming in his room in this case, his business was to satisfy the demands of the first covenant, in behalf of his seed. These demands were now run up high, quite beyond what they were to innocent Adam: the penalty was become payable, as well as the principal sum. Wherefore the first covenant being ingrossed in the second, is declared broken; and the principal and penalty being summed up together, the clearing of the whole is laid upon the last or second Adam, as the condition of the second covenant.

4. The promise of the covenant to be, upon that condition, performed by the party-contractor on Heaven's side, is implied in these words, "I have made a covenant with" (in the original, to) "my chosen;" that is, "I have made a covenant, binding and obliging myself by solemn promise to my chosen One, for such and such benefits, upon the condition therein stated and agreed to." Compare the following clause, "I have sworn unto David my servant." The nature of this promise will be inquired into in the due place.

5. *Lastly,* The administration of this covenant is put into the hands of the party-contractor on man's side: "The last Adam was made a quickening spirit." Each of the contracting parties being God, it was not possible that either party should fail, or that the last Adam should break, as the first had done. Wherefore the time

of Christ's fulfilling of the condition of the covenant being prefixed by the Father, God took Christ's single bond for sufficient security, and thereupon constituted him administrator of the covenant. Those whom he represented, were considered as being under death, which in the language of the covenant, is a very extensive term: the Spirit and life were to be purchased by him, and did belong to the promise of the covenant. So, upon the credit of his fulfilling the condition of the covenant in due time, the fulness of the Spirit, and eternal life, were lodged in him, to be communicated by him: Rev. iii. 1, "These things saith he that hath the seven Spirits of God." 1 John v. 11, "God hath given to us eternal life: and this life is in his Son." John xvii. 2, "As thou hast given him power over all flesh, that he should give eternal life." Thus was he made a quickening spirit.

Now the DOCTRINE of these texts thus compared and explained, is,

That the covenant of grace for life and salvation to lost sinners of mankind, was made with Jesus Christ the last Adam; and he constituted administrator of it.

In handling of this weighty subject, I deem it not necessary to insist to prove that there is a covenant of grace; the being of which is obvious from the texts, and many other Scriptures, such as, Isa. xlii. 6; xlix. 8; and liv. 10; Heb. viii. 6; and xiii. 20. But the following account of it shall be ranged under these six heads: namely,

1. The parties in the covenant of grace.
2. The making of that covenant.
3. The parts of it.
4. The administration of it.
5. The trial of a saving personal inbeing in it.
6. The way of instating sinners personally and savingly in it.

HEAD I.

THE PARTIES IN THE COVENANT OF GRACE.

In all covenants, of whatsoever nature they be, whether covenants of absolute promise, or conditional ones, there must needs be distinct parties: for howbeit one may decree, resolve, or purpose with himself, without another party; yet one's covenanting or bargaining, vowing or promising, speaks an obligation thence arising to another distinct party. Accordingly, in the covenant of grace there are three parties to be considered; 1. The party-contractor on heaven's side; 2. The party-contractor on man's side; and, 3. The party contracted and undertaken for. Of which in order. And,

I. OF THE PARTY-CONTRACTOR ON HEAVEN'S SIDE.

As it was the covenant of works in this point, so it is likewise in the covenant of grace; the party upon the one side is God himself, and he only. There was no need of any other to see to the interests of heaven in this covenant; and there was no other when it was made, being made from eternity, before the world began, Tit. i. 2. This is plain from the words of the covenant, "I will be their God," Jer. xxxi. 33.

But whether God is herein to be considered personally or essentially, is not quite so clear. Some divines think, that the Father, personally considered, namely, as the first person of the glorious Trinity, is the party-contractor on heaven's side; others, that God, essentially considered, that is, as Father, Son, and Holy Ghost, is that party-contractor. But however we conceive of that matter, we are assured from the holy oracles, that these three are one God; and judge, that, according to the Scripture, it may be safely said, that God essentially considered, was the party-contractor in the person of the Father. Hereby it is owned, that the Son and the Holy Ghost have their part in the covenant, on heaven's side, as the party offended by man's sin; and, in the meantime, a peculiar agency in this great work of power and authority, on that side, is attributed to the Father; as there is unto the Son, on man's side.

And that of the party-contractor on heaven's side we may conceive aright in this matter, these two things are, in the first place, to be taken notice of. 1. He from all eternity decreed the creation of man after his own image, and the making of the covenant of works with him, in time. All things brought forth in time, lay from eternity in the womb of God's decree; in virtue whereof they have their being in time: for which cause the decree is said to bring forth, as a woman doth a child, Zeph. ii. 2. And the creation of angels and men, with the providence about them, made many lines in the volume of the sealed book of the decrees. God self-sufficient needed neither man nor angel: but, for the manifestation of his own glory, he purposed from eternity to create them; and moreover, to enter into such a covenant with man, as one should therein represent the whole family; sovereign pleasure meanwhile taking another method with the angelic tribe: but withal purposing to give both the one and the other a sufficient ability to stand in their integrity, if they would. Thus, from eternity, the covenant of works, in all the parts and appurtenances thereof, was before the eternal mind; though being made with a mere man, it could not actually be entered into, till once man was created. But, " Known unto God are all his works from the beginning of the world," Acts xv. 18. 2. He decreed also from eternity, to permit the first man, the representative of the whole family, to fall, and so to break the covenant, and involve himself, and all his posterity in ruins. It is evident from the spotless holiness of God, and the nature of the thing, that the divine permission was not the cause of man's fall; and from the necessary dependence of the creature upon the Creator, that without it, he could not have fallen. But the sovereign Lord of the creatures, permitted the fall of man for his own holy ends, purposing to bring about good from it.

Now, God, the party contractor on heaven's side in the covenant of grace, is to be considered in that matter in a threefold view.

1. He is to be considered in it as an offended God; offended with all the sins of all mankind, original and actual. Looking upon the children of men, the whole mass of mankind appeared in the eyes of his glory corrupt and loathsome, the very reverse of his holiness: he saw them all gone aside, together become filty, none doing good, no not one, Psalm xiv. 2, 3. In the first covenant, God contracted with man himself as a friend, without the interposition of a Mediator: but in the second covenant it was not so, and it could not be so; for in it man was considered as a fallen creature, a transgressor of the law, and an enemy to God; and it is a covenant of reconciliation, a covenant of peace, for those who had been at war with heaven.

2. But withal God is to be considered herein as a God purposeing and decreeing from eternity to manifest the glory of his free grace, love, and mercy, in the salvation of some of mankind lost. Accordingly, we are said to be saved in time, "according to his own purpose and grace given us in Christ Jesus, before the world began," 2 Tim. i. 9. Without such a purpose of grace in God, there could never have been such a covenant of grace. But the sovereign Lord of the creatures overlooking the fallen angels as to any purpose of mercy, entertained thoughts of love and peace towards fallen mankind, purposing in himself to make some of them everlasting monuments of his free grace and mercy, partakers of life and salvation; and so set on foot the covenant of grace.

3. *Lastly,* Yet we are to consider him also in this matter as a just

God, who cannot but do right, give sin a just recompence, and magnify his holy law, and make it honourable, Gen. xviii. 25; Heb. ii. 2; Isa. xlii. 21. Upon the motion for extending mercy to sinners of mankind, the justice of God interposeth, pleading that mercy cannot be shewn them, but upon terms agreeable to law and justice. And indeed it was neither agreeable to the nature of God, nor to his truth in his word, to erect a throne of grace on the ruins of his exact justice, nor to shew mercy in prejudice of it. Now, the justice of God required, that the law which was violated, should be fully satisfied and the honour thereof repaired by suffering and obedience: the former such as might satisfy the penal sanction of the law, and the latter, the commanding part of it. The which being quite beyond the reach of the sinners themselves, they behoved to die without mercy, unless another, who could be accepted as a sufficient surety, should undertake for them, as a second Adam, coming in their room and stead, as they lay ruined by the breach of the covenant of works.

Thus stood the impediments in the way of mercy to fallen man, quite insuperable to him, or any of his fellow creatures; and the covenant of grace was made for removing those impediments out of the way, and that it might be the channel wherein the whole rich flood of saving mercy might flow freely, for the quickening, purging, sanctifying, and perfecting of lost sinners of mankind, who were under the bands of death and the curse, through the breach of the first covenant by the first Adam.

From what is said on this point, we may draw this inference, to wit, That the redemption of the soul is precious. The salvation of lost sinners was a greater work than the making of the world: the powerful word commanded, and this last was done; but the former was not to be compassed, but with more ado.

II. OF THE PARTY-CONTRACTOR ON MAN'S SIDE.

We have seen, that upon the one side, in the covenant of grace, is God himself. Now, upon the other side is Jesus Christ the Son of God, with his spiritual seed, Heb. ii. 13, "Behold, I and the children which God hath given me:" the former, as the party-contractor and undertaker; the latter, as the party contracted and undertaken for: a good reason for his name "Immanuel, which being interpreted, is, God with us," Matt. i. 23.

The party-contractor then with God, in the covenant of grace, is our Lord Jesus Christ. He alone managed the interests of men in this eternal bargain: for at the making of it none of them were in being; nor, if they had been, would they have been capable of affording any help.

Now, Jesus Christ the party-contractor on man's side, in the covenant of grace, is, according to our texts, to be considered in that matter as the last or second Adam, head and representative of a seed, lost sinners of mankind, the party contracted for. And thus he sisted himself Mediator between an offended just God, and offending men guilty before him. In which point lay one main difference betwixt the first Adam and the last Adam: for there is one Mediator between God and men, the man Christ Jesus; who gave himself a ransom," 1 Tim. ii. 5, 6. And so the covenant of grace, which could not be made immediately with sinners, was made with Christ the last Adam, their head and representative, mediating between God and them; therefore called Jesus the Mediator of the new covenant, to whom we come by believing, Heb. xii. 22, 24.

The term Mediator is not, to my observation, applied in the holy Scripture to any other except Moses, Gal. iii. 19, "The law—was ordained by angels in the hand of a Mediator." And of him, a typical mediator, it is worth observing, that he was not only an inter-messenger between God and Israel; but in God's renewing his covenant, in a way of reconciliation, after the breaking of the tables, the covenant was made with him, as their head and representative, Exod. xxxiv. 27, "And the Lord said unto Moses, Write thou these words: for after the tenor of these words I have made a covenant with thee and with Israel." This refers unto the gracious answer made to Moses' prayer, ver. 9, "Pardon our iniquity and our sin, and take us for thine inheritance." Ver. 10, "And he" namely, the Lord, "said, Behold, I make a covenant: before all thy people I will do marvels," &c. Ver. 28, "And he wrote upon the tables" to wit, the new ones, "the words of the covenant, the ten commandments." Now, Moses was alone on the mount with God during the whole time of this transaction; and in it the Lord speaks of him and the people as one, all along.

For clearing of this purpose anent the party-contractor on man's side, I shall, 1. Evince, that the covenant of grace was made with Christ as the last Adam, head and representative of a seed; and, 2. Shew why it was so made.

First, That the covenant of grace, the second covenant, was made with Christ as the last or second Adam, head and representative of a seed, to wit, his spiritual seed, appears from the following considerations.

1. Covenants typical of the covenant of grace were made or established with persons representing their respective seed. Thus

it was in the typical covenant in our text, the covenant of royalty made with David, an undoubted type of the covenant of grace. In it David was God's servant, having a seed comprehended with him therein, Psalm lxxxix. 3, 4. He was an eminent type of Christ; who is therefore called David, Hos. iii. 5, "Afterwards shall the children of Israel return, and seek the Lord their God, and David their king." And the benefits of the covenant of grace are called the sure mercies of David, Isa. lv. 3. Thus was it also in the covenant of the day and night, (Jer. xxxiii. 20,) established with Noah and his sons, representatives of their seed, the new world, Gen. ix. 9, "Behold, I establish my covenant with you, and with your seed after you." And that this covenant was a type of the covenant of grace, appears, from its being made upon a sacrifice, chap. viii. 20, 21, 22; and from the sign and token of it, the rainbow, chap. ix. 13, appearing round about the throne, Rev. iv. 3; but especially from the nature and import of it, to wit, that there should not be another deluge, Gen. ix. 11; the substance of which is plainly declared, Isa. liv. 9, "As I have sworn that the waters of Noah should no more go over the earth; so have I sworn that I would not be wroth with thee, nor rebuke thee." Ver. 10, "For the mountains shall depart, and the hills be removed, but my kindness shall not depart from thee, neither shall the covenant of my peace be removed, saith the Lord, that hath mercy on thee." And such also was the covenant of the land of Canaan, made with Abraham representing his seed, Gen. xv. 18, and afterwards confirmed by oath, chap. xxii. 16, 17. In all which he was an eminent type of Christ, the true Abraham, father of the multitude of the faithful, who, upon God's call, left heaven his native country, and came and sojourned among the cursed race of mankind, and there offered up his own flesh and blood a sacrifice unto God, and so became the true heir of the world, and received the promises for his spiritual seed; the sum whereof is given by Zacharias in his account of the covenant with Abraham, Luke i. 72, "To remember his holy covenant:" ver. 73, "The oath which he sware to our father Abraham," ver. 74, "That he would grant unto us, that we being delivered out of the hands of our enemies, might serve him without fear," ver. 75, "in holiness and righteousness before him all the days of our life." And finally, thus it was in the covenant of everlasting priesthood made with Phinehas, another type of the covenant of grace. In it Phinehas stood a representative of his seed, Numb. xxv. 13, "And he shall have it, and his seed after him, even the covenat of an everlasting priesthood; because he was zealous for his God, and made an atonement for the children of Israel." And therein he typified Jesus Christ, representing his spiritual seed in the covenant of grace: for it is evident, that it is in Christ, who made the great atonement for sinners, the everlasting priesthood promised to Phinehas, hath its full accomplishment: his spiritual seed partaking of the same in him; according to Psalm cx. 4, "Thou art a priest for ever." Rev. i. 6, "And hath made us kings and priests unto God and his Father."

Now, forasmuch as these typical covenants were made or established with parties standing therein as public persons, heads, and representatives of their seed; it natively follows, that the covenant of grace typified by them, was made with Christ as the head and representative of his spiritual seed: for whatsoever is attributed to any person or thing as a type, hath its accomplishment really and chiefly in the person or thing typified.

2. Our Lord Jesus Christ being, in the phraseology of the Holy Ghost, the last Adam, the reason hereof cannot be taken from the nature common to the first Adam and him; for all mankind partake of that; but from their common office of federal headship and representation, in the respective covenants touching man's eternal happiness; the which is peculiar unto Adam, and the man Christ. Accordingly, Adam is called the first man, and Christ the second man, 1 Cor. xv. 47; but Christ is no otherwise the second man, than as he is the second federal head, or the representative in the second covenant; as Adam was the first federal head, or the representative in the first covenant. Agreeable to which, the apostle represents Adam as the head of the earthy men, and Christ as the head of the heavenly men, ver. 48; the former being those who bear Adam's image, namely, all his natural seed; the latter, those who partake of the image of Christ, namely, his spiritual seed, ver. 49. All this is confirmed from Adam's being a figure or type of Christ, which the apostle expressly asserts, Rom. v. 14; and from the parallel he draws betwixt them two, namely, that as by Adam's covenant-breaking, sin and death came on all that were his, so by Christ's covenant-keeping, righteousness and life come to all that are his, vers. 17, 18, 19. Wherefore, as the first covenant was made with Adam, as the head and representative of his natural seed; so the second covenant was made with Christ, as the head and representative of his spiritual seed.

3. As the first man was called Adam, that is to say, man; he being the head representative of mankind, the person in whom God treated with all men, his natural seed in the first covenant; and, on the other hand, all men therein represented by him, do, in the language of the Holy Ghost, go under the name of Adam, Psalm xxix. 5, 11. "Surely every man" in the original it is, all Adam "is va-

nity:" so Christ bears the name of his spiritual seed, and they on the other hand bear his name; a plain evidence of their being one in the eye of the law, and of God's treating with him as their representative in the second covenant. Israel is the name of the spiritual seed, Rom. ix. 6; and our Lord Jesus Christ is called by the same name, Isa. xlix 3. "Thou art my servant, O Israel, in whom I will be glorified;" as several learned and judicious commentators do understand it; and is evident from the whole context, vers. 1, 2, 4—9. The truth is, Christ is here so called with a peculiar solemnity; for the original text stands precisely thus, "Thou art my servant; Israel, in whom I will glorify myself:" that is, thou art Israel representative, in whom I will glorify myself, and make all mine attributes illustrious; as I was dishonoured, and they darkened, by Israel the collective body of the spiritual seed. And this leads us to a natural and unstrained interpretation of that passage, Psalm xxiv. 6. This is the generation of them that seek him, that seek thy face, O Jacob;" that is, in other words, that long for the appearing (Prov. vii. 15; Gen. xxxii. 30.) of the Messias the Lord whom the old testament church did so seek; a pledge of whose coming to his temple. (Mal. iii. 1.) was the bringing in of the ark into the tabernacle that David had erected for it, on which occasion that Psalm was penned. Accordingly it follows immediately, ver. 7, "Lift up your heads, O ye gates, and be ye lift up, ye everlasting doors, and the King of glory shall come in." And in another Psalm penned on the same occasion, and expressly said to have been delivered on that very day into the hand of Asaph, 1 Chron. xvi. 1, 7, that is the expression found, ver. 11, "Seek his face continually;" justly to be interpreted, agreeable to the circumstances of the main thing which David through the Spirit had in view that day, namely, the coming of the Messias. Thus, Christ bears the name of his spiritual seed; and they, on the other hand, bear his name too: 1 Cor. xii. 12, "For as the body is one, and hath many members, and all the members of that one body, being many, are one body; so also is Christ."

4. The promises were made to Christ as the second Adam, the head and representative of his seed: Gal. iii. 16, "Now to Abraham and his seed were the promises made. He saith not, And to seeds, as of many; but as of one, And to thy seed, which is Christ." I own, that here, even as in the text immediately before cited, is meant Christ mystical, the head and members. It is to them that the promises are here said to be made; but primarily to the head, secondarily to the members in him; even as the promise of life in the first covenant, was primarily made to Adam as the head, and

secondarily to all his natural seed in him. Thus, in the typical covenant with Abraham, the promises of the earthly inheritance were primarily made to Abraham himself, and secondarily to his seed according to the flesh. And even so the promise of the eternal inheritance plainly stands made to Christ, Tit. i. 2, "In hope of eternal life, which God that cannot lie, promised before the world began;" when there was none but Christ to whom that promise could be made personally. Accordingly the covenant is said to be made with the house of Israel, namely, the Spiritual Israel; yet are the promises of it directed, not to them, but to another person, Heb. viii. 10, "I will be to them a God, and they shall be to me a people." The reason of which plainly appears, in the promises being made to Christ as their head and representative. Now, forasmuch as these promises belong to the covenant of grace, which is therefore called the covenants of promise, Eph. ii. 12, it is manifest, that if they were made to Christ as the head and representative of a seed, the covenant of grace was made with him as such; and he to whom they were primarily made, was surely the party-contractor therein.

5. *Lastly*, This federal headship of Christ, and his representing his spiritual seed in the covenant of grace, appears from his suretiship in that covenant, the better testament, whereof Jesus was made a surety, Heb. vii. 22. Now, he became surety for them in the way of satisfaction for their debt of punishment and obedience; and that taking the whole burden on himself, as for persons utterly unable to answer for themselves. This will afterwards fall in to be cleared. Meanwhile, such a surety is a true representative of the party he is surety for, and one person with them in the eye of the law. Hence, not only is Christ said to have been made sin for us, 2 Cor. v. 21, to have had the iniquity of us all laid on him, Isa. liii. 6, and to have died for us, Rom. v. 8; but also we are said to have been crucified with Christ, Gal. ii. 20, to be made the righteousness of God in him, 2 Cor. v. 21, yea, to be raised up together, and glorified, being made to sit together in heavenly places in Christ Jesus, Eph. ii. 6, and to be made alive in Christ, as we die in Adam, 1 Cor. xv. 22. All which necessarily requires this his headship and representation in the covenant.

And thus it appears, that the second covenant was made with Christ as the last or second Adam, head and representative of his spiritual seed.

Secondly, We are to inquire, wherefore the second covenant, the covenant of grace, was so made? And this shall be accounted for in the following particulars.

1. The covenant of grace was made with Christ as the last Adam, head and representative of his spiritual seed, that infinite love might have an early vent, even from eternity. The special love of God to the spiritual seed took vent in the covenant of grace. And that love and that covenant are of the same eternal date: as the love was everlasting or eternal, Jer. xxxi. 3, so was the covenant, Heb. xiii. 20; Tit. i. 2. But since the seed are but of yesterday, the covenant of grace behoved to be like the covenant of works, a yesterday's covenant, a time-covenant, if it was not made with Christ as their representative; it could not otherwise have been an eternal covenant. The promise of eternal life, which is undoubtedly a promise of the covenant of grace, could not otherwise have been of so ancient a date, as before the world began, as the apostle says it is, Tit. i. 2. How could an eternal covenant be originally made with creatures of time, but in their eternal head and representative? Or how could an eternal covenant be personally made with them, by way of personal application to them, had it not been from eternity made with another as their head and representative? But in this method of infinite wisdom, free love took an early vent; not waiting the slow motion of its objects creeping out of the womb of time, in which many of them lie wrapt up, even to this day. But as princes sometimes do, by proxy, marry young princesses, before they are marriageable, or capable to give their consent; so God, in his infinite love, married to himself all the spiritual seed, in and by Jesus Christ as their representative, not only before they were capable of consenting, but before they were at all. The which they do afterwards, in their effectual calling, approve of by faith, and give their consent personally to; and so they enjoy God as their God, and God hath them as his people: John xx. 17, "I ascend unto my Father and your Father, and to my God and your God."

2. Otherwise it could not have been made at all a conditional covenant answering the design of it. This covenant taking place only upon the breach of the first covenant, the great design of it was, that dead sinners might have life, as was before observed. Now, in order to this, a holy just God stood upon conditions, without performing of which that life was not to be given: and they were high conditions, Psalm xl. 6, "Sacrifice and offering thou didst not desire." 1 Thess. v. 9, 10, "Jesus Christ, who died for us, that—we should live." But how could an effectual conditional covenant for life be made with dead sinners, otherwise than in a representative? Dead souls cannot perform any condition for life at all which can be pleasing to God. They must needs have life before they can

do any thing of that nature, be it never so small a condition: therefore a conditional covenant for life, could not be made with sinners in their own persons; especially considering, that the conditions for life were so high, that man at his best state was not able to perform them. Wherefore, if such a covenant was made at all, it behoved to be made with Christ as their representative, Rom. viii. 3. 4.

3. It was so ordered, to the end it might be unto us poor sinners a covenant of grace indeed. It is evident from the holy Scriptures, that this covenant was designed for exalting the free grace of God; and that it is so framed, as to be a covenant of pure grace, and not of works, in respect of us, whatever it was in respect of Christ: Rom. iv. 16, "Therefore it is of faith, that it might be by grace." Eph. ii. 9, "Not of works, lest any man should boast." And at this rate, indeed, it is a covenant of pure grace; and all ground of boasting is taken away from us; the Lord Jesus Christ himself, as representative, being sole undertaker and performer of the conditions thereof. But it is not so, if it is made with the sinner himself, standing as principal party, contracting with God, and undertaking and performing the conditions of the covenant for life: for how low soever these conditions, undertaken and wrought by the sinner in his own person, are supposed to be, the promise of the covenant is made to them; and so, according to the Scripture-reckoning, it is a covenant of works, Rom. iv. 4, "Now to him that worketh, is "the reward not reckoned of grace, but of debt;" and betwixt Adam's covenant and such a covenant, there is no difference, but in degree, which leaves it still of the same kind.

4. This method was taken, that the communication of righteousness and life might be in as compendious a way, as the communication of sin and death was: "As by one man's disobedience many were made sinners; so by the obedience of one shall many be made righteous," Rom. v. 19. The covenant of works having been made with Adam, as a representative of his natural seed, upon the breaking thereof, sin and death are communicated to them all from him as a deadly head. This being so, it was not agreeable to the method of divine procedure with men, to treat with those predestinate unto salvation severally, as principal parties, each contracting for himself in the new covenant for life; but to treat for them all with one public person, who, through his fulfilling the covenant, should be a quickening head to them, from whence life might be derived to them, in as compendious a way, as death was from the first Adam. For his mercies are above all his other works.

5. *Lastly*, The covenant of grace was so made, that it might be a

sure covenant; even to the end the promise might be sure to all the seed, Rom. iv. 16. The first covenant was made with a mere creature, as a principal party, and contractor: and though he was a holy and righteous man, yet was he so fickle and unstable, that he failed of performing the condition he undertook; and so the benefit of the promise was lost: wherefore fallen men were not at all fit to be principal parties, or parties-contractors, in the new covenant, wherein the promise was to be sure, and not to miss of an accomplishment. They being then wholly a broken company, not to be trusted in the matter, Jesus Christ the Son of God was constituted head of the new covenant, to act for, and in name of the spiritual seed: and that to the end, the covenant being in this manner sure in point of the fulfilling of the condition, might be also sure in point of the accomplishment of the promise. And this is the very hinge of the stability of the covenant of grace, according to the Scripture: Psalm lxxxix. 28, "My mercy will I keep for him for evermore, and my covenant shall stand fast with him." Ver. 22, "The enemy shall not exact upon him;" or, as others read it, and I think justly, "The enemy shall not beguile him," namely, as he did the first Adam. The original phrase is elliptical, *q. d.* The enemy shall not beguile (his soul, Jer. xxxvii. 9.) in him.

Before I leave this point, I offer the following inferences from it.

Inf. I. The covenant of redemption and the covenant of grace, are not two distinct covenants, but one and the same covenant. I know that many divines do express themselves otherwise in this matter; and that upon very different views, some of which are no ways injurious to the doctrine of free grace. But this I take to be Scripture truth, and a native consequent of the account given of the covenant of grace in our Larger Catechism, to wit, "That the covenant of grace was made with Christ as the second Adam, and in him with all the elect as his seed:" Gal. iii. 16. "Now to Abraham and his seed were the promises made. He saith not, And to seeds, as of many; but as of one, And to thy seed, which is Christ," Rom. v. 15, to the end. Isa. liii. 10, 11, "When thou shalt make his soul an offering for sin, he shall see his seed, he shall prolong his days, and the pleasure of the Lord shall prosper in his hand. He shall see of the travail of his soul, and shall be satisfied," &c. So the covenant of redemption and the covenant of grace are but two names of one and the same second covenant, under different considerations. By a covenant of redemption is meant a bargain of buying and selling: and such a covenant it was to Christ only; for as much as he alone engaged to pay the price of our redemption, 1 Pet. i. 18, 19. By a covenant of grace, is meant a bargain whereby all is to be had freely: and such a covenant it is to us only, to whom the whole of it is of free grace; God himself having provided the ransom, and thereupon made over life and salvation to us, by free promise, without respect to any work of ours, as the ground of our right thereto.

To confirm this, consider, (1.) That, in Scripture reckoning, the covenants for life and happiness to man are but two in number, whereof the covenant of works is one: Gal. iv. 24, "These are the *two covenants*; the one from the mount Sinai, which gendereth to bondage," namely, generating bond children, excluded from the inheritance, ver. 30. This is a distinguishing character of the covenant of works; for such are indeed the children of that covenant, but not the children of the covenant of grace under any dispensation thereof. These two covenants are called, the old covenant, and the new covenant; and the old is called the first, which speaks the new to be the second: Heb. viii. 13, "In that he saith, A new covenant, he hath made the first old." This is agreeable to the two ways unto life, revealed in the Scripture; the one by works, the other by grace, Rom. xi. 6. The one is called the law, the other grace, chap. vi. 14. The former is the law-covenant with the first Adam representing all his natural seed; made first in paradise, and afterward repeated on Mount Sinai, with the covenant of grace: the latter is the covenant of grace, made with the second Adam representing his spiritual seed: 1 Cor. xv. 47, 48. (2.) It is evident, that the salvation of sinners is by the blood of the covenant, which is the blood of Christ, Heb. x. 29; 1 Cor. xi. 25. And the Scripture mentions the blood of the covenant four times; but never the blood of the covenants: therefore the covenant, the blood whereof the Scripture mentions, and our salvation depends upon, is but one covenant, and not two. Now, that covenant is Christ's covenant, or the covenant of redemption: for it was through the blood of it he was brought again from the dead; namely, in virtue of the promise made therein to be fulfilled to him upon his performing the condition thereof, Heb. xiii. 20. And it is also his people's covenant, or the covenant of grace, Exod. xxiv. 8, "Behold, the blood of the covenant which the Lord hath made with you." It is expressly called their covenant, Zech. ix. 11, "As for thee also, by the blood of *thy* covenant, I have sent forth thy prisoners out of the pit, wherein is no water." The words expressing the party here spoken to, being of the feminine gender in the first language, make it evident, that this is not directed to Christ, but to the church: so the covenant is proposed as their covenant. And the spiritual prisoners are delivered, in virtue of this their covenant, which certainly must be the covenant of grace. By all which it appears, that the covenant of grace is the very same covenant that was made with Christ, in respect of whom it is called the covenant of redemption.

Inf. 2. Like as all mankind sinned in Adam, so believers obeyed and suffered in Christ the second Adam. For as the covenant of works being made with Adam as a public person and representative, all sinned in him, when he broke that covenant; so the covenant of grace being made with Christ, as a public person and representative, all believers obeyed and suffered in him, when he so fulfilled this covenant. This is the doctriue of the apostle, Rom. v. 19, "As by one man's disobedience many were made sinners: so by the obedience of one shall many be made righteous." Chap. viii. 3, "God sending his own Son, in the likeness of sinful flesh, and for sin condemned sin in the flesh;" ver. 4, "That the righteousness of the law might be fulfilled in us." 2 Cor. v. 21, "That we might be made the righteousness of God in him." Gal. ii. 20, "I am crucified with Christ." And it affords a solid answer for believers, unto the law's demand of obedience and suffering for life and salvation.

3. Believers are justified immediately, by the righteousness of Christ, without any righteousness of their own intervening; even as all men are condemned, upon Adam's sin, before they have done any good or evil in their own persons: Rom. v. 18, "As by the offence of one, judgment came upon all men to condemnation; even so by the righteousness of one, the free gift came upon all men unto justification of life." And thus believers are righteous before God with the self same righteousness which was wrought by Jesus Christ, in his fulfilling the covenant. The which righteousness is not imputed to them in its effects only; so as their faith, repentance, and sincere obedience, are therefore accepted as their evangelical righteousness, on which they are justified: but it is imputed to them in itself, even as Adam's sin was.

4. The covenant of grace is absolute, and not conditional to us. For being made with Christ, as representative of his seed, all the conditions of it were laid on him, and fulfilled by him. Wherefore all that remains of it to be accomplished, is, the fulfilling of the promises unto him and his spiritual seed; even as it would have been in the case of the first covenant, if once the first Adam had fulfilled the condition thereof.

5. The covenant of grace is a contrivance of infinite wisdom and love, worthy to be embraced by poor sinners, as well ordered in all things and sure, 2 Sam. xxiii. 5. O admirable contrivance of help for a desperate case! Wonderful contrivance of a covenant of God with them who were incapable of standing in the presence of his holi-

ness, or of performing the least condition for life and salvation! A new bargain for the relief of lost sinners made on the highest terms with those who were not able to come up to the lowest terms! Infinite wisdom found out the way, to wit, by a representative. The love of the Father engaged him to propose the representation; and the love of the Son engaged him to accept of it. Thus God had one, with whom he might contract with the safety of his honour; and who was able to fulfil the covenant, to the reparation of the injuries done to his glory: and sinners also had one able to act for them, and to purchase salvation for them at the hand of a holy just God. So a sure covenant was made, and a firm foundation laid, upon which God laid the weight of his honour, and on which sinners may safely lay their whole weight: "Therefore thus saith the Lord God, Behold, I lay in Zion a sure foundation: he that believeth, shall not make haste," Isa. xxviii. 16; "shall not be ashamed," Rom. ix. 33.

6. *Lastly*, The way to enter personally into the covenant of grace so as to partake of the benefits thereof, unto salvation, is, to unite with Christ the head of the covenant by faith. Being thus ingrafted into him, ye shall partake of all that happiness which is secured to Christ mystical, in the everlasting covenant: even as through your becoming children of Adam, by natural generation, ye are personally entered into the first covenant, so as to fall under that sin and death which passed upon all men, by the breach thereof, Rom. v. 12.

III. OF THE PARTY CONTRACTED AND UNDERTAKEN FOR.

As the party contractor and undertaker on man's side, in the covenant of grace, was a representative; so the party contracted and undertaken for, was represented by him. And that these two, namely, the represented, and those contracted for, are of equal latitude, is plain from the nature of the thing: for these whom one represents in a covenant, he contracts for in that covenant; and those for whom one contracts in a covenant made with him as representative, are represented by him in that covenant. Thus it was in the covenant of the first Adam, who was a figure of Christ the head of the second covenant. In it, those whom Adam contracted for, he represented; and those whom he represented, he contracted for: he represented his natural seed only, and for them alone he contracted: therefore those whom the second Adam contracted for, he represented; and whom he represented, he contracted for.

Now, the party represented and contracted for, by our Lord Jesus Christ, in the covenant of grace, was the elect of mankind; being a certain number of mankind, chosen from eternity to everlasting life; "children partakers of flesh and blood, which God gave to Christ," Heb. ii. 13, 14. In their person he stood, making this covenant with his Father; in their name he acted, striking this bargain with him, as a surety to obey the law, and satisfy justice.

And this I shall, in the first place, confirm; and then shall inquire how the elect were considered in this covenant and federal representation.

First, That the elect were the party represented, or contracted and undertaken for, in the covenant of grace, appears from the following grounds.

1. The party with whom the covenant was made, is in the text called God's chosen; as representing and contracting for all the chosen or elect: even as the first man was called Adam or man, as representing and contracting for all mankind in his covenant. For, as the apostle teacheth, Heb. ii. 11, "He—and they—are all of one;" not only of one nature, but also of one body, to wit, the election; Christ is the head elect, Isa. xlii. 1, they the body elect, Eph. v. 23. Therefore they go under one name, principally belonging to him, and then to them by participation with him. Thus he is also called Abraham's seed, as representing all the spiritual seed of Abraham, that is, the elect, Gal. iii. 16, "And to thy seed which is Christ;" and the seed of the woman, as opposed to the serpent's seed; and under that name also the elect are comprehended; they, and they only, being the party betwixt whom and the serpent with his seed, God puts the enmity, according to the promise, Gen. iii. 15.

2. Those whom Christ represented and contracted for in the covenant of grace, are the heavenly men: 1 Cor. xv. 47, 48, "The first man is of the earth, earthy: the second man is the Lord from heaven. As is the earthy, such are they also that are earthy; and as is the heavenly, such are they also that are heavenly." Now, the heavenly men, belonging to Christ the second man, are none other but the elect. For they are contra-distinguished to the earthy men, belonging to the first man; to wit, all mankind taken into the first covenant in Adam: and therefore they are the elect men, taken into the second covenant, in the second Adam. Again, the heavenly men are those who shall bear the image of the heavenly man Christ, ver. 49; and such are the elect, and they alone. And, finally, they are those to whom Christ is, in respect of efficacy, a quickening spirit: for "as is the heavenly, such are they also that are heavenly." As Adam's deadly efficacy goes as wide as his representation did in the first covenant, reaching all mankind his natural seed, and them only; so Christ's quickening efficacy goes as wide as his representa-

tion did in the second covenant, reaching all the elect, his spiritual seed, and them only: and if it did not, some would be deprived of the benefit which was purchased and paid for, by the surety, in their name: the which is not consistent with the justice of God.

3. They whom Christ represented and contracted for in the covenant, are his seed, his spiritual seed: Gal. iii. 16. "Now to Abraham and his seed were the promises made. He saith—and to thy seed, which is Christ." Psalm lxxxix. 3, 4, "I have sworn unto David my servant. Thy seed will I establish for ever." In the covenants typical of the covenant of grace, the parties represented were the seed of the representatives they were made with, as was cleared before: and in the first Adam's covenant, his natural seed were the represented. Wherefore, in the second Adam's covenant, his spiritual seed are the represented. Now, Christ's spiritual seed are the elect, and none other; for they are those whom he begets with the word of truth, Jam. i. 18. and are born again (1 Pet. i. 23.) unto him in their regeneration; whom therefore he sees as his seed, with his own image on them, Isa. liii. 10. They are the travail of his soul, who, sooner or later, are, all of them, justified, ver. 11. They are the seed that shall serve him, Psalm xxii. 30; which shall be established and endure for ever, namely, in a state of happiness, Psalm lxxxix. 4, 29, 36.

4. *Lastly*, Christ was in the covenant of grace Israel-representative, according to that text, Isa. xlix. 3, "Thou art my servant, O Israel, in whom I will be glorified." Now, Israel the collective body, is the elect, Rom. ix. 6, "They are not all Israel which are of Israel:" therefore the elect were the party represented and contracted for in the covenant. So those whom Christ took with him into the bond of his covenant, are described to be the seed of Abraham: Heb. ii. 16, "For verily he took not on him the nature of angels; but he took on him the seed of Abraham:" or rather as it is read in the margin of our Bibles, more agreeable to the original, "He taketh not hold of angels, but, of the seed of Abraham he taketh hold." The original word signifies, to take hold of a thing running away, or falling down; and in the same manner of construction, it is used of Christ's catching hold of Peter sinking in the water, Matth. xiv. 31. Fallen angels and men were both run away from God, and sinking in the sea of his wrath: and Christ with the bond of the covenant, takes hold of men; but not of the fallen angels; them he leaves to sink unto the bottom. All the seed of Adam was sinking, as well as the seed of Abraham, which is but a part of the seed of Adam, even some of all mankind: but Christ is not said to have taken hold of the seed of Adam, that is, all man-

kind; but of the seed of Abraham, that is, all the elect, or the spiritual Israel, called the house of Jacob, Luke i. 33. Accordingly it is observable, that the first time the covenant of grace was heard in the world, the discourse was directed to the serpent, by way of narration, Gen. iii. 14, 15; not to Adam, as the first covenant was, chap. ii. 16, 17, that Adam might know, he was to come in here as a private person only, and not as a public person with his seed. And for this cause also, our Lord Jesus is not simply called Adam, or man; but the last Adam, and the second man, whose seed differs from that of the first man, as Abraham's seed from Adam's seed: but he is simply called Israel, without any epithet at all: and his seed is plainly determined to be the elect, Isa. xlv. 25, "In the Lord shall all the seed of Israel be justified;" even as in the first man all the seed of Adam was condemned, Rom. v. 18. For as the first man was simply called Adam or man, because, in the first covenant, he was a compend of all mankind; he was all men in law-reckoning, they being all represented by him: so Jesus Christ was a compend of all Israel, that is, all the elect; he was all Israel in law-reckoning, they being all represented by him. And thus we have the true ground of the universality of that expression, Isa. liii. 6. "The Lord, hath laid on him the iniquity of us all;" *i. e.* of all Israel that is to say, all the elect. The which is confirmed by a parallel text, bearing the type, whereof this hath the antitype, viz. Lev. xvi. 21, "And Aaron shall lay both his hands upon the head of the live-goat, and confess over him all the iniquities of the children of Israel, and all their transgressions in all their sins, putting them upon the head of the goat." For as Israel was a people entertained with types, so they themselves were indeed a typical people.

Secondly, We are to inquire, how the elect were considered in this covenant and federal representation. And therein they came under a threefold consideration.

1. They were considered as sinners, lost, ruined, and undone in Adam; lost sheep of the house of Israel, Matt. xv. 24. In the first covenant, the whole flock of mankind was put under the hand of one shepherd, to wit, Adam; but he, losing himself, lost all the flock, and was never able to recover so much as one of them again. God had, from all eternity, put a secret mark on some of them, whereby he distinguished them from the rest, 2 Tim. ii. 19, "Having this seal, The Lord knoweth them that are his." And them also he saw among others, gone away from their pasture, wandering as waifs and strays, a prey to every devourer: but, in order to their being sought out, and returned, and kept in safety for ever, the new covenant was entered into with another shepherd, even our

Lord Jesus Christ: and they are put under his hand, as the shepherd of Israel. In Adam's representation in the covenant of works, the party represented was considered as an upright seed, Eccl. vii. 29: but in Christ's representation in the covenant of grace, the party represented was considered as a corrupt sinful mass, laden with guilt, under the wrath of God and curse of the law. And who would have represented such a company, putting himself in their room and stead? But free love engaged our Lord Jesus to it. So the holy one of God represented wretched sinners; the beloved of the Father represented the cursed company.

2. They were considered also as utterly unable to help themselves, in whole or in part; as being without strength, Rom. v. 6. They were debtors, but quite unable to pay off one farthing of the debt: they were criminals, but quite unable to bear their own punishment, to the satisfaction of justice: had it lain on them to have paid the debt, or borne the punishment, they behoved to have sunk under the load for ever. So it was necessary they should have one to represent them, taking the burden upon him for them all.

3. *Lastly*, They were considered withal as the objects of eternal, sovereign, and free love, given to Christ by his Father. The Father loved them, John xvii. 23, and therefore gave them to Christ, ver. 6. The Son loved them, Eph. v. 2; and accepting of the gift, represented them in the covenant, as a father his own children, Isa. ix. 6, "His name shall be called—The everlasting Father." Compare Heb. ii. 13, "Behold, I, and the children which God hath given me." It was owing to this free love, and mere good pleasure, that they, and not others in the same condemnation, by the breach of the first covenant, were represented and contracted for by Jesus Christ, in the second; that their names were put in the eternal contract, while the names of others were left out. They were his Father's choice, and his own choice; so he became their representative.

From what is said concerning the party represented and contracted for, we make the following inferences.

Inf. 1. There is a sovereign freedom of the love of God appearing in the second covenant, the covenant of grace. And it appears especially in two things, (1.) In that there was a love towards fallen man, and not towards fallen angels, Tit. iii. 4, whereby it came to pass, that men, and not devils, were taken hold of, represented, and contracted for, by Jesus Christ, in the covenant, Heb. ii. 16. Doubtless he could have contracted for the one, as well as for the other: but sovereignty passed by fallen angels, and caught hold of men; howbeit the former were, in their own nature, the more worthy and excellent creatures. But in all the dispensation of grace, there is no respect to creature-worth; all is owing to the mere good pleasure of God, who hath mercy on whom he will have mercy. (2.) It appears in that there was an electing love of men; whereby it came to pass, that some men, and not all men, were represented and contracted for in the covenant. All men were alike by nature; and there was nothing in one more than in another, to recommend him: but free love pitched on objects altogether unlovely; and sovereign love pitches on some such objects, passing by others of the same condition: "Even so, Father, for so it seemed good in thy sight," Matth. xi. 26. The vessels of honour and the vessels of dishonour, are both made of the same sinful lump: a mystery that must be resolved into sovereign will and pleasure, Rom. ix. 21, "Hath not the potter power over the clay, of the same lump to make one vessel unto honour, and another unto dishonour?" But say not, that this disparageth the federal representation of the second Adam, that he represented only some of mankind, whereas the first Adam represented all mankind. For as it is more to be surety for a vast sum, for one man who neither hath, nor can give any thing at all wherewithal to pay his debt, than to be surety for a hundred such as have abundance of their own; so it was more for Jesus Christ to contract and undertake for one sinner, than for Adam to contract for a righteous world. And still it holds true, that where sin abounded, grace did much more abound, Rom. v. 20, for it is more by far to save one than to ruin many. Meanwhile those represented by Christ in the second covenant, are "a great multitude, which no man could number," Rev. vii. 9, even as "the stars of heaven," Gen. xv. 5. Rom. iv. 18.

Inf. 2. There is no universal redemption, nor universal atonement. Jesus Christ died not for all and every individual person of mankind; but for the elect only. The contrary doctrine may consist with the opinion which holds the covenant of redemption, and the covenant of grace, to be two distinct covenants; the former made with Christ, and the latter with believers; the condition of the one undertaken and performed by him, the condition of the other undertaken and performed by us. Accordingly that opinion concerning the covenant, is readily embraced by Universalists of different denominations. But that doctrine is utterly inconsistent with this account of the covenant, which doth at once overthrow universal redemption or atonement, together with the federal conditionality of our holiness and good works, in the covenant of grace. For if the covenant of grace was made with Christ as a representative, and the elect only were the party represented by him in it; then surely the conditions of the covenant, his doing and dying, were accomplished for them only; and he died for no other: as when one hath entered into a bond of suretyship, his payment of that bond can never be reckoned a payment of their debt, whose names were not in the bond, and whom he was not surety for.

Inf. 3. and *last*, Whoever they be that reject the covenant of grace offered to them in the gospel, and so perish; all God's elect shall infallibly be entered personally into it, and be saved. Like as all those whom Adam represented in the covenant of works, have been, are, or shall be brought personally into that covenant, and sin and death pass upon them, Rom. v. 12; even so all those whom Christ represented in the covenant of grace, have been, are, or shall be brought personally into this covenant, and partake of righteousness and life, vers. 18, 19. Our Lord Jesus has fulfilled the conditions of the covenant for them whom he represented; and it would neither be suitable to the justice of God, nor to the wisdom of Christ the party contracting with him, that he should represent, contract, and fulfil the conditions, for any who shall never enjoy the benefit of the contract. Wherefore, since there are who, by a purpose of God that cannot be frustrated, shall, without peradventure, be brought personally into this covenant; and ye who hear the gospel, having the means for compassing that end used towards you, do stand as fair for it as any; this may encourage you to come to Christ, and take hold of the covenant. Bestir yourselves therefore, O sinners, to take hold of the covenant of grace, which is offered to you in the gospel; and come ye to Christ by faith, thereby winding yourselves personally into the bond of this covenant, and the communion thereof.

Objection. "But I fear I am none of those whom Christ represented in the covenant of grace; how then can I take hold of it by believing?" Answer. Though your name were the first name that the Lamb wrote down in his book of life; yet you nor no man can know, that it is there at all until that you have by believing taken hold of the covenant. 2 Pet. i. 10, "Make your calling and election sure;" but first your calling, and then your election. And, on the other hand, though you were a monster of all manner of wickedness, and had all the desperate marks of a castaway about you, except that one only, the sin against the Holy Ghost, you nor no man can know that you were not represented in the covenant: Matt. xii. 31. "All manner of sin and blasphemy shall be forgiven unto men: but the blasphemy against the Holy Ghost shall not be forgiven unto men." Wherefore that matter is an absolute secret to you, which, in this case, you are not to meddle to determine in: for "the secret things belong unto the Lord our God: but those things which are revealed, belong unto us," Deut. xxix. 29. Neither does your warrant to believe and to lay hold on the covenant, any manner of way depend on it: for the reprobate have as good and fair a revealed warrant to believe and take hold of the covenant of grace as the elect have, else they could not be condemned for unbelief, and not taking hold of the covenant. Be what you will, since you are certainly a sinner of mankind, your warrant is uncontestable, according to the word: "For God so loved the world, that he gave his only begotten Son, that whosoever believeth in him, should not perish, but have everlasting life," John iii. 16. "This is his commandment, that we should believe on the name of his Son Jesus Christ," 1 John iii. 23. Wherefore believe ye, and take hold of the covenant for yourselves; so shall ye know your election, and your representation in the covenant, by the effects thereof.

This difficulty cast in the way of a sinner sensible of his need of Christ, to beat him off from believing on Christ, is a dangerous device and temptation of the devil. But do you repel it, saying, O enemy of my salvation, it is true, I do not know whether Christ represented me or not, in the eternal covenant; neither am I obliged nor concerned to know it, in order to my taking hold of that covenant: but one thing I know assuredly, namely, that the covenant, in the free promise of life and salvation, upon the ground of Christ's obedience and death allenarly, is held out to me, even to me, to be believed, trusted to, and rested upon, by me, even by me; and therefore I will believe, and lay hold on it; and, upon the infallible ground of the faithfulness of God in the promise, "Whosoever believeth, shall not perish, but have everlasting life," I will assuredly conclude, that it shall be made out to me.

Question. But are there no marks or signs whereby a poor sinner may know himself to be one of those who were represented by Christ in the second covenant, and whose names he put in the bond of suretiship that he gave to his Father from eternity? Answer. Yea, there are: but then they are such, as although the having of them will prove a man to have been represented by Jesus Christ in the eternal covenant; yet the want of them will not prove a man not to have been represented therein, forasmuch as what one has not now, he may come to have afterwards. And, under this limitation, I offer these two marks of the thing in question.

Mark 1. A deliberate and cordial complacency in the covenant. As it was with the representative from eternity; so it is in time, in that matter, with the represented, when once by grace they become capable of personal consenting: there is a deliberate and cordial complacency in the covenant being proposed, Psalm xl. 7, "Then said I," ver. 8, "thy law is within my heart." The children of men discover themselves to be Adam's natural seed, represented by him in the covenant of works, by the inclination and bent of their hearts towards that covenant. There is such a bias to that covenant hung upon the minds of men naturally, that do and live, or work and win, is the religion of all natural men, so far as they have any practical religion at all: and they cannot be brought off from it but by the power of renewing grace. Even so the elect of God discover themselves to be Christ's spiritual seed, represented by him in the covenant of grace, by their deliberate and cordial complacency in this covenant. The heart touched with divine grace says of it, "This is all my salvation, and all my desire," 2 Sam. xxiii. 5. The new bias hung on their minds by renewing grace, carries them to a hearty approbation, relish and liking of the new covenant held forth in the gospel; they are well pleased with the parties-contractors, the representative and representation in it; the conditions and promises of it; the administrator, the administration, and order thereof. In a word, the covenant is in their eyes a faultless contrivance; there is nothing in it they would have out, and there is nothing out of it they would have in. So there they cast anchor for their own souls. But it is not so with others: 1 Pet. ii. 7, "Unto you therefore which believe he is precious: but unto them which be disobedient, the stone which the builders disallowed, the same is made the head of the corner;" ver. 8, "and a stone of stumbling, and a rock of offence, even to them which stumble at the word, being disobedient, whereunto also they were appointed.

Mark 2. The image of Christ begun to be drawn on the soul, together with a longing for the perfecting thereof; 1 Cor. xv. 48. "As is the heavenly, such are they also that are heavenly." Ver. 49, "And as we have borne the image of the earthy, we shall also bear the image of the heavenly." Like as all whom Adam represented, when he entered into the covenant of works in paradise, do afterwards, every one in his time, personate Adam, looking as like him as ever child was like a father, acting even as he acted, as I shewed elsewhere: so all whom Christ represented in the covenant of grace from eternity, do in time put on Christ, Gal. iii. 27, personating him, and representing him in another sense, namely, bearing his image, and "walking even as he walked," 1 John ii. 6. It is a promise of the covenant to our Lord Jesus, Isa. liii. 10, "He shall see his seed," to wit, as one sees a new-born babe. But do not others so see them too? Yea, indeed they do. Satan and wicked men see them, as rebels and traitors do with grudge and hatred see a new-born prince heir to the crown. The godly see them, as in that case the princesses do with a particular satisfaction see their new-born brother. But our Lord Jesus Christ himself sees them, as the king, the father of the babe, does with a peculiar satisfaction see him as his own son, and his own picture. Meanwhile, as Adam's children do not open out all at once what of old Adam is in them, but by degrees as they grow up; but they are still longing for the perfection thereof, when they shall be grown men, so Christ's children are but imperfect in this life as in the state of childhood; but they are longing to arrive at "perfection, at the measure of the stature of the fulness of Christ, the principle of which they have in them, Eph. iv. 13.

Thus far of the first head, the parties in the covenant of grace.

HEAD II.

THE MAKING OF THE COVENANT OF GRACE.

Having considered the parties in the covenant of grace, we come now to take a view of the making of that covenant betwixt the parties contracting therein. And here we find ourselves at the fountain-head of the salvation of lost sinners, the origin and rise of the glorious plan, laid from eternity in the secret council of the ever-blessed Trinity, for remedy of man's misery. And this is a manifold mystery, the several folds of which we are not able fully to discover. With God it was all one piece, if I may so phrase it; for with all things are together and at once; and not one thing before, and another after, as with us. Howbeit, we cannot conceive of it but in parcels; first one piece of the mystery and then another; and that because of the weakness of our capacity, as we are creatures; and much more, as we are creatures under much spiritual darkness. Wherefore we must of necessity address ourselves to the consideration of it in parcels; but still remembering, we are in the eternal mystery, transacted in the eternal decree of the holy Trinity all at once, by one eternal act of the divine will; in which, nevertheless, we are allowed to conceive a certain order, since otherwise we cannot take up the mystery.

We have already seen, that the Father, the party-contractor on Heaven's side, is in that matter to be considered as an offended God; but purposing to manifest the glory of his mercy in the salvation of some of mankind lost; yet withal as a just God, who cannot but give sin a just recompense: and also, that Jesus Christ, the party-contractor on man's side, is to be considered therein as the last or second Adam, representative of a seed. Wherefore, first of all, we are to inquire, How Christ the Son of God became second Adam? and then, How the covenant was made with him as such? the former being as it were preliminary to the latter.

First, How Christ the Son of God became second Adam? This we may take up in two things.

1. The Father willed and designed, that his own Son, the eternal Word, should, for the purpose of mercy towards mankind lost, take on their nature, and become man. He saw that sacrifice and offering would not answer the case; the debt was greater than to be paid at that rate; the redemption of souls could not be managed but by a person of infinite dignity: wherefore, having purposed that the darling attribute of mercy should be illustrated in the case of lost mankind, he willed the human nature to be united in time to the divine nature, in the person of the Son.

And hereunto the Son, as the eternal Word, the second person of the glorious Trinity, having no nearer relation to man than as his sovereign Lord Creator, readily agreed: Heb. x. 5, "Sacrifice and offering thou wouldst not, but a body hast thou prepared me."—Ver. 7, "Then said I, Lo, I come (in the volume of the book it is written of me) to do thy will, O God." The eternal Word consented to be made flesh, that all flesh might not perish: he consented to become man, to take unto a personal union with himself a human nature, to wit, a true body and a reasonable soul, according to the eternal destination of his Father. This was an instance of amazing condescension. The highest monarch's consent to lay aside his robes of majesty, to clothe himself with rags, and become a beggar, is not to be compared with it. Nay the highest angel's consent to become a worm, is not to be named in one day with the eternal Son of God, the Father's equal, his consenting to become man: for the distance between the divine nature and the human is infinite; whereas the distance between the angelic nature, and the nature of worms of the earth, is but finite.

Now, the effect of this was, that hereby the Son of God was constituted substantial Mediator, or Mediator in respect of nature, between God and man. Being from eternity God equal with the Father, he so stood related to heaven: and having from eternity consented to become man, he so stood related to earth: for though he did not actually take on him the nature of man until the fulness of time appointed by the Father; yet, forasmuch as he had from eternity consented to take it on, and it was impossible that his consent should miss to take effect, he was recokened in law, to all intents and purposes thereof, as if he had actually been incarnate. A type of this his substantial mediation was Jacob's ladder, which was "set upon the earth, and the top of it reached to heaven," Gen. xxviii. 12. A clear emblem of the divine and human nature in Christ, through whom, as substantial Mediator, there was a way opened towards a communication for peace between heaven and earth. Accordingly our Lord Jesus applies it to himself: John i. 51, "Hereafter you shall see heaven open, and the "angels of God ascending and descending upon the Son of man;" to wit, as on Jacob's ladder, Gen. xxviii. 12.

2. The Father chose him to be head of the election; to be the last Adam, federal head and representative of such as sovereign pleasure should pitch upon to be vessels of mercy, and inrolled in the book of life; a head and representative with whom he might make the new covenant for life and salvation to them.

And to this also he readily agreed, consenting to be the last or second Adam, head and representative of the election; to sustain their persons, and transact in their name: Isa. xliii. 1, "Behold—mine elect in whom my soul delighteth." Psalm lxxxx. 19, "I have exalted one chosen out of the people." 1 Cor. xv. 47, "The second man is the Lord from heaven." The breach between God and man was greater than to be done away by a mere intermessenger, who travelling between parties at variance, reconciles them with bare words. There could be no covenant of peace betwixt God and sinners without reparation of damages done to the honour of God through sin, and without honouring of the holy law by an exact obedience: but these things being quite beyond their reach, Christ the Son of God saith, "Lo, I come; I am content to take their place, and put myself in their room as a second Adam."

Now, the effect of this was, that hereby he was constituted last Adam, or the second man, 1 Cor. xv. 47; and official Mediator, or Mediator in respect of office, between God and man, 1 Tim. ii. 5, 6, "There is one God, and one Mediator between God and men, the man Christ Jesus; who gave himself a ransom for all." Being called of his Father unto that office, and having embraced the call thereto, he was invested with the office, and treated with as such, before the world began, Tit. i. 2. And indeed he, and he only, was fit for it. The two families of heaven and earth being at war, there could be no peace between them but through a Mediator. But where could a mediator be found to interpose between such parties, who would not either have been too high, or else too low, in respect of one of the parties at variance? Man or angels would have been too low, in respect of God; and an unveiled God would have been too high, in respect of sinful men, unable to bear intercourse with such heavenly majesty. Wherefore the Son of God, that he might be fit to mediate; as he being God equal with the Father, was high enough in respect of the party offended; so he consented to become low enough in respect of the party offending, by his becoming man.

Secondly, It is to be inquired, How the covenant was made with Christ as second Adam? And this also may be taken up in two things.

1. The Father designed a certain number of lost mankind, as it were by name, to be the constituent members of that body chosen to life, of which body Christ was the designed head; and he gave them to him for that end: Phil. iv. 3, "My fellow-labourers, whose names are in the book of life." John xvii. 6, "Thine they were, and thou gavest them me." These were a chosen company, whom sovereign free grace picked out from among the rest of mankind, on a purpose of love, and gave to the second Adam for a seed; on which account they are said to have been chosen in him, Eph. i. 4; being in the decree of election laid upon him as the foundation-stone, to be built upon him, and obtain salvation by him, 1 Thess. v. 9; which decree, as it relates to the members elect, is therefore called the book of life; being as it were the roll which the Father gave to the second Adam, the head-elect, containing the names of those designed to be his seed, to receive life by him.

Now, our Lord Jesus standing as second Adam, head of the election, to wit, such as sovereign pleasure should pitch upon to be vessels of mercy, did accept of the gift of the particular persons elected or chosen by his Father: John xvii. 6, "Thine they were, and thou gavest them me." Ver. 10, "And thine are mine." Like as the first Adam, in the making of the first covenant, stood alone without actual issue, yet had destinated for him a numerous issue, to be comprehended with him in that covenant, to wit, all mankind; the which Adam did at least virtually accept: so a certain number of lost mankind being elected to life, God, as their original proprietor, gave them to Christ the appointed head, to be his members, and comprehended with him in the second covenant, though as yet none of them were in being; and he accepted of the gift of them, being well-pleased to take them in particular for his body mystical, for which he should covenant with his Father. And, in token thereof, he as it were received and kept as his own the book of life containing their names, which is therefore called the Lamb's book of life, Rev. xxi. 27.

2. The Father proposed to him as second Adam, the new covenant for life and salvation to them, in the full tenor, promises, and condition thereof; treating in him with all those particular persons of lost mankind elected unto life, and given to him, even as he treated with all mankind in Adam in the first covenant. The promises therein proposed, were indeed great and glorious; but withal the condition, or terms, on which they were proposed, were exceeding high.

Howbeit, as the first Adam, standing as head and representative of all his natural seed, entered into the first covenant with God, accepting the promise thereof, upon the terms and condition therein proposed, which he engaged to fulfil; so our Lord Jesus standing as second Adam, head and representative of the particular persons of lost mankind, by name elected to life, and given to him as his spiritual seed, entered into the second covenant with his Father; accepting the promises thereof, upon the terms and condition therein proposed; consenting and engaging to fulfil the same, for them. And thus the covenant of grace was made, and concluded, betwixt the Father and Christ the second Adam, from all eternity; being the second covenant, in respect of order and manifestation to the world, though it was first in being: 1 Cor. xv. 47, "The second man is the Lord from heaven." Isa. liii. 10, "When thou shalt make his soul an offering for sin, he shall see his seed." Tit. i. 2, "In hope of eternal life, which God that cannot lie, promised before the world began." Psalm xl. 6, "Sacrifice and offering thou didst not desire, mine ears hast thou opened"—7, "Then said I, Lo, I come"—8, "I delight to do thy will, O my God: yea, thy law is within my heart."

Now, Christ the second Adam, giving this consent, took upon him a threefold character, of unparallelled weight and importance; sisting himself, (1.) The Kinsman-redeemer in the covenant, (2.) The Surety of the covenant, and, (3.) The Priest of the covenant. The mediation of Christ doth indeed run through the whole of the covenant. And there are several other parts of that mediation, which respecting the promises of the covenant, do belong to the administration thereof. But these I have now mentioned, do respect the condition of the covenant, and so belong to the making thereof; under which head we shall consider them in order.

I. CHRIST THE KINSMAN-REDEEMER IN THE COVENANT.

OUR Lord Jesus Christ, the second Adam, giving his consent to the covenant, as proposed to him by the Father, sisted himself Kinsman-redeemer in the covenant: Job xix. 25, "I know that my Redeemer liveth, and that he shall stand at the latter day upon the earth."

Under the law, when a man was not able to act for himself, to assert and use his own right, one that was akin to him, had a right to act for him, coming in his room, and standing up in his right. And such a one was called his Goel; which properly signifies a Kinsman-redeemer. Hence that word is sometimes rendered a kinsman; as Numb. v. 8, "If the man have no (Goel) kinsman to recompense the trespass unto." Ruth iii. 12, "I am thy (Goel) near kinsman: howbeit there is a (Goel) kinsman nearer than I." Sometimes it is rendered a Redeemer; as Prov. xxiii. 11, "Their (Goel) Redeemer is mighty." Isa. xlvii. 4, "As for our (Goel) Redeemer, the Lord of hosts is his name." One's acting in that capacity, is called doing the kinsman's part, or redeeming, to wit, by right of kin, Ruth iii. 13; and iv. 6. Howbeit, such a one might refuse to do the kinsman's part; as Ruth's kinsman-redeemer did, who resigned his right to Boaz, and in token thereof drew off his own shoe, and gave it him, Ruth iv. 6, 7, 8.

Now, Christ the second Adam saw sinners, his ruined kinsmen quite unable to act for themselves. Not one of them all was able to redeem himself, and far less his brother. Withal, the angels, near akin to them in the rational world, durst not meddle with the redemption; being sure they could not have missed to mar their own inheritance thereby, nor have delivered their poor kinsmen neither. If he should have declined it, and drawn off his shoe to them, or to any other of the whole creation, there was none who durst have ventured to receive it, or his foot in it. "I looked," saith he, "and there was none to help; and I wondered that there was none to uphold: therefore mine own arm brought salvation," Isa. lxiii. 5. He took on himself the character of their Kinsman-redeemer; and of him as such Job speaks in the forecited passage, which I conceive to be thus expressed in the original: "I know, my Kinsman-redeemer liveth: and the latter one he shall stand up upon the dust." In which words Job comforts himself with a view of Christ as his Kinsman-redeemer living, even in his day, in respect of his divine nature; and as the latter or second one, (in opposition to the former or first, Exod. iv. 8, 9; Deut. xxiv. 3, 4.) namely, the latter or second Adam Redeemer, in opposition to the former or first Adam destroyer; firmly believing, that the one uniting to himself a human nature, should as sure stand up upon the dust of the earth, and do the kinsman's part for him; as the other, having the breath of life breathed into his nostrils, stood up upon it, and ruined all.

Now, there were four things the kinsman- redeemer was to do for his kinsman, unable to act for himself; all which Christ the second Adam undertook in the covenant.

1. He was to marry the widow of his deceased kinsman, to raise up seed to his brother. Hereof Boaz was put in mind by Ruth, chap. iii. 9, "I am Ruth thine handmaid; spread therefore thy skirt over thine handmaid, for thou art a near kinsman." Compare ver. 10—13; chap. iv. 10; and Ezek. xvi. 8. I spread my skirt over thee—and thou becamest mine." Our nature was in a comfortable and fruitful condition, while the image of God impressed thereupon in Adam, remained with it; but that image being removed, in the spiritual death caused by his sin, there ensued an absolute barrenness, as to the fruits of holiness, in our nature thus left. But our Kinsman-redeemer consented to marry the widow. Being to take to himself a human nature he undertook to take on our human nature in particular, taking his flesh of Adam's family. Thus was it provided, that his body should not be made of nothing, nor of any thing whatsoever that was not derived from Adam as its original. It was a low match indeed for him; and would have been so, even if the family of Adam had been in its primitive state and splendour: but now it was considered as in the depth of poverty and disgrace. Yet, being necessary for our redemption, he consented thereto, as our Kinsman-redeemer. Accordingly, in the fulness of time, he was made of a woman, a daughter of Adam's family, Gal. iv. 4, and so was a son of Adam, Luke iii. 23—38. Thus was a foundation laid for the mystical marriage of believers with him; which mystical marriage doth not belong to the condition and making of the covenant properly so called, but to the promise and administration of it, being a sinner's personal entrance thereinto. And the great end, in subordination to the glory of God, for which this more intimate union and match with our nature was gone into by our Kinsman-redeemer, was to render it again fruitful in the fruits of true holiness: and without it our nature had for ever remained under absolute barrenness in that point, even as the nature of fallen angels doth.

2. He was to redeem the mortgaged inheritance of his poor kinsman, Lev. xxv. 25, "If thy brother be waxen poor, and hath sold away some of his possession, and if any of his kin come to redeem it, then shall he redeem that which his brother sold;" or rather, "then shall come in his kinsman-redeemer, that is near unto him; and he shall redeem that which his brother sold." Our father Adam waxing poor through the deceitful dealing of the tempter with him, quite sold away the inheritance of eternal life for a mor-

sel of forbidden fruit: and his children waxing poorer still, through their own personal fault, had set themselves farther and farther from it. They could not have raised amongst them all, what would have redeemed so much as one man's part of it. Howbeit, except it was redeemed, they could never have had access to it. Wherefore the second Adam, as Kinsman-redeemer, took the burden of the redemption on himself, and agreed to pay the price of that purchase; "dying for us, that we might live together with him," 1 Thess. v. 10.

3. He was to ransom his poor kinsman in bondage, paying the price of his redemption: Lev. xxv. 47, "If thy brother wax poor, and sell himself," ver. 48, "After that he is sold, he may be redeemed again; one of his brethren may redeem him." Ver. 52, "According unto his years shall he give him again the price of his redemption." Being sold in the loins of our first father, we were brought into bondage under the curse of the law. So we are by nature the law's bond-men, and consequently slaves to sin and Satan, never to have been released without a ransom, the full worth of so many souls. This ransom was stated in the covenant; to wit, that the Kinsman-redeemer should give himself a ransom for his poor kinsmen: and he agreed to it, for purchasing their liberty, 1 Tim. ii. 5, 6. The ransom was great, soul for soul, body for body; a person of infinite dignity for his poor kinsmen in bondage. But he consented to take on him the form of a servant, that he might be set free; to have his ear bored at the law's door-post, that they might be delivered out of their bondage.

4. *Lastly*, He was to avenge the blood of his slain kinsman on the slayer: Deut. xix. 12, "The elders of his city shall send and fetch him thence, and deliver him into the hand of the (Goel) avenger of blood, that he may die." Our Kinsman-redeemer saw all his poor kindred slain men. And the devil was the murderer, John viii. 44. He had ministered poison to them in the loins of their first parent; yea, he had smitten them to death, killed them with an arrow shot through the eye. But no avenger of their blood could be found, till the second Adam, as their Kinsman-redeemer, did, in the second covenant undertake the avenging of it. Meanwhile, the murderer had the power of death, Heb. ii. 14; and "the sting of death is sin, and the strength of sin is the law," 1 Cor. xv. 56. Wherefore there was no disarming and destroying of the murderer, without taking the sting out of death which he had the power of. And that was not to be done, but by removing the guilt of sin, whereby sinners were bound over to death: neither was this to be done, but by satisfying the law, whose awful sanction of death strongly kept fast

the guilt of death on the sinners. These were the iron gates to be broke through, ere the Kinsman-redeemer, the avenger of blood, could get at the murderer. But the mighty Redeemer undertook, by his own death and sufferings, to satisfy the law; and by that means to remove the strength of sin; and by this means again, to take away the sting of death: and so by his own death to destroy the murderer that had the power of death; and thus to avenge the blood of his slain kinsman upon him, Heb. ii. 14. So did Samson, a type of our Kinsman-Redeemer, avenge Israel of the Philistines their oppressors, pulling down the house on the Philistines, and dying himself to destroy them, Judg. xvi.

II. CHRIST THE SURETY OF THE COVENANT.

Christ the second Adam consenting to the covenant, sisted himself also surety of it: Heb. vii. 22, "By so much was Jesus made a surety of a better testament;" or rather, as others read it, of a better covenant. A surety is one who undertakes for another, obliging himself whether for paying his debt, civil or criminal, or for his performing a deed. That we may then rightly understand Christ's suretiship, it is necessary we consider, 1. For whom, 2. For what he became surety in the covenant.

First, For whom Christ became surety in the covenant. I find two things advanced on this head, namely, (1.) That he became surety for God to sinners; and (2.) Surety for sinners to God. To the first of these, the Socinians restrain Christ's suretiship, denying the second; and so overthrow the foundation of our salvation. But all orthodox divines agree, in that the second of these is the main thing in it. Some of them indeed make no difficulty of admitting, that Christ became surety for God to sinners, as well as surety for sinners to God, undertaking, on God's part, that all the promises shall be made good to the seed, even to all that believe. There is no question, but God's promises are, in respect of his infallible truth and veracity, most firm and sure in themselves, and cannot miss to be performed: but we being guilty creatures, are slow of heart to believe; and therefore do need what may make them more sure to us, or assure our hearts they shall be performed to us. And for this cause he hath given us his word of promise under his hand in the holy scriptures, and an earnest of the promised inheritance, Eph. i. 14; the seal of the Spirit, ver. 13; 2 Cor. i. 22: the sacramental seals, Rom. iv. 11; yea, and his solemn oath too, in the matter, to shew unto the heirs of promise the immutability of his counsel, Heb. vi. 17. And if Jesus Christ is surety for God to us, it is no doubt for the same end.

But I doubt if the holy scripture calls Christ a surety in that sense at all. In the forecited passage, Heb. vii. 22, the only text wherein Christ is expressly called a surety, it is evident, that his suretiship therein mentioned, respects his priestly office, wherein he deals with God for us; ver. 20, "And in as much as not without an oath he was made priest," 21. (—"by him that said unto him, The Lord sware, and will not repent, Thou art a priest for ever after the order of Melchisedec)" ver. 22, "By so much was Jesus made a surety of a better testament." But his suretiship for God to us, cannot relate to his priestly office, but to his kingly office, in respect of which all power is given to him in heaven and in earth; and consequently a power to see that all the promises be performed to his people. And therefore his suretiship mentioned in that text, is for us to God, and not for God to us. It is but in other two texts only, as far as I have observed, that we read of suretiship relative to the case between God and a sinner: and in both of them, the suretiship is not to the sinner, but for him. They are Psalm cxix. 122, "Be surety for thy servant for good;" and Job xvii. 3. "Put me in a surety with thee." The original phraseology or expression, is the same in the latter text as in the former; and the same in them both, as in the case of Judah's suretiship for Benjamin, to his father, Gen. xliii. 9; and xliv. 32. Now, unless the sacred oracles go before us, in proposing Christ as a surety for God to us, I see no reason, why the being of such a thing at all should be yielded to the adversaries, who make such a pernicious use of it. As for the comfort that might arise from it to us, the same is fully secured, in that the whole administration of the covenant is committed into the hand of our Lord Jesus Christ; and he is the Trustee and Testator of the covenant or covenant-benefits; as shall be shown in due place.

But, without all peradventure, Christ the Mediator and second Adam, being surety in the covenant, for sinners to God; as the scriptures do abundantly declare: Psalm lxxxix. 19, "I have laid help upon one that is mighty." 1 Tim. ii. 5, "One Mediator between God and men, the man Christ Jesus;" ver. 6, "Who gave himself a ransom for all." 2 Cor. v. 21, "He hath made him to be sin for us, who knew no sin." Isa. liii. 6, "The Lord hath laid on him the iniquity of us all." Gal. iii. 13, "Christ hath redeemed us from the curse of the law, being made a curse for us." Isa. liii. 5, "He was wounded for our transgressions, he was bruised for our iniquities." The covenant of grace was made with the spiritual seed in Christ the second Adam, taking burden for them upon himself as their surety. And without a surety it could not have been made with them. For they were a company of broken men, owing a thousand times more than they were all worth: and their word in a new bargain for life and salvation was worth nothing; there could be no regard had to it in heaven. There was neither truth nor ability left them after the first covenant was broken. Behold their character in point of truth or veracity, Rom. iii. 4, "Let God be true, but every man a liar:" and in point of ability, chap. v. 6, "When we were yet without strength, in due time Christ died for the ungodly." The demands in this covenant were high, and quite above their ability to answer: and, besides, they themselves were false and fickle. They brake their word in the first covenant when able to have kept it; how could they be trusted in this new bargain, when their ability was gone? So there was an absolute necessity of a surety for them in it. And Jesus Christ became surety for them; so the new covenant, on which depends all their salvation, was made, and made sure.

Solomon tells us, That "he that is surety for a stranger, shall smart for it: and he that hateth suretiship, is sure," Prov. xi. 15. Our Lord Jesus knew very well, the burden he took on himself in his suretiship for sinners; the character of those whom he became surety for; and that he could have no relief from them; but his love to his Father's glory, and the salvation of sinners, engaged him in it, being perfectly sure to smart for it, as will appear from considering,

Secondly, For what he became surety in the covenant. Suretiship, in respect of the subject-matter of it, is of two sorts. 1. There is a suretiship for paying one's debt: Prov. xxii. 26, "Be not thou one of them that strike hands, or of them that are sureties for debts." 2. A suretiship for one's performing of a deed: chap. xx. 16, "Take his garment that is surety for a stranger; and take a pledge of him for a strange woman;" that is of him who is surety for her good behaviour; for she will leave them in the lurch.

Now, our Lord's suretiship for sinners was of the first sort. Christ as the second Adam consenting to the covenant, sisted himself surety for the debt of the seed represented by him. Their debt was by God's eternal fore-knowledge, stated from the broken covenant of works, in the whole latitude of the demands it had on them; and he became surety for it, striking hands with his Father to pay it completely, And,

1. He became surety for their debt of punishment, which they as sinners were liable in payment of, as the original phraseth it, 2 Thess. i. 9. That was the debt owing to the divine justice, for all and every one of their sins, original or actual. The demerit of their sins, as offences against an infinite God, was an infinite punishment.

They were liable to bear the pains of death, in the full latitude thereof; to suffer the force of revenging wrath, to the complete satisfaction of infinite justice, and full reparation of God's injured honour. This was their debt of punishment: a debt which they themselves could never have cleared, though paying to the utmost of their power, through the ages of eternity. But this their debt Christ became surety for, obliging himself to lay down his life for theirs which was lost in law: Psalm xl. 6, 7, "Sacrifice and offering thou didst not desire, mine ears hast thou opened—Then said I Lo, I come." John x. 15, "I lay down my life for the sheep." Ver. 18, "I lay it down of myself; I have power to lay it down, and I have power to take it again. This commandment have I received of my Father." Here is a suretiship that never had a match! David in a transport of grief for the death of his son Absalom, wishes he had died for him 2 Sam. xviii. 33; Reuben will venture the life of his two sons for Benjamin, Gen. xlii. 37; and Judah will venture his own for him, chap. xliii. 9, while yet there was hope that all would be safe: but our Lord Jesus deliberately pledgeth his own life for sinners, when it was beyond all peradventure, the precious pledge would be lost in the cause, and that the death he would suffer, would be a thousand deaths in one. Some have offered themselves sureties in capital causes, and embraced death, for their country or friends: and "peradventure for a good man some would even dare to die. But God commendeth his love towards us, in that while we were yet sinners, (and enemies), Christ died for us," Rom. v. 7, 8, 10.

Now, in the second Adam's suretiship for the criminal debt of his spiritual seed, there was not an ensuring of the payment thereof one way or other, only; as in simple cautionary: but there was an exchange of persons in law; Christ substituting himself in their room and taking the whole obligation on himself. This the free grace of God the creditor did admit, when he might have insisted, that the soul that sinned should die: and, a delay being withal granted as to the time of the payment, God thus manifested his forbearance, celebrated by the apostle, Rom. iii. 25. And, in virtue of that substitution, Christ became debtor in law, bound to pay that debt which he contracted not; to restore that which he took not away, Psalm lxix. 4. For, becoming surety for them, to the end there might be laid a foundation, in law and justice, for exacting their debt of punishment from him, there guilt was transferred on him, Isa. liii. 6. "The Lord laid on him the iniquity of us all." This was pointed at, in the laying of the hand on the head of the sacrifices under the law, especially on the head of the scape-goat, Lev. xvi. 21. "And Aaron shall lay both his hands on the head of the live goat, and confess over him all the iniquities of the children of Israel, and all their transgressions in all their sins, putting them upon the head of the goat." All the sins of all the elect were at once imputed to the surety, and so became his, as his righteousness becomes ours, namely, in law-reckoning, 2 Cor. v. 21. "For he hath made him to be sin for us who knew no sin; that we might be made the righteousness of God in him." And he himself speaks so of them, Psalm xl. 12. "Mine iniquities have taken hold upon me;" as several valuable interpreters do understand it, according as the apostle gives us direction, determining Christ himself to be the speaker in this Psalm, Heb. x. 5, 6, 7. He was indeed without sin inherent in him; but not without sin imputed to him, till in his resurrection he got up his discharge, having cleared the debt by his death and sufferings. Then was he justified in the Spirit, 1 Tim. iii. 16, and so shall appear the second time, without sin, Heb. ix. 28; the sin which was upon him, by imputation, the first time he appeared, being done away at his resurrection. This relation of our sin to Christ, is necessary from the nature of suretiship for debt; in which case, no body doubts but the debt becomes the surety's, when once he hath stricken hands for it. And how else could the law have justly proceeded against Christ? How could our punishment have been, in justice, inflicted on him, if he had not had such a relation to our sin? If the law could not charge our sin on him, in virtue of his own voluntary undertaking, it could have no ground in justice to inflict our punishment on him.

2. He became surety for their debt of duty or obedience; the which also is a debt according to the style of the holy scripture, Gal. v. 3, "A debter to do the whole law." The law as a covenant of works, though it was broken by them, and they had incurred the penalty thereof, yet neither lost its right, nor ceased to exact of them the obedience which at first it required of man, as the condition of life. They were still bound to perfect obedience, and on no lower terms could have eternal life, as our Lord taught the lawyer for his humiliation, Luke x. 28, "Thou hast answered right: this do, and thou shalt live." The paying of the debt of punishment might satisfy as to the penalty of the bond; but there is yet more behind, for him who will meddle in the affairs of the broken company. How shall the principal sum therein contained, be paid; namely, the debt of obedience to the law, for life and salvation? The honouring of God could not allow the quitting of it: and they were absolutely unable to pay one mite of it, that would have been current in heaven; forasmuch as they were without strength, Rom. v. 6, and dead in trespasses and sins, Eph. ii. 1, quite as unfit for

the doing part, as for the suffering part. But Christ became surety for this debt of theirs too, namely, the debt of obedience to the law as a covenant, which was, and is the only obedience to it for life; obliging himself to clear it by obeying in their room and stead, and fulfilling what the law could demand of them in this kind: Psalm xl. 7, 8, "Then said I, Lo, I come, I delight to do thy will, O my God: yea, thy law is within my heart." Matth. iii. 15, "Thus it becometh us to fulfil all righteousness." Chap. v. 17, "Think not that I am come to destroy the law, I am not come to destroy, but to fulfil."

And here also there was an exchange of persons in law, Christ substituting himself in their room, and taking their obligation on himself: in virtue of which, he became the law's debtor for that obedience owing by them; and this he himself solemnly owned, by his being circumcised, Luke ii. 21, according to that of the apostle, Gal. v. 3, "I testify again to every man that is circumcised, that he is a debtor to do the whole law." For becoming surety for them in this point also, he transferred on himself their state of servitude, whereby the law had a right to exact that debt of him, which they, upon the breach of the covenant of works, were liable in payment of.

For clearing of this, it is to be considered, that all mankind was by the first covenant, the covenant of works, constituted God's hired servants; and actually entered into that their service, in their head the first Adam. And in a token hereof, we are all naturally inclined in that character to deal with God; though by the fall we are rendered incapable to perform the duty of it, Luke xv. 19, "Make me as one of thy hired servants." The work they were to work, was perfect obedience to the holy law; the hire they were to have for their work, was life, Rom. x. 5, "The man that doth those things, shall live by them." The penalty of breaking away from their master, was bondage under the curse, Gal. iii. 10, "Cursed is every one that continueth not in all things which are written in the book of the law to do them." But violating that covenant of hired service, they brake away from their Lord and Master: so they not only lost all plea for the hire, but they became bond-men under the curse; still obliged to make out their service, and that, furthermore, in the misery of a state of servitude or bondage, Gal. iv. 24, "These are the two covenants; the one from the mount Sinai, which gendereth to bondage." Their falling under the curse inferred the loss of their liberty, and constituted them bond-men; as appears from the nature of the thing, and instances of the cursed in other cases, as Gen. ix. 25, "Cursed be Canaan; a servant of servants shall he be." Josh. ix. 23, "Now therefore ye" (namely, the Gibeonites) "are cursed, and there shall none of you be freed from being bond-men." The very ground being cursed, (Gen. iii. 17.) falls under bondage, according to the scripture, Rom. viii. 21.

Now, Christ saw all his spiritual seed in this state of servitude; but unable to bear the misery of it, or to fulfil the service: and he put himself in their room, as they were bond-men; transferring their state of servitude on himself, and so sisting himself a bond-servant for them.

The holy scripture sets this matter in a clear light. That is a plain testimony unto it, Phil. ii. 6, 7, 8, "Who being in the form of God—took upon him the form of a servant—and became obedient unto death, even the death of the cross." The form of a servant which he took upon him, was the form of a bond-servant. For so the word in the original properly signifies; being the same word that is constantly used in that New Testament phrase, which we read bond or free, or bond and free, 1 Cor. xii. 13; Gal. iii. 28; Eph. vi. 8; Col. iii. 11; Rev. xiii. 16. and xix. 18. And the apostle leads us to understand it so here, telling us, that this great surety-servant became obedient unto death, even the death of the cross. The which kind of death was a Roman punishment, called by them, the servile punishment, or punishment of bond-servants; because it was the death that bond-men malefactors were ordinarily doomed unto; freemen seldom, if ever, according to law. And forasmuch as his being in the form of God, denotes his being very God, having the very nature or essence of God; for the form is that which essentially distinguisheth things, and makes a thing to be precisely what it is; and this form is, according to the apostle, the foundation of his equality with God his Father, which nothing really different from the divine essence, can be: therefore his taking upon him the form of a bond-servant, must necessarily denote his becoming really a bond-servant, as really as ever man did, who was brought into bondage, or a state of servitude.

The Father solemnly declares the transferring of our state of servitude on Christ, speaking to him under the name of Israel, as was cleared before, Isa. xlix. 3, "Thou art my servant, O Israel, in whom I will be glorified." As if the Father had said to him, "Son, be it known, it is agreed that I take thee in the room and place of Israel, the spiritual seed, to perform the service due in virtue of the broken original contract: Thou in their stead art my servant; my bond-servant," as the word is rendered, Lev. xxv. 39, and elsewhere: "it is from thy hand I will look for that service." Agreeable hereunto is the account we have of our redemption from the curse, Gal. iii. 13. namely, that it was by Jesus Christ being made a "curse for us: for it is written, Cursed is every one that hangeth on a tree:" the which Christ did, dying on a cross, the capital punishment of bond-men.

Behold the solemnity of the translation, Psalm xl. 6, "Sacrifice and offering thou didst not desire, mine ears hast thou opened." The word here rendered opened, properly signifies digged, as may be seen in the margin of our Bibles: and so the words are, "Mine ears thou diggedst through;" that is, boredst, as it is expressed in our paraphase of the Psalms in metre, "Mine ears thou bor'd." This has a manifest view to that law concerning the bond-servant, Exod. xxi. 6, "Then his master shall bring him unto the judges; he shall also bring him to the door, or unto the door-post: and his master shall bore his ear through with an awl; and he shall serve him for ever;" that is, in the language of the law, till death. This is confirmed from Hos. iii. 2, "So I bought her to me for fifteen pieces of silver;" which was the half of the stated price of a bond-woman, Exod. xxi. 32. In the original it is, "So I digged her through me;" the same word being here used by the Holy Ghost, as Psalm xl. 6. It is a pregnant word, which is virtually two in signification; and the sense is, I bought her, and bored her ear to my door-post, to be my bond-woman: according to the law, Deut. xv. 17, "Thou shalt take an awl, and thrust it through his ear unto the door, and he shall be thy servant for ever: and also unto thy maid-servant thou shalt do likewise." That the boring of her ear as a bond-woman, was no-ways inconsistent with the prophet's betrothing of her to himself, Hos. iii. 3, appears from Exod. xxi. 8.

Joseph was an eminent type of Christ, as the Father's servant. And it is observable, that he was first a bond-servant, and then an honorary servant. In the former state, being sold for a servant, Psalm cv. 17, he was a type ofChrist, a bond-servant in his state of humiliation; whose most precious life was accordingly sold by Judas for thirty pieces of silver, the stated price of the life of a bond-servant; Exod. xxi. 32, "If the ox shall push a man-servant; or maid-servant; he shall give unto their master thirty shekels of silver, and the ox shall be stoned." In the latter state, being made ruler over all the land of Egypt, Psalm cv. 21, 22; Gen. xli. 40, he was a type of Christ, in that most honourable and glorious service or ministry, which was conferred on him in his state of exaltation, wherein he was constituted a servant, for whose law the isles shall wait, Isa. xl. 1, 4; God having given him a name which is above every name, that at the name of Jesus every knee should bow, Phil. ii. 9, 10. This latter service of Christ belongs to the promise of the covenant: but the former, to wit, the bond-service, being his surety-service, belongs to the condition of the covenant. Wherefore, rising from the dead, having fulfilled the condition of the covenant, paid the debt for which he became surety, and got up the discharge, he put off for ever the form and character of a bond-servant, "and rose and revived, that he might be Lord both of the dead and living," Rom. xiv. 9.

And hence it clearly appears, how the obedience of the man Christ comes, in virtue of the covenant, to be imputed to believers for righteousness, as well as his satisfaction by suffering: for that kind of obedience which he performed as our surety, was no more due by him, antecedently to his contract of suretiship, than his satisfaction by suffering. It is true, the human nature of Christ, being a creature, owed obedience to God in virtue of its creation; and must owe it for ever, forasmuch as the creature, as a creature, is subject to the natural law, the eternal rule of righteousness: but Christ's putting himself in a state of servitude, taking on him the form of a bond-servant, and in the capacity of a bond-servant, performing obedience to the law, as it was stated in the covenant, for life and salvation was entirely voluntary. Obedience to the natural law was due by the man Christ, by a natural tie; but obedience to the positive law, binding to be circumcised, baptized and the like, which is supposed guilt on the party subjected thereto, was not due, but by his own voluntary engagement. And the obedience of a son to the natural law, he owed naturally: but obedience to that or any other law, in the character of a bond-servant, and thereby to gain eternal life and salvation, he owed not but by compact. The human nature of Christ had a complete right to eternal life, and was actually possessed thereof in virtue of its union with the divine nature; so that there was no occasion for him to gain life to himself by his obedience. Wherefore, Christ's taking on him the form of a bond-servant and in that character obeying the law for life and salvation, were a mere voluntary work of his, as surety for sinners; wherein he did that which he was no otherwise bound to, than by his own voluntary undertaking. Now, forasmuch as the obedience of Christ imputed to believers for righteousness, is his obedience of this kind only; there is a clear ground for its imputation to them according to the covenant.

And thus we have seen Christ's suretiship in the covenant to be of a suretiship for paying one's debt; and what the debt was which he became surety for.

If it be inquired, Whether or not Christ's suretiship is also of the nature of suretiship for one's performing of a deed? or, Whether Christ became surety in way of caution to his Father, that the elect should believe, repent, and perform sincere obedience? I answer, Though the elect's believing, repenting, and sincere obedience, are infallibly secured in the covenant; so that whosoever, being subjects capable of these things, do live and die without them, shall undoubtedly perish, and are none of God's elect: yet I judge, that Christ did not become Surety in the covenant, in way of caution to his Father, that the elect should perform these deeds, or any other; and that that way of speaking doth not so well agree with the scripture-account of the covenant. Because,

1. It doth somewhat obscure the grace, the free grace, of the covenant; whereas the covenant is purposely so ordered, as to manifest it most illustriously, being of faith, that it might be by grace, Rom. iv. 16. For such a suretiship, or cautionary for the elect's performing of these things, must needs belong to the condition of the covenant, properly so called; as being a deed of the Mediator, whereby he promiseth something to God, and engageth that it shall be performed by them: and so these things performed by them accordingly, must be a part of the condition of the covenant. But that sinners themselves perform any part of the condition of the covenant, properly so called, cannot be admitted without prejudice to the grace of the covenant: for so far as we perform, in our own persons, any part of the condition, the reward is not of grace, but of debt; for "to him that worketh, is the reward not reckoned of grace, but of debt," Rom. iv. 4. But the reward is wholly of grace to us, as it is of debt unto Christ; for "to him that worketh not, but believeth on him that justifieth the ungodly, his faith is counted for righteousness," ver. 5. Chap. xi. 6, "And if by grace, then is it no more of works; otherwise grace is no more grace." Suppose a man is surety for a thousand pounds for his neighbour, who is thereupon to have a right to a certain valuable benefit; and that this man absolutely becomes surety for the whole sum, excepting only an hundred pence; for which hundred pence also he becomes cautioner, that it shall be paid by the principal: it is evident, that the condition of this bargain is divided between the surety and the principal, though indeed their shares are very unequal: but however unequal they are, as far as the hundred pence which the principal pays in his own person, do reach, so far the benefit is of debt to him. Or put the case, A surety engageth for the whole of the sum payable; and, besides, is surety for the principal's good behaviour; it is evident, that in this case the

good behaviour of the principal is a part of the condition of the bargain, as well as the payment of the money; since caution for it is required by him who is to communicate the benefit. At this rate, the condition is still divided between the surety and principal; and the latter performs a part of it as well as the former: and so the reward is, in part, of debt unto him, as well as to the surety. The application hereof to the case in hand is obvious. The sum of the matter lies here: If Christ did in the covenant become Surety in way of caution for his people's performing some deed; the performing of the condition of the covenant, properly so called, is divided betwixt Christ and them, however unequal their shares are: and if the performing of the condition is divided betwixt Christ and them, so far as their part of the performance goes, the reward is of debt to them, which obscures the grace of the covenant.

2. According to the Scripture, the elect's believing, repenting, and sincere obedience, do belong to the promissory part of the covenant. If we consider them in their original situation, they are benefits promised in the covenant by God unto Christ the Surety, as a reward of his fulfilling of the condition of the covenant. And so they are, by the unchangeable truth of God, and his exact justice, insured beyond all possibility of failure: Psalm xxii. 27, "All the ends of the world shall remember and turn unto the Lord." Ver. 30, "A seed shall serve him." Ver. 31, "They shall come, and shall declare his righteousness unto a people that shall be born." Psalm cx. 3, "Thy people shall be willing in the day of thy power." See Isa. liii. 10. with ver. 1; Ezek. xxxvi. 26, 27, 31; Heb. viii. 10, 11. If it be asked, To whom are these promises made, and the promises of the like nature through the Bible? it is evident, that several of them are made to Christ expressly; and the apostle answers as to them all Gal. iii. 16, "To Abraham and his seed were the promises made.—To thy seed which is Christ." And whereas there are found promises wherein Christ himself is the undertaker, as John vi. 37, "All that the Father giveth me, shall come to me;" they are not to be taken for Christ's engaging to his Father, as cautioner for a deed to be done by the seed: but therein he speaks to men, as administrator of the covenant, intrusted with the conferring on sinners the benefits purchased by his obedience and death, and made over to him by the promise of the Father: Matt. xi. 27, "All things are delivered unto me of my Father." Ver. 28, "Come unto me, all ye that labour, and are heavy laden, and I will give you rest." Luke xxii. 29, "And I appoint [or dispone] unto you a kingdom, as my Father hath appointed [or disponed] unto me." Thus far of Christ's suretiship in the covenant.

III. Christ the Priest of the Covenant.

As it was necessary for Christ the second Adam his doing the part of a Kinsman-redeemer, that he should become Surety in the covenant; so it was necessary to his performing of what he became Surety for, that he should be a Priest. And accordingly, consenting to the covenant, he became the Priest of the covenant, Heb. ix. 11, "Christ being come an High Priest of good things to come." A priest is a public person, who deals with an offended God in the name of the guilty, for reconciliation by sacrifice, which he offereth to God upon an altar, being thereto called of God, that he may be accepted. So a priest speaks a relation to an altar, an altar to a sacrifice, and a sacrifice to sin.

Those whom Christ represented in the covenant being sinners, he became their Priest, their High Priest, appearing before God in their name, to make atonement and reconciliation for them: and this was the great thing that the whole priesthood under the law, and especially the high priesthood, did typify and point at. Their nature was the priest's garments he put on, to exercise his priestly office in; the same being pure and undefiled in him: and in their nature he sustained their persons, representing them before God, as their great High Priest. A lively type hereof was Aaron's bearing before the Lord, the names of the children of Israel, the twelve tribes, upon his two shoulders, in the shoulder-pieces of the ephod; these names being engraven on two onyx-stones set therein by divine appointment, Exod. xxviii. 9, 10, 12: as also his bearing them in the breastplate, being engraven on twelve stones set therein, ver. 15—29. Thus Aaron the high-priest was all Israel representatively; an illustrious type of Christ the Priest of the covenant, the spiritual Israel representative, Isa. xlix. 3.

The necessity of Christ the second Adam his becoming a Priest, appears in these following things jointly considered.

1. Those whom he represented, were sinners: and there could not be a new covenant without provision made for removing of their sin; and that required a priest. The first covenant was made without a priest, because then there was no sin to take away; the parties therein represented, as well as the representative, were considered as innocent persons. But the second covenant was a covenant of peace and reconciliation between an offended God and sinners, not to be made but by the mediation of a priest, who should be able to remove sin, and repair the injured honour of God: Zech. vi. 13, He shall be a priest upon his throne, and the counsel of peace shall

be between them both." And there was none fit to bear that character but Christ himself. No man was fit to bear it; because all men were sinners themselves, and such an high priest became us, as was undefiled, separated from sinners, Heb. vii. 26. It is true, the elect angels were indeed undefiled; but yet none of them could be priest of the covenant; because,

2. Sin could not be removed without a sacrifice of sufficient value, which they were not able to afford. The new covenant behoved to be a covenant by sacrifice, a covenant written in blood; and without shedding of blood, there was no remission, Heb. ix. 22. Therefore the typical covenant with Abraham was not made without the solemnity of sacrifice, Gen xv. 9; that he might know the covenant to be a covenant of reconciliation, in which a just God did not shew his mercy, but in a way consistent with the honour of his justice. Now the sacrifices of beasts, yea, and whatsoever the creatures could afford for sacrifice in this case, were infinitely below the value. But Jesus Christ becoming a priest, gave himself a sacrifice to God, for establishing the covenant; and that sacrifice was for a sweet-smelling savour, Eph. v. 2, or, as the Old Testament phrase is, a a savour of rest, Gen. viii. 21, marg. The represented being sinners, were corrupt and abominable before God; and he as it were smelled a savour of disquiet from them, they being a smoke in his nose, Isa. lxv. 6; their sin set his revenging justice and wrath astir. But the sacrifice of Christ himself, was fit to send forth such a sweet smelling savour unto God, as should quite overcome the abominable savour rising from them, and lay his revenging justice and wrath to the most calm and profoundest rest.

The necessity of a sacrifice in the second covenant, arose from the justice of God requiring the execution of the curse of the broken first covenant; whereby the sinner should fall a sacrifice for his sin, according to that, Psalm xciv. 23, "He shall bring upon them their own iniquity, and shall cut them off in their own wickedness." It was an ancient custom in making of covenants, to cut a beast in twain, and to pass between the parts of it: and that passing between the parts, respected the falling of the curse of the covenant upon the breaker: Jer. xxxiv. 18, "And I will give the men that have transgressed my covenant, which have not performed the words of the covenant which they had made before me, when they cut the calf in twain, and passed between the parts thereof;" or rather, more agreeably to the original, "I will make the men that have transgressed my covenant—the calf which they cut in twain, and passed between the parts thereof:" that is, I will make them as that calf which they cut in twain; I will execute the curse on them, cutting them asunder as covenant-breakers, Matth. xxiv. 51. Now, the covenant of works being broken, justice required this execution of the curse of it, in order to the establishing of a new covenant, the covenant of grace and peace. But had it been executed on sinners themselves, the fire of wrath would have burnt continually on them; but never would such a sacrifice have sent forth a savour smelling so sweet, as to be a savour of rest to revenging justice; forasmuch as they were not only mere creatures, whose most exquisite sufferings could not be a sufficient compensation for the injured honour of an infinite God; but they were sinful creatures too, who would still have remained sinful under their sufferings. Wherefore Jesus Christ, being both separate from sinners, and equal with God, consented in the covenant to be the sacrifice, on which the curse of the first covenant might be executed in their room and stead.

This is lively represented in the covenant made with Abraham, in which he was a type of Christ, Gen. xv. In that covenant God promised the deliverance of Abraham's seed out of the Egyptian bondage, and to give them the land of Canaan; a type of the deliverance of Christ's spiritual seed from the bondage of sin and Satan, and of putting them in possession of heaven, vers. 13, 14, 16, 18. Awful was the solemnity used at the making of this covenant. There were taken a heifer, a she-goat, and a ram, each of them of three years old; typifying Christ, who was about three years in his public ministry, ver. 9. These were each of them, divided in the midst, hacked asunder by the middle; which typified the execution of the curse of the broken first covenenant on Christ our surety and sacrifice for us, ver. 10. Abraham's driving away the fowls that came down upon the carcases, typified Christ's victory over the devils all along during the state of his humiliation, and especially his triumphing over them on the cross, ver. 11. And finally, there was a smoking furnace, and a burning lamp that passed between the pieces; which signified the revenging wrath of God seizing on Christ the sacrifice, and justice therewith satisfied, ver. 17.

3. No sacrifice could be accepted, but on such an altar as should sanctify the gift to its necessary value and designed effect, Matth. xxiii. 19. And who could furnish that but Christ himself, whose divine nature was the altar from whence the sacrifice of his human nature derived its value and efficacy as infinite? Heb. ix. 14, "How much more shall the blood of Christ, who through the eternal Spirit, offered up himself without spot to God, purge your conscience from dead works?" His blessed body suffering and bleeding to death on the cross, and his holy soul scorched and melted within him with the fire of the divine wrath, both in the meantime

united to his divine nature, were the sacrifice burning on the altar, from which God smelled a sweet savour, to the appeasing of his wrath, and satisfying of his justice fully. Not that Christ was a sacrifice only while on the cross; but that his offering of himself a sacrifice, which was begun from his incarnation in the womb, the sacrifice being led on the altar in the first moment thereof; and was continued through his whole life; was completed on the cross, and in the grave: Heb. x. 5, "Wherefore when he cometh into the world, he saith, sacrifice and offering thou wouldst not, but a body hast thou prepared me:"—ver. 6, "Then said I, lo, I come." Isa. liii. 2, "When we shall see him, there is no beauty that we should desire him." Ver. 3, "He is—à man of sorrows, and acquainted with grief." 2 Cor. v. 21, "He hath made him to be sin for us."

4. *Lastly*, There behoved to be a priest to offer this sacrifice, this valuable sacrifice, unto God upon that altar; else there could have been no sacrifice to be accepted, and so no removal of sin, and consequently no new covenant. And since Christ himself was the sacrifice, and the altar too, he himself alone could be the priest. And forasmuch as the weight of the salvation of sinners lay upon his call to that office, he was made priest of the covenant by the oath of God, Heb. vii. 20, 21. As he had full power over his own life, to make himself a sacrifice for others; so his Father's solemn investing of him with this office by an oath, gave him access to offer himself effectually; even in such sort as thereby to fulfil the condition of the condition, and to purchase eternal life for them.

INFERENCES FROM THE SECOND HEAD.

I shall close up this head, of the making of the covenant of grace, with two inferences from the whole.

Inf. 1. What remains for sinners, that they may be personally and savingly in covenant with God, is not, as parties contractors and undertakers, to make a covenant with him for life and salvation; but only, to take hold of God's covenant already made from eternity, between the Father and Christ the second Adam, and revealed and offered to us in the gospel, Isa. lvi. 4, 6. I have no design hereby to disparage our covenants made for national reformation by our godly progenitors, and commonly called the national covenant, and solemn league and covenant, on which God set the seal of his good pleasure in the experience of many. These and the like are covenants of duties, consequential enough to the taking hold of God's covenant of grace. Neither would I discourage any serious souls, from taking hold of God's covenant of grace, for eternal life and salvation to themselves, with all the awful solemnity of the most express words, yea, and of writing and subscribing it with their hands; which is commonly called personal covenanting. But I would have all to beware of a practical corrupting of the covenant of grace, by making covenants of their own, upon such and such terms, which they will fulfil for life and salvation. The carnal Jews mistaking the design of the giving of the law, did so corrupt the covenant of grace; looking for life and salvation, not for the sake of the promised seed alone, but for their obedience, such as it was, to the moral and ceremonial laws. And thus many, thinking that eternal salvation is proposed to them in the word upon the condition of faith, repentance, and sincere obedience to God's law, do consent to these terms, and solemnly undertake to perform them: just binding themselves to such and such duties, that God may save their souls: and so they make their covenant. And while they can persuade themselves, that they perform their part of the covenant, they look for life and salvation thereupon. This doth quite overturn the nature of the covenant of grace: for "to him that worketh, the reward is not reckoned of grace, but of debt," Rom. iv. 4; and "if it be of works, then it is no more grace," chap. xi. 6. The sinfulness of this practice is great, as overlooking Christ, the great undertaker and party-contractor by the appointment of the Father; and putting themselves in his room, to do and work for themselves for life. And the danger of it must needs be great, as laying a foundation to bear the weight of their salvation, which divine wisdom saw to be quite unable to bear it. The issue whereof must be, that such covenanters shall lie down in sorrow. So the apostle determines, Gal. v. 4, "Christ is become of no effect unto you, whosoever of you are justified by the law; ye are fallen from grace."

Our part then, in this case, is only to take hold of God's covenant made already, and offered and exhibited to us in the gospel. This hold is taken by faith; which is, in Scripture account, the hand of the soul, John i. 12. So the original expression plainly carries it, Isa. lvi. 46, "That fasten in my covenant." In which phraseology, the correlate word hand (expressed Gen. xxi. 18,) is understood; *q. d.* That fasten (their hand) in my covenant; that is to say, "Who by the hand of faith take fast hold of my covenant;" as Adonijah did of the horns of the altar, 1 Kings i. 50, wherein the same manner of expression is used. And this you do by taking hold of Christ in the free promise of the gospel; believing that he is held forth to you in particular, confiding and trusting in him as your Saviour, for your salvation from sin and wrath, upon the ground of God's faithfulness in the promise, that whosoever believeth in him, shall not perish, but have everlasting life, for he is given for a covenant to you, Isa. xlix. 8; and to receive him, is to believe on his name, John i. 12.

This is our making a covenant with God by sacrifice, which is mentioned, Psalm l. 5. The original expression is, That cut my covenant upon a sacrifice; namely, by laying their hands in faith on the head of the sacrifice, thereupon cut down in their stead: and so ceremonially transferring their guilt on the sacrifice; but really and spiritually, approving of the device of salvation by a crucified Saviour, and falling in with it as the method of salvation for them. In this way of covenanting, the free grace of the covenant is preserved pure and entire: for "to him that worketh not, but believeth on him that justifieth the ungodly, his faith is counted for righteousness," Rom. iv. 5. Here the honour of sole undertaker and party-contractor in the covenant, is, according to the Father's appointment left to Christ, the One that is mighty, Psalm lxxxix. 19. Here the second Adam builds the temple, without our laying one stone therein in our own persons; even as the first Adam laid it in ruins, without our pulling down one stone of it in our own persons: and Christ bears the personal glory of the reparation, even as Adam the personal blame of the ruin, Zech. vi. 13. And at this rate the soul doth in time, for her own part, give her solemn approbation of the covenant made from eternity, and a personal consent to what Christ from everlasting consented to in her name: even as the princess married by proxy in her childhood, ratifies all when she is come to age, by receiving her husband. Like as all Adam's children, as such, taking salvation to heart, and therefore covenanting with God, do in effect repeat the covenant of works made with Adam their representative; so all the second Adam's seed, as such, taking salvation to heart, and therefore covenanting with God, do, in effect repeat the covenant of grace made with Christ their representative. In the making of the covenant before the world began, the Father proposed to Christ as second Adam, their head and representative, that he should take the burden upon him for them, and be their Kinsman-redeemer, their Surety for their debt of punishment and duty, and their Priest; and Christ consented thereto from eternity. Amen, for my part, says the elect soul in time, in the covenanting day; it is infinitely well ordered: I am a lost sinner, a debtor to divine justice, a guilty creature; he is, with my whole heart and soul, *my* Kinsman-redeemer, *my* Surety, *my* Priest: my part of the punishment incurred, and of the duty owing, is a vast and exceeding great part of that debt; but my soul is well content with and rests in that method of paying it: 2 Sam. xxiii. 5, "He hath made with me an everlasting covenant," (Heb. He hath put to me an everlasting covenant)—" This is all my salvation and all my desire." The Father said to Christ as their representative, For thy so doing and suffering, " I will be their God, and they shall be my people." Amen, said Christ from eternity, " All mine are thine," John xvii. 10. Amen, for my part, says the elect soul in the time of personal covenanting. This heart of mine must have some God, I must belong to one or other; and too long have I been for another: but now, timber of the house, and stones of the wall, bear witness, my soul is content with, consents to, and rests in this method of disposing of me; namely, that the God and Father of our Lord Jesus Christ be my God in Christ, and I one of his people from henceforth and for ever.

This manner of covenanting is inconsistent with a purpose or desire of continuing in sin; even as one's committing himself for cure into the hands of a physician who cures infallibly, is inconsistent with a desire to keep his disease hanging about him. Christ being " made of God unto us wisdom, righteousness, sanctification, and redemption," 1 Cor. i. 30; it necessarily carries along with it, a taking of Christ for a Prophet, and a King, and Lord unto us; as such a one doth necessarily yield himself to the physician's management. In it one joins himself to Christ as his covenant head, who also is the Administrator of the covenant; and so subjects himself to his teaching and government. And it is such a way of covenanting, as no profane person, nor hypocrite, continuing so, ever did or can fall in with. For, (1.) It speaks a heart content to part with all sin, well pleased with Christ's whole salvation, whereof the principal part is to save his people from their sins, Matth. i. 21; whereas unsound covenanters are always offended with some one thing or other in Christ, chap. xi. 6. (2.) It speaks a soul carried out of all confidence in itself, its own working and doing for life and salvation, and bottomed only upon Christ's doing and suffering for that end. And thus, such a covenanter, being poor in spirit, Matth. v. 3, and rejoicing in Christ Jesus, and having no confidence in the flesh, Phil. iii. 3, is distinguished from the presumptuous hypocrite, whose confidence for life and salvation is ever upon his own doing and working, either in whole or in part; as also from the despairing unbeliever, who hath no confidence, neither in Christ, nor in himself that he shall have life and salvation, however he may believe firmly that others shall. So this faith, this covenanting, is quite another thing, than either the false faith of the presumptuous profane, and presumptuous hypocrite, or the no-faith of the desperate, or the wavering doubter, who can never fix in greater or lesser measure of confidence in Christ, for salvation to himself; Jam. i. 6, "But let him ask in faith, nothing wavering: for he that wavereth, is like a wave of the sea, driven with the wind, and tossed." Ver. 7, "For let not that man think that he shall receive any thing of the Lord."

If any think this to be an easy way of believing or covenanting, either they mistake it, or try it not. To believe upon some ground we see in ourselves, is very natural, but to believe merely upon a ground in another, namely righteousness in Christ, and faithfulness in God, while all in ourselves tends to make us dispair, is above the reach of nature. A conscience thoroughly awakened, will convince a sinner, that it is a matter of greatest difficulty.

Inf. 2. Justifying faith, though it receives Christ in all his offices, as Prophet, Priest, and King; yet as it enters us personally into the covenant, and justifies, it eyes him in his priestly office particularly; namely, as the great high priest, who hath made atonement for sin, by the sacrifice of himself; as the surety, who undertook and completed the payment of the debt of punishment and duty; and as the kinsman redeemer, who having married our nature to the divine nature in himself, redeemed the mortgaged inheritance with his own blood, gave himself a ransom for us, to deliver us from our spiritual bondage, and by his death destroyed him that had the power of death; Rom. iii. 25, "Whom God hath set forth to be a propitiation, through faith in his blood." Chap. v. 11, "Our Lord Jesus Christ, by whom we have now received the atonement." The comfort for a wounded conscience, sick with the guilt of sin, lies here. This is that office of Christ to which the convinced sinner, standing trembling before the just Judge of the world, lifts his eyes and makes his recourse for safety: for there, and only there, can one see a ransom, a righteousness, an atonement. In his prophetical and kingly office, he administrates the covenant; but in his priestly office, he performed the condition of it. So it is the foundation of the other two. It was by the sacrifice of himself, that the word and Spirit of the covenant, whereby he teacheth sinners, were purchased: and thereby also he obtained his kingdom. And his intercession is founded upon his oblation. So his priestly office and that considered particularly in point of his offering his sacrifice, doth, as the foundation stone, bear the weight of the salvation of sinners, and of the honour of God and the Mediator therein. Wherefore it is not strange, that his investiture with the priestly office was confirmed by the oath of God; a solemnity not used in the case of his prophetical and kingly offices.

And thus far of the making of the covenant.

HEAD III.

THE PARTS OF THE COVENANT OF GRACE.

THE parts of the covenant of grace, being the things therein agreed upon betwixt God and Christ the second Adam, are two, to wit, the conditionary part, and the promissory part. These comprehend the whole of the covenant, and of them we shall treat in order.

The first part of the covenant, namely, the conditionary part.

The condition of a covenant or bargain, properly and commonly so called, is, that part of a covenant or bargain, upon the performing of which one's right to the benefit promised is founded, and his plea for it is stated, as becoming due to him for his performance, according to, and in virtue of the agreement between the parties. This is a federal condition, a covenant-condition, or the condition of a covenant; and what all men, in common conversation understand by a condition of a covenant or bargain. As for instance, the paying of such a sum of money for such a commodity, according to the agreement between the parties, in the condition of a covenant of commerce, sale, or traffic: the working of such a piece of work, or doing of such a deed, for such a reward agreed upon by the parties, is the condition of a covenant of service on hire.

Besides this, there is also what is called a condition of connection or order in a covenant; whereby one thing necessarily goes before another, in the order of the covenant without being the ground upon which one's right and title to that other thing is founded. As in the former instances, the buyer's receiving of the commodity, and the hireling's receiving of the reward, covenanted or bargained for, must needs go before their profession or enjoyment of them; but it is evident, that that receiving is not the thing upon which the buyer's right and title to the commodity, or the hirling's right and title to the reward, is founded: therefore, though it may be called a condition of connection in the respective covenants, yet it cannot, in any propriety of speech, be called the condition of them.

Now, to apply these things to our purpose: in the order of the covenant of grace, forasmuch as the having of the Spirit must go before faith, faith before justification, justification before sanctification, holiness before heaven's happiness; these may be called conditions in the covenant of grace, to wit, conditions of certain connection; and this belongs to the established order of the promises of the covenant, which are contradistinguished to the condition of the covenant. Howbeit such conditions can in no proper sense be called the condition or conditions of the covenant of grace, more than the buyer's receiving of the commodity can be called the condition of the covenant or bargain of sale. But the condition of the covenant of grace, properly so called, is, Christ in the form of a bond-servant, as last Adam, Representative, Kinsman-redeemer, Surety, and Priest, his fulfilling all righteous owing, in virtue of the broken covenant of works, unto God by his spiritual seed: Matth. iii. 15, "Thus it becometh us to fulfil all righteousness."

For clearing of this purpose, I shall, (1.) Evince this to be the condition of the covenant; (2.) Explain and unfold that righteousness, the fulfilling whereof was made the condition of the covenant.

First, To evince that this is the condition of the covenant of grace consider,

1. Christ's fulfilling all right eousness as second Adam is what the Father proposed unto him, as the terms on which his seed should be saved, and upon which he founded his promise of eternal life to be given them; and not any work or deed of theirs: Isa. liii. 10, "When thou shalt make his soul an offering for sin, he shall see his seed." Ver. 11, "He shall see of the travail of his soul, and shall be satisfied: by his knowledge shall my righteous servant justify many; for he shall bear their iniquities." Luke xxii. 20, "This cup is the new testament in my blood, which is shed for you." And the same is that which Christ as the second Adam did from eternity consent unto, undertake, and bind himself for; and which he did in time, according to agreement perform. Thus he himself represents it, Matth. iii. 15, "Thus it becometh us to fulfill all righteousness;" namely, as it becometh a person of honour and credit to fulfill his bargain. Luke xxiv. 26, "Ought not Christ to have suffered these things?" to wit, as one ought to perform the condition of a covenant or bargain he has agreed to.

2. This is the only ground of a sinner's right and title to eternal life; and upon nothing else can he safely found his plea before the Lord for life and salvation; Eph. i. 7, "In whom we have redemption through his blood, the forgiveness of sins, according to the riches of his grace." Phil. iii. 8, 9, "That I may win Christ, and be found in him, not having mine own righteusness—but—the righteousness which is of God by faith." Surely upon the condition of the covenant fulfilled, one may found his plea before the Lord for the benefits promised in the covenant: but no man may found his plea before the Lord for these on any work or deed of his own whatsoever, no not on faith itself; but only on Christ's fulfilling all righteousness: therefore no work nor deed of ours whatsoever, no not faith itself, can be the condition of the covenant of grace pro-

perly so called; but only Christ's fulfilling all righteousness. The sinner standing in the court of conscience, trembling before the Lord, flees in under the covert of that righteousness fulfilled by the Mediator, and dare oppose nothing but it to the condemning sentence of the law, giving up with all other pleas for life and salvation. Believing in Christ is the pleading upon that ground, not the ground of the sinner's plea: it saith, "My Lord and my God" in the promise, upon the ground of Christ's fulfilling all righteousness allenarly, as the condition of the covenant. If any will make it the ground of their plea, they must needs produce it as a work of a law, that is, as a deed done by them, whereby they have fulfilled and answered a law, and whereupon they crave the benefit promised: which will, according to the scripture, be found a dangerous adventure, Rom. iii. 20; Gal. ii. 16; and v. 4.

3. It is by this, and this alone, the salvation of sinners becomes a debt: therefore this alone is the condition of the covenant. For the reward is of debt to him, and him only, who fulfills the condition of a covenant: to him that worketh, not to him that worketh not, but believeth, Rom. iv. 4, 5. And so it is of debt to Christ alone, not to us; and therefore it was he that fulfilled the condition of the covenant; we fulfil no part of it. This is confirmed from the primitive situation of mankind with reference to eternal life, in the first Adam's covenant, duly considered. The condition thereof was perfect active obedience. And, according to the nature of that covenant, if this obedience had been fulfilled by Adam, eternal life to him and his would thereupon have become a debt to him. And the plea of his posterity for life, in that case, would not have been founded on their personal obedience coming after that fulfilment; since it would not have been the performance of the condition, but the fruit of the promise, of the covenant: but it would have been founded on that performance of Adam their representative; forasmuch as, in the case supposed, it would have been the only obedience whereby the condition of that covenant was fulfilled; and so they would have obtained life, not for any personal work or deed of theirs, but for the obedience of the first Adam their representative, to which God did graciously make the promise of life, in the first covenant.

4. Faith and obedience are benefits promised in the covenant, upon the condition of it, as hath been already evinced; and, in virtue of the promises of the covenant, they are produced in the elect: therefore they cannot be the condition of the covenant. And elect infants are saved, though they are neither capable of believing nor of obeying: howbeit, the condition of the covenant must needs

be performed, either by themselves who are saved, or else by another in their stead. Therefore Christ's fulfilling all righteousness, which is the only obedience performed in their stead, must be the alone proper condition of the covenant.

5. *Lastly,* The covenant of grace doth so exclude our boasting, as the covenant of works did not. This is clear from Rom. iii. 27, "Where is boasting then? It is excluded. By what law? of works? Nay: but by the law of faith." But if any deed or work of ours be the condition of the covenant of grace, in whole or in part, our boasting is not excluded, but hath place therein, as in the covenant of works; the difference being at most but in point of degrees: for, according to the scripture, it is working, or fulfilling the condition of a covenant, that gives the ground of boasting; forasmuch as to him that worketh, the reward is reckoned of debt: and life being of or by works in the covenant of works, though not in the way of proper merit, but in the way of paction or compact only, this gave men the ground of boasting in that covenant, according to the scripture. Therefore, so far as life and salvation are of or by any work or deed of ours, as fulfilling the condition of the covenant of grace, our boasting is not excluded, but hath place therein, as in the covenant of works. Wherefore, since the covenant of grace is so framed, as to leave no ground for our boasting, no work nor deed of ours, but Christ's fulfilling all righteousness, even that alone, is the condition of the covenant of grace: and our life and salvation are neither of works, nor by works, as fulfilling the condition of the covenant: Tit. iii. 5, "Not by works of righteousness, which we have done, but according to his mercy he saved us." Eph. ii. 9, "Not of works, lest any man should boast."

God forbid we should go about to justle faith and obedience out of the covenant of grace: those who do so in principle or practice, will thereby justle themselves out of the kingdom of heaven: Matt. v. 19, "Whosoever shall break one of these least commandments, and shall teach men so, he shall be called the least in the kingdom of heaven;" that is, he shall be treated as he treated that one of these commandments, he shall be judged unworthy of the fellowship of that kingdom. Faith is necessary savingly to interest us in Jesus Christ the head of the covenant: and none can attain to eternal happiness, without actual believing, who are subjects capable of it; nor can any attain it without the Spirit of faith indwelling in them. Obedience is necessary, as the chief subordinate end of the covenant, being that whereby God hath his glory he designed therein: and without obedience begun here, none who are subjects capable of it, can see heaven. But withal it is necessary, that they be kept in the place and station assigned them in the covenant by the Father and the Son from eternity. By faith we personally embrace the covenant, consent to, and rest in the condition of the covenant fulfilled by Christ; and so are justified and brought into a state of salvation: John x. 9, "I am the door; by me if any man enter in, he shall be saved." Compare John i, 12; and iii. 16; and xiv. 6. By evangelical repentance and gospel-obedience, we testify our thankfulness to God, and evidence the truth of our faith, and our being within the covenant: 1 Pet. ii. 9, "Ye are a chosen generation, a royal priesthood, an holy nation, a peculiar people; that ye should shew forth the praises of him who hath called you out of darkness into his marvellous light:" ver. 10, "Which in time past were not a people, but are now the people of God: which had not obtained mercy, but now have obtained mercy." Compare Rom. vi. 13. and xii. 1, 2; 1 Cor. vi. 20.

This the prophet taught the Jewish church of old, Mic. vi. 8, "He hath shewed thee, O man, what is good; and what doth the Lord require of thee, but to do justly, and to love mercy, and to walk humbly with thy God?" In the sixth verse, a most important question is put, concerning the acceptance of a sinner with God, how it may be obtained, "Wherewith shall I come before the Lord?" and several costly expedients for that purpose are proposed by the sinner, even to the giving of "the fruit of his body for the sin of his soul," ver. 6, 7. But the prophet answers that question in a word, tacitly upbraiding them with gross stupidity, in their groping for the wall in broad day-light, even as in the night: "He hath shewed thee, O man, what is good;" that is, what is goodly, valuable, and acceptable, in the sight of God, for that purpose, even for a sinner's obtaining pardon and acceptance with God; namely, the Messias, Jesus Christ sacrificed for sinners. This was what God had all along, by his prophets, and by the whole ceremonial law, pointed out to them, and set before them, as the good for that purpose, that they might by faith look thereunto, and be saved, Isa. xlv. 22. And, in the style of the Holy Ghost, Christ crucified is elsewhere spoken of under the same notion: 2 Chron. xxx. 18, "The good Lord pardon every one that prepareth his heart to seek God." Orig. "Jehovah the good make atonement for," &c. Psalm lxxxv. 12, "The Lord shall give that which is good;" or, shall give the good. Compare John iv. 10, "If thou knewest the gift of God, and who it is." Isa. lv. 2, "Eat ye that which is good." Compare John vi. 55, "My flesh is meat indeed." Job xxxiv. 4, "Let us know among ourselves what is good." Ver. 5, "For Job hath said, I am righteous." Now, being thus accepted of God, what doth he require of thee in point of gratitude, but to do justly, as one accepted not without a righteousness answering the demands of justice and judgment: and to love mercy, as one who hath obtained mercy; and to walk humbly with thy God, as one who is free grace's debtor? In the same manner of expression doth Moses address himself to the people secured of the possession of Canaan by the oath of God, and being just to enter upon it, Deut. x. 11, 12, "And now, Israel, what doth the Lord thy God require of thee, but to fear the Lord thy God," &c.? namely, in point of gratitude, for his giving thee that good land.

Inf. From what is said it appears that your life and salvation entirely depend on your special interest in Christ's righteousness. If ye are possessed of it your salvation is secure; if not, salvation is far from you. If you were never so full of your own righteousness, works, doings, and sufferings, all is but filthy rags in this case, and cannot give you a right or title to life: and although you can see nothing of your own in yourselves, which you can lean to before the Lord, yet if the righteousness of Christ is yours in possession, by faith, your life and salvation are firm as a rock.

Case. How then shall I know that Christ's righteousness is indeed mine in possession? Answ. The Lord himself gives a distinguishing character of such happy possessors, Isa. li. 7, "Hearken unto me, ye that know righteousness, the people in whose heart is my law." They that know righteousness, are, in the style of the Scripture, those whose it is, agreeable to the phrase, Matth. xxv. 12, "I know you not," *q. d.* Ye are none of mine, I acknowledge you not as mine. So this character consists of two parts. (1.) They are such as acknowledge Christ's righteousness as their only righteousness in the sight of God, and look to it alone for life and salvation, renouncing all their own righteousness: Isa. liii. 11. "By his knowledge shall my righteous servant justify many;" that is by the knowledge or acknowledgement of him, which is by faith. (2.) They have the law of God in their hearts. The righteous people, righteous by faith, are a holy people. They make conscience of internal obedience; for the holy law rules within them, even there whither no eye reacheth, but the eyes of God and their own consciences. So they are distinguished from hypocrites, who are "like unto whited sepulchres, beautiful outward, but within full of all uncleanness." They make conscience of external obedience too; for as the candle burning within the lanthorn will shine through it, so the law of God ruling in the heart, cannot miss to rule in the life and conversation too: Matth. vi. 22, "If therefore thine eye be single, thy whole body shall be full of light." And so they are distinguished from the profane, whose unholy lives declare them to have neither part nor lot in this righteousness: Psalm xxiv. 3, 4, "Who shall stand in his holy place? He that hath clean hands." And the law is not only in their minds by its light, to drive them to obedience; as in the case of legalists, who work like slaves; but it is in their hearts and affections, discovering to their souls the beauty of holiness; and so drawing them to all obedience, and causing them to work like sons to a father. Their hearts are reconciled to the purity of the holy law, and they delight in it after the inward man, Rom. vii. 22, and would fain reach a full conformity unto it, saying from the heart, "O that my ways were directed to keep thy statutes!" Psalm cxix. 5.

Secondly, To unfold that righteousness, the fulfilling of which was made the condition of the covenant of grace, we shall view it in the several parts thereof. That righteousness, forasmuch as it was to be fulfilled in the room and stead of sinners, was and must be stated from the law, or broken covenant of works, which they were lying under; for the law, or broken covenant of works, was so far from being neglected in the new bargain, that whatsoever it had to charge upon, or demand of the parties contracted for in the new covenant, was summed up, and set down therein, to be fully cleared by Christ their surety contracting for them. Now, stating that righteousness from thence, it will be found to consist of three parts making so many conditionary articles of the covenant of grace: to wit, holiness of nature, righteousness of life, and satisfaction for sin. Of the which in order.

ARTICLE I.

HOLINESS OF NATURE.

The law required holiness of nature as a condition of life, inasmuch as condemning original sin, saying "Thou shalt not covet," it concluded all men to be by nature children of wrath. For God being essentially holy, holy by necessity of nature, nothing can be so contrary to God as an unholy nature; because, howbeit persons or things of a like nature may be contrary in some points, yet they can never be so contrary one to another, as those of quite opposite natures. But the parties contracted for in the covenant of grace, having their nature wholly corrupted, and being incapable to purify it, or make their heart clean, Prov. xx. 9; it is evident, they could by no means answer this demand of the law by themselves. Wherefore, for the satisfaction of the law in this point, it was settled as a conditionary article of the covenant of grace, "That Christ the second Adam, representing them, should be a man of a perfectly holy, pure and untainted nature, fully answering for them the holiness and perfection of nature required by the law." "For such an high priest became us, who is holy, harmless, undefiled, separate from sinners," Heb. vii. 16. And this article contains two clauses.

I. "That he, as the second Adam, should be conceived and born holy, for and instead of them corrupt in their nature, conceived and born in sin." There was a holy nature given to Adam as the root of mankind, to be by him kept and transmitted to his posterity, in the way of natural generation. And upon this ground, the law requires all men to be born holy, pronouncing them unclean and children of wrath, in the contrary event, Job xiv. 4; Eph. ii. 3. But how could this demand be answered by sinners? They are born in sin: they cannot enter again into their mother's womb, and be born a second time, without sin. No, they cannot: yet the law will not bate of that demand for life. Wherefore it is provided, that Christ, as a public person, representing his spiritual seed, should be born perfectly holy; that, whereas they brought a sinful corrupt nature into the world with them, he should bring a holy human nature into the world with him. And so he was the last Adam, 1 Cor. xv. 45, holy and undefiled, Heb. viii. 26, "that holy thing born," Luke i. 35. And the effect thereof with respect to that law-demand for life is, that all believers are, in law-reckoning, born holy in the second Adam, even as they were created holy in the first Adam. Hence they are expressly said to be crucified in him, Col. ii. 11, which plainly presupposeth their being born in him. And it is in virtue of their being legally born holy in Christ, when he was born, that, being united to him in the time of loves, they are really born again, and at length perfected; even as in virtue of their being legally defiled in Adam, when he sinned, they are actually and really defiled in their own persons, coming into the world: the holy nature being actually communicated to them from Christ their spiritual head, in whom they were legally born holy; even as the corruption of nature is actually conveyed to them from Adam their natural head, in whom they sinned in law-reckoning.

2. The other clause is, "That Christ, as the second Adam, should retain the holiness of nature inviolate unto the end, for them and in their name." The law, or covenant of works, required, as a condition of life, that the holiness of nature, given to mankind in Adam, should be preserved pure and incorrupt. But it was lost: and put the case, that it had been restored, they could not have retained it,

in their own persons, unstained amidst so many snares. Wherefore, to satisfy the law-demand in this point, it was provided, that in the man Christ, as a public person representative of his seed, their nature should be kept perfectly holy unto the end, without the least stain or defilement: Isa. xlii. 4, "He shall not fail;" or, "he shall not wax dim," or wrinkle, as the skin doth when the moisture is exhausted. Therein the first Adam failed. He shone in purity of nature, as he came from the Creator's hand: but he failed, he waxed dim; the holiness of his nature being exhausted by sin, all mankind in him lost their spiritual beauty, and wrinkled. But now that the second Adam failed not, but preserved the holiness of human nature in him unstained, not in the least darkened, even to the end of his life; the remains of the corruption of nature in believers are not imputed to them, Rom. iv. 8; but as defiled as they are in themselves, through those remains cleaving to them, yet in Christ their beauty is fresh, and not marred in the least, according to that, Cant. iv. 7, "Thou art all fair, my love, there is no spot in thee."

ARTICLE II.

RIGHTEOUSNESS OF LIFE.

This also the law insisted upon as a condition of life; and justly: for God gave to Adam, and all mankind in him, a law to be obeyed in all points; not only in virtue of the tie of natural duty, but in virtue of the bond of a covenant for life: but it was never fulfilled by them. The first Adam began indeed the course of obedience; but he quickly fell off from it, with all his natural seed in him. Now, it being inconsistent with the honour of the law, that the prize, to wit, eternal life, should be obtained without the race was run; it still insisted, saying, "If thou wilt enter into life, keep the commandments," Matth. xix. 17. Howbeit, we were weak, moveless, without strength for running that race. Wherefore it was settled as another conditionary article of the covenant, "That Christ, as a public person, represented those whom he contracted for, should begin and perfect the course of obedience to the law in righteousness of life." And accordingly, he became obedient unto death, Phil. ii. 8.

The law, which was the rule of this obedience, exacted of him, was the same law of the ten commands, that was given to Adam, and binding on us as under it: for he was made under the law, to redeem them that were under the law, Gal. iv. 4, 5. It extended to all divine institutions which the second Adam found in being, whether obliging men as men, or as members of the church of God on earth: even as the rule of the first Adam's obedience, extended to the positive law touching the forbidden fruit, which was in being when he was set to fulfil his covenant-obedience.

That we may the more distinctly comprehend this article, it may be observed to bear these three things following.

1. "That he, as the second Adam, should obey the whole law, in the name of those he represented." This was a debt owing by them all; and was required of them by the law, as a condition of life: Gal. iii. 10. "Cursed is every one that continueth not in all things which are written in the book of the law to do them." But the answering of this demand was quite beyond their reach. Man, by the fall, having lost much of his knowledge of the law, had lost sight of many of the duties required therein: howbeit, ignorance of the law excuseth no man. His heart was averse to and enmity against the law, Rom. viii. 7. And he was without strength to perform the duties therein required of him, chap. v. 6. So that by reason of ignorance, aversion, and impotency in that matter, the obedience of the whole law was not to be had from them. Wherefore it was provided, that Christ, as their representative, should give obedience to the whole law for them; that both tables of the law, and each command of each table, should have the due obedience from him; that the law being laid before him in its spirituality and full extent, he should fully answer it, in internal and external obedience, in his mind, will, and affections, in thought, word, and deed; that he should conform himself to the whole natural law, and to all divine institutions, ceremonial or political, so as to be circumcised, keep the passover, to be baptized, to be a servant of or subject to rulers, pay tribute to whom it was due, and the like: in one word, that he should perform the whole will of God, signified in his law; so that with the safety of the law's honour, his people might have life. What the first Adam failed in, the second Adam was to do. And this I take to be represented unto us, in the case of the first and second king of Israel, to wit, Saul and David, Acts xiii. 22. "I have found David the son of Jesse, a man after mine own heart, which shall fulfil all my will;" Gr. "all my wills." In which there is a plain view to Saul, who was partial in his obedience to the will of God, (1 Sam. xv.) and upon that score lost the kingdom for him and his.

2. "That every part of that obedience should be carried to the highest pitch and degree." This the law required of them, as a condition of life; as our Lord himself shewed unto the lawyer, Luke x. 27, "Thou shalt love the Lord thy God with all thy heart, and

with all thy soul, and with all thy strength, and with all thy mind; and thy neighbour as thyself." Ver. 28, "This do, and thou shalt live." But it was a demand they could never have answered, since Adam had squandered away their stock of ability, and left them without strength. They might as soon have reached up their hands to the sun in the firmament, so far above, as have attained to the perfection of obedience demanded of them by the law. Wherefore it was agreed, that Christ should in their name obey the law in that perfection, being made under the law, as they were under it, Gal. iv. 4, 5; that every action of his should bear, not only a goodness of the matter, but of the manner too, and that in perfection; that love to God and man should flame in his holy human soul, to the utmost pitch required by the law; and so that debt owing by his seed, might be cleared by him, acting as a public man in their name.

3. *Lastly*, "That all this should be continued to the end, without the least failure in one jot of parts or degrees of obedience." This also was a condition of life stated in the first covenant; Gal. iii. 10, "Cursed is every one that continueth not in all things which are written in the book of the law to do them." But it was a demand they could by no means answer; man's nature being so vitiated by the fall, that if a thousand hells were lying upon it, the best on earth could not keep perfectly right one hour. Wherefore it was agreed, that the second Adam should, in the name of those he represented, continue in all things written in the law to do them, even to the end; that he should not fail in his begun course of obedience, but run to the end of the race set before him; that from the womb to the grave, his heart and life should shine in perfection of holiness. All which he did accordingly fulfil, being obedient unto death, Philip. ii. 8.

ARTICLE III.

SATISFACTION FOR SIN.

THE former two were in the condition of Adam's covenant: but this was not in it; for while there was no sin, there was no place for satisfaction for sin. But the new covenant behoved to be settled on the condition of a satisfaction for sin; because the broken law or covenant of works, insisted for it as a condition of life to sinners, in virtue of its penalty by them incurred. Howbeit, it was quite beyond their power to answer this demand of the law. If then the

Mediator will have a seed brought from the state of death, into a state of life and salvation, he must buy them from the hand of justice, telling down a price for every soul of them, 1 Cor. vi. 20. Accordingly, all the sins of every one of them, from the first sin they should be convinced and born in, to the last sin they should expire with, being foreseen of God from eternity, were summed up as so many breaches of the law or covenant of works: and it was made another conditionary article of the covenant, "That Christ, as a public person, should satisfy fully and completely for them all:" Isa. liii. 6, "The Lord hath laid on him the iniquity of us all; compared with Lev. xvi. 21, "All the iniquities of the children of Israel, and all their transgressions in all their sins."

Now, in this article there were three things established.

First, "That Christ, as a public person, should satisfy for them by suffering:" Luke xxiv. 26, "Ought not Christ to have suffered?" Sinners were liable to suffer for the satisfaction of justice: and nothing but suffering could be accepted, as a compensation of the injury done by sin, to the honour of God, in the violating of his holy law. Thousands of rams, and ten thousands of rivers of oil, were at the Mediator's command; all the silver and gold, and the precious things of the earth and seas, were at his disposal: but none of these could be of use in this bargain; they were all of no value in a treaty for the redemption of the soul, Mic. vi. 6, 7, 8; 1 Pet. i. 18. His own suffering could only avail here. That the Son of God should suffer, was indeed an amazing proposal; but it was necessary, in order to satisfy for our sin.

Secondly, "That he should suffer the same punishment they should have suffered in virtue of the penalty of the broken covenant of works;" and that was death in its full latitude and extent. This appears from the penalty of that covenant, from which the debt of satisfaction was stated, "In the day thou eatest thereof, thou shalt surely die," Gen. ii. 17; compared with Christ's dying for, that is, in the room and stead of sinners, so often mentioned in the Scriptures, Rom. v. 6, 8; 2 Cor. v. 14, 15; 1 Thess. v. 10. And it is confirmed from that the Scripture teacheth, that the all for whom Christ died, died in him, 2 Cor. v. 14, "If one died for all, then were all dead;" or, then the all died, to wit, in him; even as they sinned, and became liable to death, in Adam. So saith the apostle, "I am crucified with Christ," Gal. ii. 20.

For clearing this purpose, two things are to be distinguished in that death which was the penalty of the covenant of works. 1. What was essential to it, wrapt up in the very nature of the thing itself called death in the stile of that covenant. And that may be compromised in these two: (1.) The curse, (2.) Infinite execution: the former making the death legal, the latter making it real and satisfactory. 2. What was accidental to it, arising, not from the nature of the thing in itself, but from the nature of the party dying that death. And this is of two sorts. (1.) There is something arising from the nature of the dying party, as he is a mere creature; such as the eternity of the punishment and despair of life. (2.) Something arising from the nature of the dying party, as he is a sinful creature, or subject of inherent sin; such as the extinction of the saving relation betwixt God and the soul, the divesting it of God's image, and the corruption and dissolution of the body.

Now, the essentials of that death we should have suffered in virtue of the penalty of the broken covenant of works, were laid, as a part of the condition of the covenant of grace, on Jesus Christ, to be suffered by him, for us. For he was "made a curse for us," Gal. iii. 13, and "gave himself for us, an offering and a sacrifice to God for a sweet smelling savour," Eph. v. 2, that is, a sacrifice equalling the infinite offence arising from our sin; whence he is said, "by one suffering" to have "perfected for ever them that are sanctified," Heb. x. 14. But the accidentals of that death were no part of the condition of the covenant laid on him: nor could they at all have place in him; since he was neither a subject of inherent sin, nor yet a mere creature. Nevertheless, it was still the same death that we should have suffered; forasmuch as the essentials were the same. Thus the bodies of the saints, which are now weak and corruptible, shall at the resurrection be powerful and incorruptible, yet still the same bodies; since these qualities are but accidental to a human body. So in the case of clearing of debt, though, the borrower could not pay it, but in a great quantity of copper-money, and that advanced by little and little for a long time: which withal would ruin him: yet, if his rich cautioner should pay all at once, in a little gold; it is evident, it would be the payment of the same debt, providing only that it fully equalled the sum borrowed. Nay, confining our view to death itself, which is the general proper notion of the thing in question, let us put the case, that two men, equally guilty of the same crime, are laid under one and the same sentence of death; and it is execute on them both: but the one is by a miracle raised to life again, the other lies and rots in the grave. It is evident in this case, that the death they died, is the same death, answering the very same estimate which the law made of the crime; and that therefore the death of the former satisfies the law, as well as the death of the latter, so that it cannot reach his life again for that crime: howbeit, it is no less evident, that there is a huge difference between the death of the one and the other, in accidentals, particularly in the duration or continuance of it. Wherefore, we conclude, that as Christ gave the same active obedience to the law which we should have given in virtue of the condition of the covenant of works; so he suffered the same punishment of death that we should have suffered in virtue of the penalty of that broken covenant: forasmuch as, whatever difference there was in accidentals, the essentials were the same; it being laid on him, in the new covenant, to suffer death for us, equalling the infinite offence arising from our sins, being fully proportionate to the estimate the law and justice of God had made of our crime.

And thus, according to what is said, two grand points were established in the conditionary part of the covenant.

1. "That the curse of the law due to us for our sin, should be transferred on him as the second Adam, our representative; whereby he should instantly be a man dead in law for his seed." Either he or they behoved to bear the curse: for it is written, "Cursed is every one that continueth not in all things written in the law." Since God had annexed the threatening of death to his first covenant, saying, "In the day thou eatest thereof, thou shalt surely die;" the truth of God secured the curse its taking place, as soon as sin should enter. Now, they were not able to bear it, without being ruined thereby. But that it might be borne, and they withal saved, it was provided, that he should be laid under it, in their room and stead; that as he was made sin for them, so he should also, in consequence thereof, be made a curse for them, Gal. iii. 13.

The curse is the sentence of the broken law passed upon a person, binding him over to the revenging wrath of God, to the full satisfaction of justice. So that awful and tremendous mystery lies here. Christ must stand before the tribunal of the holy law, as a sinner; answerable for all the sins of all the elect, by virtue of his bond of suretiship registrate in the records of heaven: and sentence must pass upon him, adjudging and binding him over to suffer all that revenging wrath which their sins deserved. The Lamb of God said, "Lo, I come:" so it was done, he was made a curse for us. In token hereof, being convened before the Jewish sanhedrim, he was judged a blasphemer, and worthy of death; and compearing before Pilate the Roman governor, he was by him sentenced to die, and that upon the cross.

Behold the stupendous result of this awful transaction, the transferring of the curse on Christ the second Adam! 1. Hereby he was made the separated one of the elect society, separated unto evil, as the immediate effect of the curse is described, Deut. xxix. 21. He was made the devoted head, devoted to pay for all the rest. He was set up as the mark against which all the arrows of revenging wrath should be aimed. He was appointed to be the common receptacle of all the floods of vengeance, issuing from incensed justice towards the whole body of the elect, to swallow them up; here the current of all these was turned, that they should together flow in upon him. Hence he cries, Psalm lxix. 2, "I am come into deep waters, where the floods overflow me." 2. Hereby he became the resting-place of revenging justice, where it was to prey, till it should be satisfied to the full; Isa. liii. 10, "Thou shalt make his soul an offering for sin." In token hereof, when the officers came to apprehend him, he said, "If ye seek me let these go their way." Justice leaves the chase of the rebel-multitude, seeks him, and him only; since he was made a curse for them. Thus he was designed to be the sacrifice for all his seed, which the fire of revenging wrath should burn up, till it sent forth a sweet-smelling savour, a savour of rest to the incensed justice of an offended God.

2. Another grand point established here, was, "That the curse transferred on him, should be infinitely executed upon him as the second Adam, our representative; whereby he should die really for his seed, to the full compensation of all the injuries done to the honour of an infinite God, by all their sins." Vain is that curse which takes not effect: as the curse of the holy law was not causeless, so it could not miss of coming on, in its infinite weight, for the satisfaction of justice. Now, had it so come on them, they would have been eternally satisfying, but could never have ended their satisfaction. But coming on him, the church of God was purchased with his own blood, Acts xx. 28, and "the blood of Jesus Christ his Son cleanseth us from all sin," 1 John i. 7, the infinite dignity of the person dying, making the execution of the curse on him unto death to be infinite in value, fully compensating the infinite wrong, according to the estimate made of it by law and justice.

And here it was settled and agreed, "That the curse should be executed on the whole man;" that being their due; and therefore that he should "become poor," and "not have where to lay his head," that he should suffer hunger, for want of meat; thirst, for want of drink: that his name and reputation should be sunk, loaded with vile reproaches and slanders; his very friends going about to lay hands upon him as a mad-man; that he should be accounted a worm and no man; a reproach of men, and despised of the people: his whole lot in the world afflicted, persecuted, and exceeding low; and that in end, being stripped of his garments, he should be hung up naked before the sun, between two malefactors, as if the worst of the three.

More particulary, here it was stipulated and agreed to,

1*st*, "That the curse should be executed on his blessed body;" forasmuch as their bodies were liable to it, as being instruments of sin and dishonour to God: that he should be hanged on a tree, that all the world might therein read the anger of God against the breaking of the first covenant, by eating of the forbidden tree; and his being made a curse for us, since it is written, "Cursed is every one that hangeth on a tree;" that the curse should go over, and death pass through, every part of that blessed body: that his head should be disgracefully wounded with a crown of thorns put upon it; his visage marred more than any man; his back given to the smiters; his cheeks to them that plucked off the hair; his face not hid from shame and spitting; his tongue made to cleave to his jaws; his hands and feet pierced, nailed to a cross; all his bones drawn out of joint; his heart like wax, melted in the midst of his bowels; his blood shed; his strength dried up; and that in end it should expire and die, be separate from his soul, pierced with a spear, and laid in the dust of death.

2*dly*, "That it should be executed on his holy soul, in a special manner;" forasmuch as their souls were the principal actors in sin: that he should undergo the wrath of God in it, being all along his life a man of sorrows, and acquainted with grief: and that towards the latter end, there should be an hour and power of darkness, wherein the malice of men, the power and rage of devils, should be jointly engaged against him, making their utmost efforts on him; and then the full floods of Heaven's revenging wrath should come rolling in upon his soul: that they should so overflow it, as to strike him with sore amazement, fill him with trouble, load him with heaviness, and overwhelm him with exceeding sorrow: that there should be such a pressure of divine wrath on his holy soul, as should put him into an agony, even to his sweating great drops of blood; and should bring over it a total eclipse of comfort, and as it were melt it within him; that so, while he was dying a bodily death on the cross, he might die also a spiritual death, such as a most pure and holy soul was capable of.

Here was the death determined in the covenant, for the second Adam our representative; a death in virtue of the curse transferred on him, long-lasting and exquisite, for the full satisfaction of revenging justice. (1.) It was long-lasting death. He was a-dying, in the style of the covenant of works, not only upon the cross, but all along the time of his life; the death that was the penalty of that covenant, working in him from the womb, till it laid him in the grave. Wherefore he behoved to be conceived of a woman of low estate; and born in the stable of an inn, no room for him in the inn itself; laid in a manger, no cradle to receive him; his infant-blood shed in his circumcision, as if he had been a sinner; yea, his infant-life sought by a cruel persecutor, and his mother obliged to run her country with him, and go to Egypt. Returning, he behoved to live an obscure life in an obscure place, from which nothing great nor good was expected, John i. 46; and coming out of his obscurity, to be set up as the object of the world's ill-will and spite, obloquy and maltreatment, till by the hand of Jew and Gentile he was put to death on the cross. (2.) It was an exquisite death. No pity, no sparing in it: but the curse carried it to the highest pitch. No sparing from an angry God, Rom. viii. 32. No sparing from wicked men let loose on him, pushing him like bulls, roaring on him and devouring him like lions, and rending him like dogs, when once their hour and power of darkness was come, Psalm xxii. 12, 13, 16. Not a good word spoken to him in the midst of his torments, by those that stood by; but cruelly mocked and insulted by them. Much less a good deed done him. Not a drink of water allowed him, but vinegar offered him, in his thirst caused through the fire of divine wrath drinking up his spirits and moisture. Nay, the very face of the heavens was lowring on him: the sun must not give him its light, but wrap up itself from him in darkness; because "light is sweet, and it is a pleasant thing to behold the sun."

Lastly, In this article it was established, "That he should suffer all this voluntarily, submissively, and resignedly, out of regard to the wronged honour of God." Accordingly, speaking of his life, he saith, "No man taketh it from me, but I lay it down of myself," John x. 18, compare Psalm xl. 6, 7, 8. This the law demanded of them whom he suffered for, condemning all murmuring and impatience, and binding them to obedience and suffering conjunctly. But how could they have so borne the load of revenging wrath, who cannot bear a sharp fit of the gout or gravel, without some degree of impatience in the eye of the holy law? Wherefore it was provided, that Christ, as their representative, should bear their punishment voluntarily, and with perfect patience and resignation: that he should go "as a lamb to the slaughter," quietly resigning his human will to the divine will; and make his obedience in his sufferings, as conspicuous as his sufferings themselves: that, in midst of the extremity of his torments, he should not entertain the least unbecoming thought of God, but acknowledge him holy in them all, Psalm xxii. 3: nor yet the least grudge against his murderers; in token of which, he prayed for them while he was on the cross, saying, "Father forgive them; for they know not what they do," Luke xxiii. 34.

Thus far of the conditionary articles.

INFERENCES FROM THE CONDITIONARY PART OF THE COVENANT.

Thus, as we have shown, stood the important condition of the covenant of grace; and from thence the following inferences are fairly deducible.

Inf. 1. The redemption of the soul is precious. Is it not? Look to the price of the purchase, the ransom of souls, as stated in the covenant; the holy birth, righteous life, and satisfactory death of the Son of God; and ye must conclude it to be a costly redemption. Turn hither your eyes, (1.) Ye who value not your own souls. See here the worth of those souls ye sell for a thing of nought, for satisfying a corrupt passion, a pang of lust of one sort or another. Costly was the gathering of what ye thus throw away. Ye let them go at a very low price; but Christ could not have one of them at the hand of justice, but at the price of his precious blood. Ye cannot forego the vanities of a present world for them, nor spend a serious day or hour about them; but he, after a life-time of sorrows underwent a most bitter death for them. What think ye? Was he inconsiderate and too liberal in his making such a bargain for the redemption of souls? He was infinitely just, who proposed the condition; and he was infinitely wise, who went in to it. He was a Father that exacted this ransom for souls; and he was his own Son that paid it. Be ashamed and blush, to make so low an estimate of those souls, which Heaven set such a high price on. (2.) Ye who have cheap thoughts of the pardom of sin, and of salvation, correct your mistake here. You fearlessly run on in sin, thinking all may soon be set to rights again, with a God forgive me, have mercy on my soul; so as you may leap out of Delilah's lap into Abraham's bosom. O fearful infatuation! Is the mean and low birth, the sorrowful life, and the bitter death of Jesus the Son of God, not sufficient to give men a just and honourable notion of the pardon of sin? Look into the condition of the covenant for pardon, written in the blood of the Lamb of God, and learn the value a just God puts upon his pardons and salvation. See, O sinner, that it is not words, but deeds; not promises and resolves to do better, but perfection of holiness and obedience; not drawing of sighs and shedding of tears, but shedding of blood; and not thy blood neither, but blood of infinite value, that could procure the pardon of sin, and salvation. And if thou have not upon thee by faith all that righteousness Christ fulfilled, to be presented unto God for a pardon, thou shalt never obtain it. Particularly, ye are apt to think light of the sin ye were born in, and the corruption cleaving to your nature; but know, that God does not think light of these. It behoved to be an article of the covenant, that Christ should be born holy, and retain the holiness of human nature in him to the end; else the unholy birth and corrupt nature we derived from Adam, would have staked us all down eternally under the curse. (3.) Ye that have mean thoughts of the holy law, rectify your dangerous mistake by the help of this glass. Ye make no bones of transgressing its commands; ye neglect and despise its curse: as it is a law, ye shew not so much regard to it as to the laws of men; and as it is a covenant, ye look upon it as out of date, being in no concern how it may be satisfied for you. And shall the honour of the holy law lie in the dust, in your case? Rather than it should so lie in the case of Sodom and Gomorrah, God would have them laid in ashes with fire and brimstone. Yea, for vindicating the honour of the law, this whole world shall be burnt to ashes, and all the unholy cast out from the presence of the Lord for ever. And in the case of them that are saved, God would have the curse of the law executed upon his own Son as their Surety, and the commands of it perfectly obeyed in all points by him in their name. Sure, if you are possessed of any share herein, it will be great and honourable in your sight, as it is in the sight of God.

Inf. 2. The law is no loser, in that life and salvation are bestowed on believers in Christ. It is so far from being made void through faith, that it is established thereby, as the apostle witnesseth, Rom. iii. 81. God would never dispense his pardons at the expence of the honour of his law; nor declare one righteous, without the righteousness of the law being fulfilled, either by him, or in him by another, Rom. viii. 4. Wherefore, life and salvation being designed for the elect, the law's whole accounts of all it had to charge on them for life, were taken in; and an infallible method was laid down for clearing them, the burden of the payment being transferred on Christ their surety. By this exchange of persons the law had no loss. Nay, it was more for the honour of the law, that he was made under it, and satisfied it, in virtue of the claim it had upon him by the second covenant, than if they, being mere creatures, had satisfied it in all points. But the truth is, they being sinners, could never by any means have fully satisfied it; though it had eternally pursued them and exacted of them, it would never have had enough from them; whereas now, by Christ's taking their debt on him, it was paid to the utmost farthing.

Inf. 3. Faith hath a broad and firm bottom to stand on before the Lord. The believer hath a strong plea for life and salvation, which cannot miscarry; namely, the condition of the covenant fulfilled by Jesus Christ, even all righteousness: Having therefore, brethren, boldnesss to enter into the holiest by the blood of Jesus—let us draw near with a true heart, in full assurance of faith," Heb. x. 19—22. The broken boards of uncovenanted mercy, and men's own works, which presumption fixeth upon, cannot but fail, since the law admits no life for a sinner on these grounds. But forasmuch as there a gift of Christ and his righteousness proclaimed in the gospel is by the authority of heaven, he who by faith receiveth that gift, and makes the same his only plea before the Lord, cannot miss of salvation: Rom. v. 17, "They which receive (Gr. the) abundance of grace, and of the gift of righteousness, shall reign in life by one, Jesus Christ;" where the abundance mentioned, relates not to different degrees of the grace or gift, but to the offence, as appears from ver. 20: As if he had said, "Who receive the grace and gift of righteousness which abound beyond Adam's offence saving them out of the gulf of ruin it plunged them into." Faith uniting a sinner to Christ the head of the second covenant, makes him partaker of Christ's righteousness, as really as ever his covenant-relation to Adam made him partaker of his guilt. So having all that Christ was, did, or suffered, for fulfilling the condition of the second covenant, to plead for life and salvation; it is not possible the claim can miscarry, justice as well as mercy befriending the plea of faith, as a righteous thing with God, 2 Thess. i. 6, 7.

Inf. 4. *lastly*, All who are in Christ the head of the covenant of grace, and so brought into it personally, are inherently righteous, or holy. For like as though Adam alone did personally break the first covenant by the all-ruining offence, yet they to whom his guilt is imputed, do thereupon become inherently sinful, through the corruption of nature conveyed to them from him; so, howbeit, Christ alone did perform the condition of the second covenant, yet those to whom his righteousness is imputed, do thereupon become inherently righteous, through inherent grace communicated to them from him by the Spirit. So teacheth the apostle in the forecited passage, Rom. v. 17, "For if by one man's offence, death reigned by one; much more they which receive the abundance of grace, and of the gift of righteousness, shall reign in life by one, Jesus Christ." How did death reign by Adam's offence? Not only in point of guilt, whereby his posterity were bound over to destruction; but also in point of their being dead to all good, dead in trespasses and sins: therefore the receivers of the gift of righteousness must thereby be brought to reign in life, not only legally in justification, but also morally in sanctification, begun here, and perfected hereafter.

Accordingly, answerable to the three parts of the condition of the covenant of grace, undertaken and performed by the second Adam, to wit, holiness of nature, righteousness of life, and satisfaction for sin; there are three characters to be found in all capable subjects, who being personally brought into the covenant, have the righteousness of Christ upon them, and imputed to them.

Char. 1. They are all born again, and so made partakers of a new and holy nature: 2 Cor. v. 17, "Therefore," (namely, since he died for all, ver. 15,) "if any man be in Christ, he is a new creature." Christ's being born holy, secured a holy new birth to them in him: so they are all new creatures, "created in Christ Jesus unto good works," Eph. ii. 10; new made in Christ, as sure as they were marred in Adam. And how can it be otherwise? Can a man be ingrafted in the true vine, and not partake of the sap and juice of the stock, that is, the Spirit and grace of Christ? No, surely: "If any man have not the Spirit of Christ, he is none of his," Rom. viii. 9. Or, can the Spirit and grace of Christ be in any, and yet no change made on their nature, but it still remain unrenewed? No, indeed: "If Christ be in you, the body is dead, because of sin; but the Spirit is life, because of righteousness," ver. 10. Consider this, ye who pretend to rely on the righteousness of Christ, but are very easy in this point, whether ye are born again, or not; whether there is a holy nature derived from Christ to you, or not. Believe it, sirs, if it be not so, ye have no saving interest, part, nor lot in Christ's righteousness. Ye may on as good grounds pretend, that howbeit the guilt of Adam's sin was imputed to you, yet there was no corrupt nature derived from him to you; as pretend, that Christ's righteousness is imputed to you, while yet ye are not born again, your nature is not changed, by the communication of sanctifying grace from Christ, unto you. Deceive not yourselves; ye must be regenerate, else ye will perish: for "except a man be born again, he cannot see the kingdom of God," 1 John iii. 3.

Char. 2. They are all righteous and holy in their lives; Isa. lx. 21, "Thy people also shall be all righteous." Chap. lxii. 12, "And they shall call them the holy people." How did ungodliness, unrighteousness, and profanity, enter into the world, the which are now overflowing all banks? Was it not by one man, by Adam's sin, which is imputed to all mankind? Rom. v. 12. Then be sure, if the second Adam's righteousness be imputed to you, holiness of life will come along with it: 1 Cor. vi. 11, "But ye are washed, but ye are sanctified, but ye are justified." Does sanctification then go before justification? No: but it hath a necessary dependence on justification, and evidenceth it to the world, and to one's own conscience. Unjustified, unsanctified; and unsanctified, unjustified. Did our blessed Saviour come into the world, and in our nature lead a holy righteous life, that men might live as they list? Nay, quite the contrary; even that we being delivered out of the hands of our enemies, might serve him without fear, in holiness and righteousness before him, all the days of our life," Luke i. 74, 75. If then Christ lived for you, assuredly ye shall live for him. Consider this, ye who are far from righteousness of life, living in the neglect of the duties either of the first or second table, or both. Your ungodly and unrighteous life declares you to be yet in your sins, under the curse, and far from righteousness imputed. There is indeed a righteousness of Christ; but alas! it is not upon you: ye are naked for all it, and stand exposed to revenging wrath.

Char. 3. The old man is crucified in them all: Gal. v. 24, "They that are Christ's, have crucified the flesh, with the affections and lusts." Therefore I say to you in the words of the apostle, Rom. viii. 13, "If ye live after the flesh, ye shall die: but if ye through the Spirit do mortify the deeds of the body, ye shall live." When our Saviour hung on the cross, he hung there as representative of all that are his, with all their sins on him by imputation, that the body of sin might be destroyed in his sufferings for it, Rom. vi. 6. He hung there as the efficient meritorious cause of their mortification, that by his death they might destroy the power of death in them; which appears not in any thing more, than in living lusts preying on their souls: Hos. xiii. 14, "I will redeem them from death: O death, I will be thy plagues." See Tit. ii. 14; Rom. vi. 6, 7; Eph. v. 25, 26. And he hung there as the exemplary cause of their mortification; so that all who are his, and have sinned after the similitude of Adam's transgression, are likewise crucified and die to sin, after the similitude of his crucifixion and death; being crucified with him, Gal. ii. 20; planted together (with him in the likeness of his death, Rom. vi. 5; the fellowship of his sufferings making them conformable unto his death, Phil. iii. 10. Will ye then live after the flesh, not wrestling against, but fulfilling the lusts thereof; living in sin and to sin, instead of being mortified to it; and yet pretend that the satisfaction of Christ is imputed to you for righteousness? Truly you may on as good grounds say, that the blood of Christ shed for you, hath proven ineffectual; and that he hath so far missed of his aim and design in suffering for you; or that he died for you, that you might live in your sin without danger. These would make a blasphemous profession. Accordingly, your presumptuous sinful life and practice, is a course of practical blasphemy against the Son of God, making him the minister of sin; and evidenceth your pretensions to the imputation of his satisfaction to be altogether vain. Nay, of a truth, if ye have any saving interest in the death of Christ, your old man is crucified with him, Rom. vi. 6; and ye are dead with him, ver, 8; dead with him to sin, to the world, and to the law.

(1.) If ye have a saving interest in Christ's death, ye are dead with him to sin: Rom. vi. 10, "In that he died, he died unto sin once." Ver. 11, "Likewise also reckon ye yourselves to be dead indeed unto sin." While our Lord Jesus lived in the world, the sins of all the elect, as to the guilt of them, hung about him, and made him a "man of sorrows" all along; when he was upon the cross, they wrought upon him most furiously, stinging him to the very soul, till they killed him, and got him laid in the grave. Then they had done their utmost against him, they could do no more. So dying for sin, he died unto it, he was delivered from it: and in his resurrection he shook them all off, as Paul shook the viper off his hand into the fire, and felt no harm; rising out of the grave, even as he will appear the second time, without sin. Wherefore, if ye do indeed know the fellowship of his sufferings, if you really have fellowship with him in them, death will have made its way from Christ the head unto you as his members; his death unto sin cannot miss to work your death unto it also. If you are dead indeed with Christ, as ingrafted into him, sin hath got its death's wounds in you; the bond that knit your hearts and your lusts together, is loosed; and ye will be shaking off the viperous brood of them into the fire, in the daily practice of mortification. But if ye are not dead, but still living unto sin, it is an infallible evidence ye are none of the members of Christ: Rom. vi. 2, "How shall we that are dead to sin, live any longer therein?" Ver. 3, "Know ye not, that so many of us as were baptized into Jesus Christ, were baptized into his death?"

(2.) If ye have a saving interest in Christ's death, ye are dead with him to the world: Col. iii. 1, "If ye then be risen with Christ, seek those things which are above." Ver. 3, "For ye are dead, and your life is hid with Christ in God." The world hated him, and used him very unkindly while he was in it; and when he died he parted with it for good and all, John xvii. 11, "Now I am no more in the world—I come to thee." The quietest lodging that ever the world allowed him in it, was a grave: and coming out from thence, he never slept another night in it. He tarried indeed forty days in it after that; as many days as the Israelites' years in the wilderness; the former an exemplar, the latter a type of the Christian life, from conversion till the removal into the other world;

nevertheless he was dead to the world still; he conversed now and then with his own, but no more with the world. Now, if ye are his, ye are dead with him unto the world too, in virtue of his death; being crucified unto it, Gal. vi. 14. Union with Christ by faith lays sinners down in death, in Christ's grave; and so separates between them and the world for ever: and withal, it raiseth them up again with Christ into a quite new manner of life; no more that manner of life which they lived before their union with him, than that which Christ lived after his resurrection, was the manner of life he lived before his death: Rom. vi. 4, "We are buried with him by baptism into death: that like as Christ was raised up from the dead by the glory of the Father, even so we also should walk in newness of life." If your title to heaven is indeed settled, by your receiving the atonement, now is your forty days before your ascension into it; now are ye no more of the world, although you be in it: your treasure and heart are no more there. Ye are no more indwellers in it, as natives: but travelling through it, as "strangers, coming up from the wilderness, leaning on the beloved," Cant. iii. 5.

(3.) *Lastly*, If ye have a saving interest in Christ's death, ye are dead with him to the law also: Gal. ii. 19, "I through the law am dead to the law." Ver. 20, "I am crucified with Christ." Our Lord Jesus took on our nature to satisfy the law therein: the whole course of his life was a course of obedience to it, for life and salvation to us; and he suffered to satisfy it in what of that kind it had to demand, for that effect: in a word, he was born to the law, he lived to the law, and he died to the law; namely, to clear accounts with it, to satisfy it fully, and get life and salvation for us with its good leave. He was "made under the law, to redeem them that were under the law," Gal. iv. 4, 5. And when once it fell upon him, it never left exacting of him, till it had got the utmost farthing, and he was quite free with it, as dead to it, Rom. vii. 4. In token whereof he got up the bond, blotted it out, yea, rent it in pieces, nailing it to his cross, Col. ii. 14. Now, Christ became dead to it, dying to it in his death on the cross: so that the holiness and righteousness of the man Christ did thereafter no more run in the channel in which it had run before, namely, from the womb to his grave; that is to say, it was no more, and shall be no more for ever, obedience performed to the law for life and salvation; these having been completely gained and secured by the obedience he gave from the womb to the grave. "Wherefore, my brethren," if ye be his, "ye also are become dead to the law by the body of Christ," which became dead to it on the cross, Rom. vii. 4. As ye will not be libertines in your life and practice, being dead to sin and the world with Christ; so ye will not be legalists in your life and practice neither, being also dead with him to the law as a covenant of works. Your obedience will run in another channel than it did before your union with Christ, even in the channel of the gospel. Ye will serve in newness of spirit, in faith and love. The frowns of a merciful Father will be a terror to you to frighten you from sin; love and gratitude will prompt you to obedience. The grieving of the Spirit of a Saviour will be a spring of sorrow to you; and his atoning blood and perfect righteousness will be the spring-head of all your comfort before the Lord; your good works but streams thereof, as they evidence your saving interest in these, are accepted through them, and glorify God your Saviour. Ye will not continue to serve in the oldness of the letter, as before; at what time the law was the spring of all the obedience ye performed; fear of the punishment of hell for your sins, and hope of the reward of heaven's happiness for your duties, being the weights that made you go, though for all them you often stopped; your sorrows springing from your ill works, under the influence of the law allenarly; and your comforts from your good works, under the same influence; ye being alive to the law and dead to Christ. Rom. vii. 6, "But now we are delivered from the law, that being dead wherein we were held; that we should serve in newness of spirit, and not in the oldness of the letter." If by faith you wholly rely on Christ's righteousness, the holiness of his nature, the righteousness of his life, and his satisfaction for sin, how is it possible but ye must be dead to the law? for the law is not of faith, Gal. iii. 12. But if you perform your obedience for life and salvation, looking for acceptance with God on the account of your works, you go in a way directly opposite to the way of faith, and either altogether reject Christ's satisfying of the law, or else impute imperfection unto his payment of the bond. And "Christ is become of no effect unto you, whosoever of you are justified by the law; ye are fallen from grace," Gal. v. 4.

Thus far of the first part of the covenant, namely the conditionary part.

The second part of the covenant, namely, the promissory part.

In every covenant, whether it be a proper or improper covenant, there is a promise. And in a proper covenant, the promissory part answers to the conditionary part; being an obligation which the party-covenanter to whom the condition is performed, comes under for some benefit to be bestowed in view of the performance of the condition. This is the promise of a proper covenant, binding on him who makes it, providing the party contracting with him do his part. In every such case, where the thing is lawful and possible, it binds in point of truth and faithfulness, by virtue of compact: in some cases it binds also in point of remunerative justice; to wit, where the condition performed is properly equivalent to the benefit promised.

The covenant of grace, made between God and Christ as the head and representative of his spiritual seed, is a proper covenant. And in it there is a promissory part, answering to the conditionary part already explained: and it is God's part of the covenant, as the other was the Mediator's. Thereby God hath obliged himself to make the benefits therein condescended on forthcoming, upon the consideration of the performing of the condition. And forasmuch as the condition performed by Christ, was strictly meritorious of the benefits promised; the promises are binding and firm, not only in respect of the truth and faithfulness, but also of the justice of God.

Of what weight and importance the promissory part of the covenant is, will appear by the following considerations.

1. The covenant hath its name from this part of it, being called the covenants of promise, Eph. ii. 12. Covenants, because, though still in itself but one covenant, yet from its first promulgation in paradise, it was often renewed, as to Abraham, Jacob, the Israelites in the wilderness, and to David: and as oft as it was renewed it was renewed in a promise. The first covenant had a promise of life: yet it is not called a covenant of promise: on the contrary, the law, or that covenant, is opposed to the promise; though not in its use, yet in its nature, Gal. iii. 18, "If the inheritance be of the law, it is no more of promise." For the law's promise of life was suspended on the condition of works, to be performed by men themselves: whereas in the second covenant, life and salvation are promised to sinners freely, for Christ's sake, without respect to any work of theirs as the condition thereof.

2. The covenant is described to us, by the Holy Ghost, as a cluster of free promises of grace and glory to poor sinners, in which no mention is made of any condition: Heb. viii. 10, "This is the covenant—I will put my laws into their mind, and write them in their hearts: and I will be to them a God, and they shall be to me a people." Ver. 11, "And they shall not teach every man his neighbour, and every man his brother, saying, Know the Lord: for all shall know me, from the least to the greatest." Ver. 12, "For I will be merciful to their unrighteousness, and their sins and their iniquities will I remember no more." These promises with their condition, having been proposed to, and accepted by Christ as second

Adam, and the condition performed by him; the covenant comes natively, in the gospel, to be set before us in them, to be by us received and embraced in and through Christ, by faith. Thus the promises are the covenant by way of eminency; even God's covenant, wherein he hath bound himself to perform his part, as the Mediator hath already performed his. And in this sense, indeed, the covenant of grace is not conditional, but consists of absolute promises; that is, promises become absolute, through the condition thereof actually performed already: but being considered in its full latitude, and in respect of Christ the covenant, and all the promises thereof, are properly and strictly conditional.

3. The promises of the covenant are the purchase of the blood of Christ; the fruit of his fulfilling all righteousness, in his birth, life, and death. As the curse came by the demerit of Adam's sin; so the promises are owing to the merit of Christ's righteousness; they are the new testament in his blood, 1 Cor. xi. 25. From the promise of the bread and water, (Isa. xxxiii. 16.), to the promise of a seat with him on his throne, (Rev. iii. 21.), they are all the purchase of his meritorious obedience even to death. Justly are they called exceeding precious promises, 2 Pet. i. 4, as being the price of his blood. Of what unspeakable weight and importance must they be, that cost such a price, between the Father and his own Son!

4. The great design and end of the covenant is accomplished in the performing of the promissory part thereof; and that is, the glory of God, and the salvation of sinners. The great glory to God, and grace to sinners, springing up from the whole of the covenant, meet together here, namely, in the accomplishment of the promises, as all the rivers meet together in the sea. The promises were the great thing the parties-contractors had in view, when they entered into the covenant: it was room for them the Father sought by his proposal of the covenant; and that was what the Son intended to purchase, by his fulfilling the condition. The condition of the covenant is the foundation of the promises; the promises the glorious superstructure reared upon that costly foundation. The administration of the covenant, is subservient to the accomplishment of the promises. The condition of the covenant was performed on earth, in the space of about thirty-three years; the promises have been a-performing more than five thousand years on earth, and will be a-performing in heaven, through the ages of eternity.

5. The happiness and comfort of all the elect, for time and eternity, depends upon the promises of the covenant. What keeps unconverted elect persons from dying in that state, and so dropping down to hell, but the promises of the covenant? What makes

grace overtake them, when they are fleeing from it, but the promise? What preserves grace in them, like a spark of fire in an ocean, that it is not extinguished, but the promise? And what is their security and comfort in the face of death, but the same promise? 2 Sam. xxiii. 5.

6. The glory of the man Christ, as Mediator, depends on the promise of the covenant. This was the security, in the faith of which he lived on earth, about the space of thirty-three years, in a very low condition; and in end died an ignominious death: Psalm xxii. 4, "Our fathers trusted in thee: they trusted, and thou didst deliver them." He paid the price of the redemption of sinners, while as yet many of the redeemed were not born, nay nor as yet are; and several of them imbrewed their hands in his blood: but he rested on the promise of the covenant. He pleaded it when he was just entering into the swelling waves of death, where he was, like Jonah, to be swallowed up. John xvii. 5, "Now, O Father, glorify me with thyself." And in the faith of the accomplishment of the promise, he completed his performance of the condition: "for the joy that was set before him" in the promise, he "endured the cross, despising the shame," Heb. xii. 2.

7. *Lastly*, God hath sworn the promise of the covenant: "I have made a covenant with my chosen: I have sworn unto David my servant." The apostle tells us, that "God willing more abundantly to show unto the heirs of promise the immutability of his counsel, confirmed it by an oath," Heb. vi. 17. A tender man will not swear a promise, but in a matter of weight. Of what unspeakable weight and importance then must the promise of the covenant be, which the God of truth hath confirmed with his oath?

Now, for clearing of this part of the covenant, we shall, 1. Consider the promises in general; and, 2. Take a more particular view of them.

OF THE PROMISES IN GENERAL.

As to the promises in general, two things are to be inquired into: 1. What are the general kinds of them? 2. To whom they are made?

I. As to the general kinds of the promises; considering the parties on whom the promises of the covenant of grace have their direct and immediate effect, they appear to be of two general kinds.

1. Some of them have their direct and immediate effect on Christ himself, the head of the covenant; such as the promise of assistance in his work, and the promise of a name above every name. So in the first covenant, there were promises which were to have their direct and immediate effect, on Adam himself, and looked not, but

mediately and indirectly, to his posterity, such of them, at least, as should have lived after the complete fulfilling of the condition of the covenant; namely, the promises of natural life continued in vigour and comfort, and of spiritual life in favour and fellowship with God, during the course of his probationary obedience.

2. Others of them have their direct and immediate effect on Christ's spiritual seed, comprehended with him in the covenant; such as the promises of regeneration, of the new heart, and cleansing from the defilement of sin. So in the first Adam's covenant, the promise of life contained a promise of the holy conception and birth of his natural seed; in respect of which the promise would have had its direct and immediate effect, not on Adam himself, but on his posterity.

II. The next thing to be considered, is, To whom they were made? And we may take up this point in two things.

First, The promises of the first sort, namely, those having their direct and immediate effect on the person of Christ, were made to Christ himself. Of this no doubt can be moved. And they were made to him as head of the covenant, the second Adam, the representative of his seed. This appears from our text, wherein he is called the Chosen, the head-elect, and representative of the election, David God's servant; in which capacity, the covenant was cut off, or made to him, by the Father. It is evident, that all the promises of assistance in his work, and of his subequent reward, were made to him in view of his performance of the condition: and therefore since he performed the condition, as head of the covenant, second Adam, and representative of his seed, these promises were made to him in that capacity.

The promises of this kind then were made to Christ only. And that was the peculiar honour put upon the head of the covenant, in the promissory part; as it was his peculiar burden to fulfil the conditionary part. So he hath the name which is above every name, and is anointed with the oil of gladness above his fellows. In the election, whereof he is the head, he shines above the rest, as the sun in his meridian brightness above the twinkling stars. He is the Benjamin at God's table with his brethren, whose mess of promises in the covenant is five times so much as any of theirs; the Joseph, who was separated from his brethren, in fulfilling the condition of the covenant, and hath a double portion in the promised land made over to him, as the first-born amongst many brethren.

Nevertheless, as the honour and prosperity of the head redound to the members, their interest, in respect of their union and communion, being a joint interest; so the glory and honour settled on

Christ by promise, are a spring of grace and glory to his members, an enriching treasure, their glory and crown. He is that head of gold which puts a glory on the body: and the ointment poured upon the head, cannot miss to go down to the skirts of his garments. And hence is, (1.) The continual cry of prayer by the whole company of the faithful, for the accomplishment of the promises made to the Mediator, Psalm lxxii. 15, "Prayer also shall be made for him continually." It is evident that psalm concerns the Messias. But prayer made continually for Christ! how can that be? Why, till the world's end, that cry in prayer shall never cease among the faithful, Thy kingdom come, Matth. vi. 10. It began with Adam's embracing the promise by faith, was carried all along the time of the Old Testament; and now it hath been sounding in the New Testament church more than sixteen hundred years, and shall not cease until the consummation of all things. (2.) Hence also the joyful acclamations of praise, by the same company, for the accomplishment of promises to the Mediator. Whensoever there appears any such accomplishment made, it is matter of joy to the church; and the more there appears of it, the joy is the more increased. Thus the church hath a song upon the fulfilling of the promise of the gathering of the nations unto him, Isa. xii. 1; of this victory over Antichrist, Rev. xix. 1; of the calling of the Jews, ver. 6. And when, the end being come, all the promises made to him shall be accomplished, that will afford them an everlasting song of praise.

Secondly, The promises of the other sort, namely, those having their direct and immediate effect on the elect, are made to Christ primarily, and to them secondarily: first, to the head; then, to the members, through him.

1. The promises having their immediate effect on the elect, are made to Christ immediately, primarily, and chiefly. God hath in the covenant promised grace and glory, all that pertains to life and godliness, unto a select company of mankind: but the promise of all these was first and chiefly made to Christ their head; so that he hath not only an interest in these promises, but the chief interest in them. This appears by several documents from the word of God.

1*st*, The apostle testifies, that the promises were made to the seed, which is Christ, Gal. iii. 16. And the promises he speaks of, are, promises of the blessings, of the Spirit, ver. 14; of the inheritance, ver. 18; the promises received through faith, ver. 14. Even these are made to Christ the head of the body. This is confirmed by those passages which shew God's covenant to be made with Christ, and in the meantime explain it by a promise of the happiness of his seed, Psalm lxxxix. 3, 4; ver. 28, and 29, ver. 35, and 36. And what is more natural, than to make a promise to a father in favour of his children?

2dly, Our Lord Jesus is constitute the heir of all things, (Heb. i. 2.), in virtue of the promise of the covenant, "I will make him my first-born," Psalm lxxxix. 27. Now, if Christ, as the second Adam, be heir of all things, by his Father's promise, the promises of all things are made to him; and, consequently, the promise of eternal life, comprehending all happiness to his people, is made to him in the first place. So Christ is the first and chief heir; and they are secondary heirs in and through him. Hence, in view of the great promise of the covenant, "I will be their God," our Saviour hath that endearing expression, "I ascend unto my Father and your Father, and to my God and your God," John xx. 17, compare Rom. 17, viii. "And if children, then heirs; heirs of God, and joint-heirs with Christ."

3dly, As in the covenant of works, God promised life to Adam's natural seed; upon condition of his perfect obedience; which is evident from death's coming on them by his disobedience: so in the covenant of grace, he hath promised life to Christ's spiritual seed, upon condition of his obedience; for "as in Adam all die, even so in Christ shall all be made alive," 1 Cor. xv. 22. But that promise of life for Adam's natural seed, was primarily made to Adam himself, while as yet none of them were in being; and they were to partake of it only through him, to whom it was made as their representative. Therefore the promise of life to Christ's spiritual seed, was made chiefly to Christ himself; and to them only in and through him. Accordingly we are told, that the promise of eternal life, upon which the hope of believers is built, was made before the world began, Tit. i. 2. And to whom could it be then made immediately and primarily, but to Christ the head of the covenant?

Lastly, These promises contain a part of the reward made over in the covenant to Jesus Christ, "who, for the joy that was set before him, endured the cross," Heb. xii. 2. A great part of which joy lay here; "He shall see his seed, the travail of his soul," Isa. liii. 10, 11. All of these promises were the price of his blood to him, the purchase of his obedience and death; therefore called the New Testament in his blood. To whom could the reward be chiefly promised, but to him who, performing the condition, wrought the work? Unto him therefore it was of debt, namely in virtue of the promise, which made it due to him upon his performing the condition. The blessings of the covenant which come on the elect, are certainly to be considered as a reward to Christ, as well as a free gift to them. And considering them in the first of these views, there is no more absurdity in the promise of the new heart's being made to Christ, than in a physician's making a promise to a father to cure his lame child, when he hath given him security for his fees: in which case, the child cannot look on the promise as made to himself at all, but secondarily, through his father, who was the party-contractor.

This is a point of considerable weight, and serves both to inform our minds, and direct our practice; for the following inferences from it are native.

(1.) The promises of the covenant are not made to the believer's good works; but to Christ's works, and to the working believer in him. Unto the believer they are absolutely free, and not of debt; and therefore are not made to his works; for "to him that worketh, is the reward not reckoned of grace, but of debt," Rom. iv. 4. There is indeed a comely order of the promises, whereby the promise of purity of heart to the elect, goes before the promise of their seeing God in heaven; the promise of humiliation, before that of lifting up; whereupon it is declared in the administration of the covenant, that the pure in heart shall see God; that they who humble themselves, shall be lifted up: and thus "godliness hath promise of the life that now is, and of that which is to come," 1 Tim. iv. 8. But the foundation of all these promises, whether of things that are our duty, or our privilege, what they all depend upon as their proper condition, is the obedience of Christ allenarly; they being all made to him in the first place, the latter as well as the former.

(2.) The first grace whereby the dead elect are quickened, and made to believe and unite with Christ, is conveyed to them in the channel of a promise, as well as the grace following faith: Ezek. xxxvi. 27, "I will put my Spirit within you." For although in their natural state they are not capable of a believing pleading of the promise; nor have they, at that time, a personal saving interest in the promises; yet the Lord Jesus knoweth them that are his, and for whom the promises were made to him; and having the administration of the covenant in his own hand, he cannot fail of seeing to the accomplishing of them, in the appointed time. Howbeit they, being dead in trespasses and sins, cannot consult their own interest; yet he having the chief interest in the promises, will not neglect his own cause, but will see them exactly accomplished.

(3.) The way to be personally and savingly interested in the promises, for time and eternity, is to unite with Christ by faith; "for all the promises of God in him are yea, and in him amen," 2 Cor. i. 20. Would ye fain know how the great and precious promises may become yours? Why, they are all his; they are all made to him. Take him, and they are yours: even as he who marries the heiress, hath a right to her portion, and all the bills and bonds wherein any of it is contained.

(4.) When through deadness and darkness of spirit, whether arising from some conscience-wasting guilt, or otherwise, your faith of the promise is failed, and you cannot again fasten your gripe upon it, because you can see no good in you; embrace Christ again, and the promise in him; notwithstanding of your seen and felt sinfulness and utter unworthiness; and by no means stand off from the promise until you be in better case; but say with the Psalmist, "Iniquities prevail against me: as for our transgressions, thou shalt purge them away," Psalm lxv. 3. For as the goodness in you was not the ground of the promise; so the evil in you doth not overturn it, and make it of none effect. The foundation of the promise stands sure in Christ, whatever alterations the frame and case of a believer's spirit do undergo. It is established as the moon, (Psalm lxxxix. 37.), which is still the same in itself, notwithstanding of the variety of its appearances to our sight, one while waxing, at another time waning.

(5.) The true way to plead the promises, is to come to God in the name of Christ, and plead the fulfilling of them to us for his sake: John xvi. 23, "Whatsoever ye shall ask the Father in my name, he will give it you." Matt. xxi. 22, "Believing, ye shall receive." Dan. ix. 17, "O our God,—cause thy face to shine upon thy sanctuary that is desolate, for the Lord's sake." To ask in Christ's name, believing, is to present one's self before the Lord, as a member of Christ, joined and cleaving to him offered unto us in the gospel; and for the sake of the head, to implore the free favour of the promise, relying on his merit for obtaining it. This is the import of that passage, Gen. xii. 3, as it relates to Christ, "In thee shall all families of the earth," to wit, that shall be blessed, "be blessed;" or rather, as the original word properly signifies, be made to kneel, namely, to receive the blessing; all that are blessed, being blessed in Christ, Eph. i. 3. Compare Phil. ii. 10. This is the method in which God dispenseth the favours of his promise: 2 Sam. vii. 21, "For thy word's sake, and according to thine own heart, hast thou done all these great things." Compare 1 Chron. xvii. 19, "For thy servant's sake, and according to thine own heart, hast thou done all this greatness;" *i. e.* for the sake of the word, thy servant, the Messias; for as both these passages are a narration of the very same thing, there is no manner of difference at all between them in the original, save that where the one hath thy word, the other hath thy servant.

(6.) Believers may hereby strengthen their faith of the accomplishment of the promises to them. Whatever easy work some have, in maintaining their presumptuous hopes of the mercy of God to eternal life; while not seeing the heinous nature of their sin, they build their hopes on something in themselves, rather than upon the free promise of the covenant in Christ Jesus; yet unto the serious godly, no small difficulty in believing doth arise, from the joint view of the greatness and preciousness of the promises, and the greatness of their sins and of their unworthiness. Hence they are ready to say, Can ever such promises be made out to such a one as I am? And truly there is nothing in them that can furnish an answer to this grave case. But here is a satisfying answer to it: The promises are all of them made to Christ chiefly, even to him who purchased them with his blood; and justice requires that they be performed to him: and being performed to him, they must needs have their effect on all his members, for whom, because in themselves unworthy, he merited them. So the soul may say, However unworthy I am, yet He is worthy for whom God should do this.

2. The promises having their immediate effect on the elect, are made to themselves secondarily, in and through Christ. As he hath the fundamental and chief interest in them, so they have a derived interest in them through him. There was from eternity a legal union between Christ and them in the covenant; whereby their debt became his, and the promises made to him became theirs. As upon the one hand, "The Lord laid on him the iniquity of us all," Isa. liii. 6; so, on the other hand, "grace was given us in Christ Jesus before the world began," 2 Tim. i. 9. In time there is a real mystical union made between him and them, upon his taking possession of them by his Spirit, and dwelling in them by faith. The former constituted a right for them unto the promises, in Christ the head; the latter vests them with a right thereto, in their own persons, through him; as being actual members of his body. In respect of the one, eternal life is said to be promised, and grace said to be "given us, before the world began," Tit. i. 2; 2 Tim. i. 9; in respect of the other, believers are called "the heirs of the promise," Heb. vi. 17; "partakers of his promise in Christ," Eph. iii. 6; and the "promise is given to them that believe," Gal. iii. 22.

Thus it appears, that these promises are made to Christ's spiritual seed, as well as to himself; though primarily to him as the representative, on whom the fulfilling of the condition was laid; and but secondarily to them as the represented, who were to receive the benefit. And hence ariseth another difference, namely, that, properly and strictly speaking, the promises were conditional to Christ, but they are absolute and free to us; even as the promise of life, in the first covenant, was conditional to Adam, which would have been absolute to his natural seed, the condition once being fulfilled. Thus Christ's merit and the free grace of God, meet together in the covenant: justice is fully satisfied, and grace runs freely, in that channel; the promises being all purchased at the full rate, but no part of the price advanced by us. Hence we obtain precious faith, with all other saving benefits, through the righteousness of God, and our Saviour Jesus Christ, (or rather, the righteousness of our God and Saviour Jesus Christ), as the proper condition of them all, 2 Pet. i. 1. And in the meantime, God "blotteth out our transgressions for his own sake," Isa. xliii. 25; and "all things that pertain unto life and godliness, are given (or gifted) unto us," 2 Pet. i. 8.

OF THE PROMISES PECULIAR TO CHRIST.

HAVING spoken of the promises in general, we come now to take a more particular view of them; and first of the promises peculiar to Christ himself. These are many, but may all be reduced to three heads; to wit, the promise of assistance, of acceptance, and of reward of his work.

First, Our Lord Jesus had a promise of assistance in his work: Psalm lxxxix. 21, "Mine arm shall strengthen him." Having undertaken the work of our redemption, he had his Father's promise, that when it came to the setting to, he would strengthen and uphold him in going through with it, Isa. xlii. 1.—4. And in the faith of this covenanted assistance, he went through the hardest pieces thereof, chap. l. 6, "I gave my back to the smiters, and my cheeks to them that plucked off the hair; I hid not my face from shame and spitting." Ver. 7, "For the Lord God will help me." Accordingly, in his heaviness in the garden, "there appeared an angel unto him from heaven, strengthening him," Luke xxii. 43. And this promised assistance was the token of his Father's good pleasure in, and liking of the work, while it was a-doing.

Secondly, He had a promise of the acceptance of his work when once done; of the acceptance thereof, as a full discharge and performance of the condition of the covenant, intitling him to the promised reward. Hence in view of the sure performance of his work the acceptance thereof was, at his baptism, proclaimed by "a voice from heaven, saying, This is my beloved Son, in whom I am well pleased," Matth. iii. 17. And it was renewed at his transfiguration, a little before his passion, chap. xvii. 5. Unto this promise of acceptance belongs the promise of his resurrection, and of his justification.

1. The promise of his resurrection from the dead: Psalm xvi. 10, "Thou wilt not leave my soul in hell; neither wilt thou suffer thine holy One to see corruption;" which is expounded of the resurrection of Christ, Acts ii. 31. God, by raising Christ from the dead, did in effect declare his acceptance of the work by him performed. It evidenced the debt to be fully cleared, that he who laid him up in the prison of the grave, did bring him out of it again; sending his angel to "roll away the stone from the door" of it, and so to dismiss him legally. For thus it was agreed in the covenant, that as Christ should give himself to the death, for the satisfaction of justice: so the Father should bring him again from the dead, in respect of that satisfaction made by his blood, Heb. xiii. 20.

2. The promise of his justification: Isa. l. 8. "He is near that justifieth me." The accomplishment of which is observed by the apostle, 1 Tim. iii. 16, "God was manifest in the flesh, justified in the Spirit." Our Lord Jesus Christ having no personal sins to be pardoned, needed no personal justification; but as he was the surety of the elect, and had the iniquities of them all laid on him, it was provided in the covenant as just, that, the work he had undertaken being performed, he should have an official justification. Having paid the debt, he had by promise a full and ample discharge thereof, under the hand and seal of heaven. And here lies the great security of his people against the law's demand of satisfaction from them.

Lastly, He had a promise of a glorious reward to be conferred on him, as a proper merit of his work done, there was a joy set before him in the promise, for which he endured the cross, despising the shame, Heb. xii. 2. Never was there such a work wrought; and never was there such a reward promised. Unto it there belongs a fivefold promise.

1. The promise of a new kind of interest in God, as his God and and Father: Psalm lxxxix. 26. "He shall cry unto me, thou art my Father, my God." Our Lord Jesus had God to his Father, by eternal birth-right: but there was a new relation constituted between God and Christ as the second Adam, head of the covenant, founded upon his undertaking and fulfilling the covenant condition; whereby he became heir of God as his heritage, according to that of the apostle, Rom. viii. 17, "Heirs of God, and joint heirs with Christ;" namely, with Christ as the primary heir. For by his obedience unto death, he purchased the enjoyment of God as a God and Father. I do not say, he purchased it for himself; the man Christ needed not to do that, forasmuch as he had it, in virtue of the personal union of the two natures: but he purchased it for sinners, who had lost all saving interest in God, but could not be happy without it.

2. The promise of a glorious exaltation, to be the Father's honorary servant, prime minister of heaven, as great administrator of the covenant: Isa. lii. 13, "Behold, my servant shall deal prudently, he shall be exalted and extolled, and be very high." Chap. xlix. 8. "I will give thee for a covenant of the people." In fulfilling the condition of the covenant, he took upon him the form of a bond-servant, and humbled himself even unto the death of the cross: wherefore God also, according to the promise of the covenant, hath highly exalted him to the prime ministry of heaven, and given him a name as great administrator of the covenant, which is above every name; that at the name of Jesus every knee should bow, Phil. ii. 7. 8, 9, 10. The nature, vast extent, and importance of this promise, will afterwards be unfolded, when we come to treat of the administration of the covenant, in virtue thereof put in the Mediator's hand.

3. The promise of a seed and offspring, numerous as the stars of heaven: Isa. liii. 10, "He shall see his seed." Gen. xv. 5, "So shall thy seed be;" namely, "as the stars of the sky in multitude," Heb. xi. 12: even the whole multitude of the elect, all of them to live by his death, and to bear his image, as a child doth that of his father. He consented to suffer the pangs of death; but they were travailing pains, to issue in a numerous birth. He was as a corn of wheat to fall into the ground, and die; but the promise secured to him, on that condition, his bringing forth much fruit, John xii. 24. It is in pursuance of the accomplishment of this promise, the gospel continues to be preached from age to age; forasmuch as, in virtue thereof, "as many as are ordained to eternal life, shall believe."

4. The promise of his inheriting all things, as primary heir; Psalm lxxxix. 27, "I will make him my first-born." So the apostle says, God hath appointed him heir of all things, Heb. i. 2. And Christ himself declares his being put in possession accordingly, Matt. xi. 27, "All things are delivered unto me of my Father." Thus he hath by promise suitable treasures for the supporting of the dignity conferred on him. But of this also more afterwards.

5. *Lastly*, The promise of victory and dominion over all his, and his people's enemies: Psalm lxxxix. 23, "I will beat down his foes before his face." He was to encounter with Satan, sin, and death, in the quarrel of the designed heirs of glory; and no sooner was he engaged against them, but the wicked world of men began a war with him too: but he had his Father's promise, for victory and dominion over them all: that, howbeit he should get the first fall, and die in the battle, yet his death should be the destruction of Satan's dominion, sin's power, and death's bands over his people;

and that whosoever should go about to support that tottering interest, should fall under him: Psalm cx. 1, "The Lord said unto my Lord, Sit thou at my right hand, until I make thine enemies thy footstool."

And thus far of the threefold promise peculiar to Christ himself, in the covenant.

OF THE PROMISE OF ETERNAL LIFE TO THE ELECT, CONSIDERED IN THREE PERIODS.

THE promises common to the elect, made in and through Christ unto them in the covenant, are also many. A particular enumeration of them I intend not, though every one of them is more precious than the gold of Ophir: but it would be profitable for serious Christians, as they read through the Old and New Testament, to mark them in their bibles, for their spiritual treasure, stored with such variety, as affords what is suitable for every case they can be in. They are all comprehended in, and may be reduced unto this one, to wit, the promise of eternal life: for which the two following texts may be viewed.

Tit. i. 2, "In hope of eternal life, which God that cannot lie, promised before the world began."

1 John ii. 25, "And this is the promise that he hath promised us, even eternal life."

In which words, three things for our purpose offer themselves to be observed. 1. The great and comprehensive promise of the covenant of grace, the sum of all the promises therein, to sinners; namely, the promise of life eternal: that is the order of the words in the original. The covenant is a covenant of life, designed for restoring dead sinners to life: and so the promise of it is a promise of life. And that life is eternal. 2. The date of this promise, before the world began. While as yet time was not, and the foundation of the world was not laid, it was made, and eternal life thereby secured to the elect. 3. The parties concerned in it. The maker of the promise was God that cannot lie; whose promise therefore must needs take effect. And, by special appropriation, it was the Father: it was HE that made it: ver. 24, "Ye also shall continue in the Son, and in the Father." Ver. 25, "And this is the promise that he hath promised us," &c. The party it was made to, is, (1.) and chiefly, Jesus Christ, the second Adam, head of the covenant: for there is no necessity to recede from the proper signifition of the word here used, which is promising, to a catachrestical one, to wit, purposing: since the promises were made to Christ, Gal. iii. 16. And he really was before the world began, and consequently then capable of having a promise made to him. (2.) The elect in him. He hath promised us, namely, us legally in him before the world began; that is the elect who apply and plead the promise then, when they believe.

And hence ariseth this truth, viz. The great and comprehensive promise to Christ's spiritual seed, in the covenant, is the promise of life eternal, made from eternity to Christ, and to them in him.

For opening of this promise of the covenant, we shall view it, (1.) More generally, (2.) More particularly.

I. In the general, it speaks two things, to wit, all true happiness and the everlastingness of that happiness.

First, It comprehends, as the matter thereof, all true happiness. For life is used for happiness in the holy language, 1 Sam. xxv. 6. So John iv. 50. And it is so used in the style of both covenants: Rom. x. 5, "The man which doth those things, shall live (*i. e.* be happy) by them." Hab. ii. 4, "The just shall live (*i. e.* be happy) by his faith." The damned have a life in hell that will last for ever: but, in the style of the Holy Ghost, they never see life, they are deprived of eternal life; because their life is not a happy life, but a miserable one. It is evident from the writings of the prophets and apostles, that the death threatened in the covenant of works, comprehended all misery, in this world and in the world to come; and, consequently, that the life therein promised, comprehended all happiness in time and eternity. Forasmuch then as the life promised in the covenant of grace, was designed for retrieving the loss sinners sustained by the fall; it must needs, in its comprehension, go as wide as the death which thereby they became liable unto. From all which we conclude, that God, in promising life to the elect in Christ, hath promised them all happiness: which accordingly goes under the name of life simply in the Scripture, 1 John v. 12, "He that hath the Son, hath life." And thus the covenant-life extends to all welfare of the whole man, and to all the means by which it is compassed.

1. The covenant-life extends to all welfare of the whole man, soul and body; the latter as well as the former. And therefore from the covenant our Lord proves the resurrection of the body, against the Sadducees, Matth. xxii. 31, 32. Though the soul is the principal part, it is not the only part, therein provided for. In virtue of the covenant, "the body is for the Lord, and the Lord for the body;" as well as the soul is for him, and he for it, 1 Cor. vi. 13. As the body had its share in the death threatened in the first cove-

nant; so it hath, and shall have its share in the life promised in the second. Since the price of the Redeemer's blood was paid for the bodies of his people, in his fulfilling the condition of the covenant; the life secured in the promise must extend to them, as well as to their souls.

2. It extends to all the means by which that welfare is to be compassed, begun, advanced, and perfected: "Whether Paul, or Apollos, or Cephas, or the world, or life, or death, or things present, or things to come, all are yours," 1 Cor. iii. 22. For the securing of the benefit itself by promise, secures all the means by which it is to be brought about. Hence the covenant descends even to the bread and the water, necessary for the support of natural life, Isa. xxxiii. 16.

Secondly, The promise comprehends the everlastingness of that happiness. It is not only life that is promised, but life eternal, life for evermore, Psalm cxxxiii. 3; which, from the moment it is given, shall never be extinguished, through the ages of time and eternity. In the style of the Scripture, eternal life is not restricted to the state of glory in heaven. But the life communicated to a sinner, in the first moment of his union with Christ, is eternal: it is the eternal life promised in the covenant, according to the Scripture, John iii. 36, "He that believeth on the Son, hath everlasting life." See chap. v. 24; 1 John v. 11, 12. Hence, from the promise of the covenant, "The just shall live by faith," the apostle proves the perseverance of the saints, Heb. x. 38. A plain evidence, that perseverance in grace, in this our state of imperfection, is a part of the eternal life promised in the covenant, as well as heaven's happiness. And thus the covenant-life extends to that which now is, and that which is to come, 1 Tim. iv. 8.

1. It extends to the life that now is in the world. And this is that eternal life begun in the several parts thereof, with respect both to soul and body. If men measure happiness by the smiles and frowns of common providence, no man indeed can be counted happy before death. But the sacred oracles teach us to take our measures of it another way, to wit, by a personal saving interest in the covenant; and do pronounce them happy, whose God is the Lord, whatever be between them and the grave, Psalm cxliv. 15. So there is promised in the covenant, happiness begun in this life, both as to soul and body; the happiness of the way to the kingdom; salvation happily begun, and infallibly to be carried on.

2. It extends to the life that is to come in the other world. And that is the same eternal life consummated and perfected, in respect both of soul and body, in heaven. There the promise of the cove-

nant is to receive its full accomplishment; of which believers now have the earnest, which is not only a part of the things promised, but an assurance of the whole.

II. For a more particular view of the promise of eternal life to the elect, it may be considered in three periods: (1.) Before their union with Christ; (2.) From their union with Christ, until death; and, (3.) From death, through eternity. Of the operation of the promise, in the first and the last of these periods, we know but little; and indeed not much of it, in the middle period. For it is like a river issuing from a hidden spring, and running far under ground; then rising above ground, and running on, till it go forth into the ocean. The hidden spring from whence the promise of eternal life to the elect issueth forth, is God's free grace, which was given us in Christ Jesus, before the world began, 2 Tim. i. 9. It runs under ground, undiscernible even to the parties themselves, till the moment of their union with Christ, in effectual calling; then rising, it runs on, as it were, above ground, in visible streams, until death; and thereafter, it runs full and perspicuous through the ages of eternity. We shall take a view of the great lines of the promise, in these its several periods.

PERIOD I.

BEFORE UNION WITH CHRIST.

If we consider the promise of eternal life to the elect, as standing in the covenant, and as accomplished to them, and having its effect on them, before their union with Christ, we may perceive two great lines in it; namely, a promise of their preservation, and a promise of the Spirit. Of which in order.

I. THE PROMISE OF PRESERVATION.

The promise of eternal life to the elect, in the covenant, comprehends a promise of their preservation, till the happy moment of their spiritual marriage with Jesus Christ, wherein they shall be settled in a state of grace: Ezek. xvi. 6, " And when I passed by thee, and saw thee polluted in thine own blood, I said unto thee when thou wast in thy blood, Live." *Heb.* " I said to thee, Live in thy blood;" as several approven versions do read it. In this illustrious passage of scripture is shewed, under the similitude of an exposed or outcast infant, the natural state and wretched condition in which God found Israel, and finds all the elect; the former being a type of the latter. There is a twofold passing by this wretched out-cast, and these at two very distant times, intimated by the Holy Ghost. The first, on the day she was born and cast out, ver. 4, 5, 6. The second, after she was grown, and become marriageable; at what time she was actually married, vers. 7, 8. The former refers to the time of the elect's coming into the world in their natural state, not only as born into it, but as beginning to act in it as rational creatures; the latter, to the time prefixed in the eternal purpose, when, by means of the law in the hands of the spirit of bondage, their breasts, as it were, are fashioned, in the work of conviction; upon which ensues their spiritual marriage with Christ. But how is the out-cast preserved in the interval, that she perisheth not in her wretched condition? Why; though no hand was laid upon her, yet a word was spoken, which secured her life in a case naturally deadly. At the first passing by her, in the day she was born and cast out, God said to her, "Live in thy blood:" that is, "Notwithstanding that thou art lying in the open field, in thy blood, thy navel not dressed, so that, according to the course of nature, thy blood and spirits must quickly fail, and this thy birth-day must be thy dying-day; yet I say unto thee, Live: thou shalt not die in that condition, but grow up in it, being preserved till the happy moment of the designed marriage." And this is the promise of the elect's preservation in their natural state. And it hath two great branches; one respecting their natural life; another respecting their spiritual death. The

First is a promise of the continuation of their natural life, till such time as they be made partakers of life in Christ Jesus. God has said it; they shall live, though in the blood of their natural state. So it is not possible they should die before that time, whatever dangers they are brought into; even though a thousand should fall at their side, and ten thousand at their right hand; for, by the promise of the covenant, there is an unseen guard about them, to defend them. It is in virtue hereof, that all along during the time they are in that state, they are preserved, whether in the womb, or coming out of it, or in all the dangers of infancy, childhood, youth, or whatsoever age they arrive at therein. This is it that, so long as they are unconverted, doth so often bring them back from the gates of death; returning them in safety, when either by diseases, or other accidents, they are past hope in their own eyes, and in the eyes of friends and physicians. Though the elect thief was, in his natural state, nailed to the cross; yet death had no power to come at him, so as to separate his soul from his body, till such time as he was once united to Christ by faith, and made partaker of a new life in him. The

Second is a promise of keeping the grave-stone from off them in their spiritual death. The grave-stone is the sin against the Holy Ghost, the unpardonable sin; which, on whomsoever it is laid, makes their case, from that moment, irrecoverable, that thenceforth they can never rise from spiritual death to life: Mark iii. 29, "He that shall blaspheme against the Holy Ghost, hath never forgiveness." But although the elect in their natural state, being dead in sin as well as others, may, through the activity of reigning and raging lusts, so rot in their graves, as to be most abominable in the eyes of God and all good men; yet, because of the promise of the covenant, it is not possible that that grave-stone should be laid on them. There is an invisible guard set on their souls, as well as on their bodies: and so it is infallibly prevented, as may be learned from that expression of our Saviour, Matt. xxiv. 24, "Insomuch that (if it were possible) they shall deceive the very elect." While they are Satan's captives, he may drive them to a prodigious pitch of wickedness. So did he with Manasseh, and Paul: but, as far as he had carried them, he could not carry them forward that step.

This promise of the elect's preservation, as it is with the rest founded on the obedience and death of Christ; whereby eternal life was purchased for them, and consequently these benefits in particular, failing which they would be ruined for ever: so it is akin to, and seems to be grafted upon the promise of assistance made to Christ in the covenant; by which a divine support was insured to him, during all the time the sins of the elect, and the wrath of God for them, should lie upon him. And at this rate, the case of the head, and of the members, was jointly provided for in the covenant.

II. THE PROMISE OF THE SPIRIT.

THE promise of eternal life to the elect, comprehends also a promise of the Spirit of life to be communicated to them, and each one of them, at the nick of time, prefixed in their cases respectively, in the eternal council; that is, the time appointed to be the time of love, the dawning of the day of grace to them, however long and dark their night may be. This promise is found, Isa. xliv. 3, "I will pour my Spirit upon thy seed." Ezek. xxxvi. 27, "I will put my Spirit within you." The elect of God being, even as the rest of mankind, dead in sin, through the breach of the first covenant, could not be recovered, but through a communication of the Spirit of life to them: but that Spirit they could not have from an unatoned God. Wherefore, in the covenant, Christ undertook to fulfil all righteousness in their name, thereby to purchase the Spirit for them; upon which was made the promise of the Spirit, the leading fruit of Christ's purchase; called therefore the Father's promise by way of eminency, Luke xxiv. 49. In token hereof the great outpouring of the Spirit was at Christ's ascension; when he, as our great High Priest, carried in the blood of his sacrifice into the most holy place not made with hands, Acts ii. For as the fire which was set to the incence on the golden altar, the altar of incense was brought from off the brazen altar, the altar of burnt-offering in the court of the temple; so the Spirit which causeth dead sinners to live, issueth from the cross of Christ, who suffered without the gate.

Now, of the promise of the Spirit there are two chief branches; namely, the promise of spiritual moral life, and the promise of faith.

1. The promise of spiritual moral life, in virtue whereof the soul morally dead in sin, is raised to life again, through the Spirit of life communicated unto it from heaven. This is the beginning, the very first of the eternal life itself promised in the covenant. It is the lighting of the sacred lamp of spiritual life in the soul, which can never be extinguished again, but burns for evermore thereafter. This promise we have, Isa. xxvi. 19, "Thy dead men shall live." And it belongs to the promise of the Spirit; as appears from Ezek. xxxvii. 14. "And shall put my Spirit in you, and ye shall live."

The effect of it is the quickening of the dead soul, by the Spirit of Christ passively received: Eph. ii. 5, "When we were dead in sins (God, ver. 4.) hath quickened us." This is the same with the renewing in effectual calling, whereby we are enabled to embrace Jesus Christ, mentioned in our Shorter Catechism on that question. And it is fitly called by some divines, the first regeneration, agreeable to the style of the holy Scripture: John i. 12, "But as many as received him, to them gave he power to become the sons of God, even to them that believe on his name:" ver. 13. "Which were born, not of blood, nor of the will of the flesh, nor of the will of man, but of God." Sinners in their natural state lie dead, lifeless, and moveless; they can no more believe in Christ, nor repent, than a dead man can speak or walk: but, in virtue of the promise, the Spirit of life from Christ Jesus, at the time appointed, enters into the dead soul, and quickens it; so that it is no more morally dead, but alive, having new spiritual powers put into it, that were lost by Adam's fall.

2. The other chief branch of the promise of the Spirit, is the promise of faith; to wit, that Christ's spiritual seed shall believe in him, come unto him, and receive him, by faith: Psalm cx. 3, "Thy people shall be willing in the day of thy power;" and Psalm xxii. 31, "They shall come." God hath promised, that, upon the shedding of the blood of his Son, for the satisfaction of justice, there shall spring up in the earth, after that costly watering, a plentiful seed, to the satisfying of his soul, Isa. liii. 10. And therefore, whoever they be that believe not, all those who were represented in the covenant, shall infallibly be brought to believe, as our Lord himself upon the credit of this promise, doth declare, John vi. 37, "All that the Father giveth me, shall come to me." Now, this also belongs to the promise of the Spirit; who is therefore called the Spirit of faith, 2 Cor. iv. 13, as being the principal efficient cause thereof, Zech. xii. 10.

The effect of this promise is actual believing, produced by the quickening Spirit in the soul, immediately out of the spiritual life given to it by the communication of himself thereto: John v. 25, "The dead shall hear the voice of the Son of God;" compared with chap. i. 12, 13; 2 Cor. iv. 13. As receiving Christ passively, the sinner that was spiritually dead, is quickened; so being quickened, he receives Christ actively. Christ comes into the dead soul by his Spirit: and so he is passively received; even as one, having a power to raise the dead, coming into a house, where there is none but a dead man; none to open the door to him, none to desire him to come in, nor to welcome him. But Christ being thus received, or come in, the dead soul is quickened, and by faith embraceth him; even as the restorer of the dead man to life, would immediately be embraced by him, and receive a thousand welcomes from him, who had heard his voice and lived. When Christ, in the womb of his mother, entered into the house of Zacharias, and she saluted Elizabeth the mother of John the Baptist, he, the babe in Elizabeth's womb, leaped as at the entrance of life: so doth the soul, in actual believing, at Christ's coming into it by his Spirit. As God breathed into the first man the breath of life, and he became a living soul, who was before but a lifeless piece of fair earth; that is, God put a spirit, a soul, into his body, which immediately showed in the man's breathing at his nostrils: so Jesus Christ, in the time of loves, puts his Spirit into the dead soul, which immediately shews itself alive, by believing, receiving and embracing him, known and discerned in his transcendent glory. And thus the union betwixt Christ and the soul is completed; Christ first apprehending the soul by his Spirit; and then the soul thus apprehended and quickened, apprehending him again in the promise of the gospel by faith.

Now, the promise of the Spirit, in both branches thereof, is granted upon the promise of a resurrection from the dead, made to Christ; and it is so interwoven therewith, that there is no separating of them. The promise of the resurrection, like the oil on Aaron's head, runs down to the skirts of his garments, in the promise of quickening his members too. Herein the Scripture is very plain, Isa. xxvi. 19, "Thy dead men shall live, together with my dead body shall they arise." Eph. ii. 5, "Even when we were dead in sins, hath quickened us together with Christ." Our Lord Jesus, in the eternal covenant, became the head of a dead body, to wit, of the body of elect sinners dead in sin; and that to the end he might restore it to life. And being legally united with that body, that so death might have access to spread itself from it unto him in due time, he had the promise of a resurrection, both for himself and his members, made unto him. The appointed time being come, death drew together its whole forces, and made an attack upon the head of the body, which alone remained alive. It stung him to the heart upon the cross, and laid him too in the dust of death: and so it had them all dead together, head and members. Thus the condition of the covenant was fulfilled. Now, the promise comes next, in its turn to be fulfilled, particularly the promise of a resurrection: namely, that, death having exhausted all its force and vigour on the head, he should be raised again from the dead; and that as death had spread itself from the members into the head, so life, in its turn, should spread itself from the head into the members, they together with his dead body arising. It was in virtue hereof, that the spirit or soul that animated Christ's body, and which he yielded up upon the cross, (Matth. xvii. 25,) shewed by his breathing out his last there, (Luke xxiii. 46, Gr.) was returned again into his blessed body; whereupon he came forth out of the grave. And it is in virtue of the same, that the Spirit of life returns into the dead souls of the elect again; upon which they live and believe. The time of the return of the Spirit, both into the head and into the members, was prefixed in the covenant, respectively; so that as it was not possible Christ should be held in the grave after three days; even so it is not possible that the elect should be held in the bonds of spiritual death, after the time prefixed for their delivery: Hos. vi. 2, "After two days will he revive us, in the third day he will raise us up, and we shall live in his sight."

And thus the promise of eternal life to the elect works in this dark period of their days; which dark period ends here. It appears now, and runs above ground ever after.

PERIOD II.

FROM UNION WITH CHRIST, UNTIL DEATH.

CONSIDERING the promise of eternal life to the elect, as it is accomplished to, and hath its effect on them, from their union with Christ until death; the great lines to be perceived therein, are the promises, 1. Of justification; 2. Of a new and saving covenant relation to God; 3. Of sanctification; 4. Of perseverance; and, 5. Of temporal benefits. Of the which in order.

I. THE PROMISE OF JUSTIFICATION.

THE promise of eternal life to the elect, comprehends the promise of justification, to be conferred on them, and each one of them, being united to Christ through the Spirit. This is found Isa. liii. 11, "By his knowledge shall my righteous servant justify many," Chap. xlv. 15, "In the Lord shall all the seed of Israel be justified." It is the leading promise of this period: and the effect of the accomplishment thereof, is, that the soul, legally dead under the sentence of the law, or curse of the broken covenant of works, is caused to live again accordingly; as it is written, "The just shall live by faith," Rom. i. 17. And this is the beginning of that life which is received from Christ by faith, and is mentioned John v. 40, "Ye will not come to me, that ye might have life." Chap. vi. 57, "He that eateth me, even he shall live by me." There is a life received from Christ before faith, whereby one is enabled to believe; of which we have already spoken: and there is a life received from Christ through faith, according to John xx. 31, "That believing ye might have life through his name." And this last is, according to the Scripture, eternal life too: chap. v. 24, "He that heareth my word, and believeth on him that sent me, hath everlasting life, and shall not come into condemnation; but is passed from death unto life."

The elect of God, lying under the breach of the first covenant, were dead in law, as being under the curse. They could not be restored to life in the eye of the law, but upon the fulfilling of the righteousness of the law; the which they not being able to do for themselves, Christ in the covenant undertook to do it for them; and thereupon was made the promise of their justification. This promise taking effect upon their believing, the curse is removed, and they are actually and personally justified. Thus they are restored to life in the eye of the law: which kind of life received by faith, is everlasting; forasmuch as, according to the covenant, the curse can never return upon them, for shorter or longer time: Isa. liv. 9, "As I have sworn that the waters of Noah should no more go over the earth; so have I sworn that I would not be wroth with thee."

Of the promise of justification there are two branches; namely, the promise of pardon, and of acceptance.

1. The promise of pardon of sin, whereby the guilt of eternal wrath is done away: Heb. viii. 12, "Their sins and their iniquities will I remember no more." The sins of the elect being, in the eternal covenant, imputed to, and laid on Christ; who becoming legally one with them, transferred their debt on himself, and undertook to pay the same; a promise was thereupon made of pardon to them, and each one of them. Now, as soon as they are mystically and really united to him by faith, by means of that union they have communion with him in his righteousness: whereupon his perfect satisfaction is imputed to them; and, upon the account of it alone, and not any deed of theirs whatsoever the free promise is accomplished, and the pardon actually bestowed on them, according to the eternal agreement: Eph. i. 7, "In whom we have redemption through his blood, the forgiveness of sins, according to the riches of his grace."

Here is life from the dead; a pardon put into the hand of the condemned man, disarming the law of its condemning power, and death of its sting, as to him: causing him to lift up his head from off the block, and go away with acclamations of praise of the King's mercy, and his Son's merit. And it is eternal life: for all his sins past, present, and to come, are pardoned, as to the guilt of eternal wrath; a formal remission of these of the two former kinds being granted, and a not imputing of these of the latter sort, as to that guilt, being secured; as the apostle teacheth, Rom. iv. 7, "Blessed are they whose iniquities are forgiven, and whose sins are covered." Ver. 8, "Blessed is the man to whom the Lord will not impute sin." And God will never revoke his pardons, chap. xi. 29, "For the gifts and calling of God are without repentance."

2. The other branch of the promise of justification, is the promise of acceptance of their persons as righteous in the sight of God; according to that, Isa. xlii. 21, "The Lord is well pleased for his righteousness' sake." Compared with Matth. iii. 17, "This is my beloved Son, in whom I am well pleased;" and Eph. i. 6, "He hath made us accepted in the beloved." A holy righteous God, whose judgment is according to truth, cannot accept sinners as righteous, without a righteousness, even a perfect righteousness. They that

are truly righteous in law, can never pass for righteous, but for unrighteous in the view of his piercing eye: "For in thy sight," says the Psalmist, Psalm cxliii. 2, "shall no man living be justified;" to wit, "by the deeds of the law," or inherent righteousness, which is imperfect, as the apostle expounds it, Rom. iii. 20. But our Lord Jesus having in the covenant undertaken to fulfill all righteousness for them, who of themselves could fulfil no righteousness; a promise was thereupon made, to accept them as righteous upon the account of his surety-righteousness, which becomes truly theirs through faith, and that by a double right. (1.) By right of free gift received: inasmuch as Christ's righteousness being made over, in the gospel, as Heaven's free gift to sinners, the gift is by faith actually claimed and received; whence it is called the GIFT of righteousness, (Rom. v. 17,) revealed unto faith, (chap. i. 17.) namely, to be believed on, and so received. (2.) By right of communion with Christ: inasmuch as sinners being united with him by faith, have thereby communion, or a common interest with him in his righteousness, Phil. iii. 9, "And be found in him, not having mine own righteousness, which is of the law, but that which is through the faith of Christ." Upon these grounds, the holiness of Christ's nature, the righteousness of his life, and the satisfaction made by his death and sufferings, being the constituent parts of that righteousness, are, according to truth, imputed to the believer, or legally reckoned his: and, upon the account thereof precisely, he is accepted of God as righteous, being "made the righteousness of God IN HIM," 2 Cor. v. 21; the righteousness of God being "UPON all that believe," Rom. iii. 22.

Here is life to the soul, righteousness unto justification of life, chap. v. 18; an everlasting righteousness, Dan. ix. 24; a garment that never waxeth old, is never rent, nay, nor sullied; but always continues in its original lustre, from the moment that it is put on. Wherefore the life must needs be ETERNAL, grace must needs reign through that "righteousness unto eternal life," Rom. v. 21; for being once put on, is never put off again for one moment, in time nor eternity.

Now, the promise of justification, in both branches thereof, is grafted upon the promise of justification made to Christ. The condition of the covenant being fulfilled, the head is justified, according to the promise; and then the members in him. First, the Mediator gets up his discharge for the whole debt; and then they, pleading it by faith for their own behoof, are discharged in their own persons.

II. THE PROMISE OF A NEW AND SAVING COVENANT-RELATION TO GOD.

The promise of eternal life to the elect, doth also comprehend the promise of a new and saving covenant-relation to God, which they, and each one of them, being justified, shall be brought into: Hos. ii. 23, "I will say to them which were not my people, Thou art my people; and they shall say, Thou art my God." Dying both morally and legally, through the breach of the first covenant, they fell under a relative death too; whereby the blessed relation between God and them was dissolved: and it could not be constituted again, while they lay under the condemnatory sentence of the law. But upon Christ's undertaking, in the covenant, to bring in an everlasting righteousness, the price of the redemption of all saving benefits, this promise was made. Wherefore they being come to Christ by faith, united with him, and justified through his righteousness, which they partake of in him; God meets them there, even in Christ the appointed meeting-place; and there, with the safety of his honour, he takes them by the hand, and joins them again in a saving relation. Thus they have a relative life, according to that, Psalm xxx. 5, "In his favour is life." The which life is eternal: forasmuch as the relation is for ever indissoluble; the bond of the second covenant being so much surer than the bond of the first, as the second Adam's undertaking was surer than the first Adam's.

Now, of this promise there are three chief branches; namely, the promise of reconciliation, of adoption, and of God's being their God.

1. The promise of reconciliation between God and them: Ezek. xxxvii. 26, "I will make a covenant of peace with them, it shall be an everlasting covenant." They were by sin in a state of enmity with God; on their part, there was a real enmity against God; on God's part, a legal enmity against them, such as a judge hath against a malefactor, whom notwithstanding he may dearly love. But Jesus Christ having undertaken, in the covenant, to expiate their guilt, by the sacrifice of himself, the Father made a promise of peace and reconciliation with them thereupon. Hence we are said to be reconciled to God by the death of his Son, Rom. v. 10; inasmuch as by his death and sufferings he purchased our reconciliation, which was promised on these terms.

Now, this promise is accomplished to the justified sinner: being pardoned, he is brought into a state of peace with God, as saith the apostle, Rom. v. 1, "Being justified by faith, we have peace with God." God lays down his legal enmity against him, never to be taken up again. And more than that, he takes him into a bond of friendship; so that he is not only at peace with God, but is the friend of God: James ii. 23, "Abraham believed God, and it was imputed unto him for righteousness: and he was called the friend of God."

This promise is grafted upon the promise of acceptance and justification made to Christ. For his sacrifice being accepted as well pleasing to God, and he discharged of the debt he became surety for; the reconciliation, as well as the pardon, of those united to him by faith, natively follows thereupon: 2 Cor. v. 19, "God was in Christ, reconciling the world unto himself, not imputing their trespasses unto them." Eph. i. 6, "He hath made us accepted in the beloved." Ver. 7, "In whom we have redemption through his blood, the forgiveness of sins."

2. Another branch of this promise, is the promise of their adoption into the family of God: Hos. i. 10, "It shall be said unto them, Ye are the sons of the living God." And this is more than the former; as it is more to be one's son, than to be his friend. We have before declared, how all mankind was, by the first covenant, constituted God's hired servants; and by the breach of that covenant, bond servants under the curse: and how Christ transferred that state of servitude of his spiritual seed on himself. Now, upon consideration of his taking on him the form of a bond servant for them, the promise of their adoption into the family of God was made. He was "made under the law, to redeem them that were under the law, that we might receive the adoption of sons," Gal. iv. 4, 5.

And being justified by faith, and reconciled to God, it is accomplished to them: forasmuch as then Christ's service is imputed to them, and a way is opened withal for their admission into the family of God, through their actual reconciliation to him: Rom. v. 1, "Being justified by faith, we have peace with God through our Lord Jesus Christ." Ver. 2, "by whom also we have access by faith into this grace wherein we stand." John i. 12, "As many as received him, to them gave he power to become the sons of God." Then are they taken as children into the family of heaven: God becomes their Father in Christ; and they his sons and daughters, to abide for ever in his house, John viii. 35. And so they have a right to all the privileges of that high relation.

Now, this promise is grafted upon the promise made to Christ of a new kind of interest in God as his Father; according to that, John xx. 17, "I ascend unto my Father and your Father." For by the Spirit of adoption we call God our Father, in the right of Jesus Christ our elder brother, spiritual husband and head.

3. The last branch is the promise of God's being their God: Heb. viii. 10, "I will be their God." This is more than reconciliation and adoption: it is the height of the relation to God, which a sinful creature could be advanced unto. They were by nature without God, Eph. ii. 12: but forasmuch as the Son of God did, in the cove-

nant, undertake to give himself for them, in their nature perfectly to satisfy the law, in his holy birth, righteous life, and exquisite death; a ransom of infinite value, quite beyond all created things whatsoever, graces, pardons, heavens; there was made, upon that consideration, a promise of God's giving himself to them, as the adequate reward of that service; which being performed by the Mediator, this reward was purchased for them. Hence God saith to Abraham, Gen. xv. 1, "I am thy exceeding great reward."

Now, to the believer being justified, reconciled, and adopted into the family of God, this heritage falls, in accomplishment of this promise, Rom. viii. 17, "And if children, then heirs; heirs of God." Gal. iv. 7, "And if a son, then an heir of God through Christ;" God himself being the heritage. He becomes their God: they have a right to him, and are possessed of him, as their own property; a property which the thought of men and angels cannot fully reach the contents of. Not only are all the works and creatures of God, in the heavens, earth, and seas, theirs, 1 Cor. iii. 22, "All are yours;" but himself is theirs: which is more than all that, as the bridegroom is more than all the marriage-robes, or his large possessions. All the attributes are theirs; his infinite wisdom to direct them, his power to afford them protection, his justice to make all the benefits purchased by Christ for them forthcoming to them, his holiness to transform them into the same image, his mercy to pity and succour them, his grace to deal bountifully with them, his faithfulness to fulfil all the promises to them in their time, and his all-sufficiency to render them completely happy. He is theirs in all his relations; their Shepherd, Provisor, Protector, King, Husband, Head, and whatever may contribute to their happiness. All the persons of the glorious Trinity are theirs: the Father is theirs, the Son is theirs, and the Holy Spirit is theirs: Isa. liv. 5, "For thy Maker is thine husband, the Lord of hosts is his name:" (Heb.) "Thy makers are thine husbands; Jehovah Sabaoth is his name."

This rich promise is grafted upon the promise made to Christ of a new kind of interest in God as his God: John xx. 17, "I ascend to my God and your God." God being the Mediator's God by purchase, he becomes our God in him. Christ having performed the condition of the covenant, falls heir to the great heritage; and we fall to it also in him, being heirs of God, joint-heirs with Christ, Rom. viii. 17.

III. THE PROMISE OF SANCTIFICATION.

In the promise of eternal life to the elect, is comprehended in like manner the promise of their sanctification: Ezek. xi. 19, "I will take the stony heart out of their flesh, and will give them an heart of flesh:" ver. 20, "That they may walk in my statutes." See Joel iii. 17, 21; Heb. viii. 10. Through the breach of the first covenant they lost the image of God: their whole faculties were so depraved, that they could neither do, speak, nor think any thing truly good, and acceptable to God: they were by nature altogether unholy; unclean, loathsome, and abominable, in their nature, heart, and life. And it was quite beyond their power to make themselves holy again: for mending of their nature could not affect it; it behoved to be renewed, Eph. iv. 23. And the curse of the law lying upon them extinguished all saving relation between God and them; and so blocked up all saving communication with heaven: for it barred, in point of justice, all sanctifying influences from thence; these being the greatest benefit they were capable of, as assimilating the creature unto God himself, or rendering it like him. The curse fixed a gulf betwixt God and them, so that sanctifying influences could not pass from him unto them; more than their unholy desires and prayers could pass from them unto him. So the fallen angels always were and the damned now are, beyond all possibility of sanctification, or of receiving sanctifying influences from heaven; there being no remedy to remove the curse, neither from the one, nor from the other. And in this case all Adam's posterity had lain for ever, had not Jesus Christ, as the head of the elect, undertaken in the second covenant to remove that bar, to fill up that gulf, and to found a new saving relation between God and them, through his own obedience and death. But upon that undertaking of the Mediator, the Father did by promise insure their sanctification; that Christ's people should be willing in the day of his power, in the beauties of holiness, Psalm cx. 3; and that a seed should serve him, Psalm xxii. 30.

And this promise, the promise of sanctification, is indeed the chief promise of the covenant made to Christ for them: among the rest of that kind, it shines like the moon among the lesser stars. Sanctification is the very chief subordinate end of the covenant of grace, standing therein next to the glory of God, which is the chief and ultimate end thereof. The promise of it, is the centre of all the rest of these promises. All the foregoing promises, the promise of preservation, the Spirit, the first regeneration or quickening of the dead soul, faith, justification, the new saving relation to God, reconciliation, adoption, and enjoyment of God as our God, do tend unto it as their common centre, and stand related to it as means to their end. They are all accomplished on sinners, on design to make them holy. And all the subsequent promises, even the promise of glorification itself, are but the same promise of sanctification enlarged and extended: they are but as so many rays and beams of light, shooting forth from it as the centre of them all.

This appears from the scriptural descriptions of the covenant, in the promissory part thereof respecting the elect: Luke i. 73, "The oath which he sware to our father Abraham." Ver. 74, "That he would grant unto us, that we being delivered out of the hands of our enemies might serve him without fear," ver. 75, "In holiness and righteousness before him all the days of our life." Here is the oath or covenant sworn to Abraham, as a type of Christ; wherein his seed's serving the Lord in holiness, is held forth as the chief thing sworn unto the Mediator by the Father; and their deliverance from their enemies, as the means for that end. See Heb. viii. 10, 11, 12, where God's writing his law in their hearts, is set on the front, as the first thing in the divine intention, though the last in execution, as appears by comparing the 10th and 12th verses. This matter is also evident from the nature of the thing. For the great thing Satan aimed at in seducing our first parents, was the ruin of the image of God in them, that so mankind might be no more like God, but like himself: and the mystery of God, for the recovery of sinners, is then finished, when holiness is brought in them to perfection in heaven, and not till then.

From all which one may plainly perceive, that the sanctification of all that shall see heaven, is secured in the covenant, upon infallible grounds, beyond all possibility of failure: and that the unholy have no saving part nor lot in the covenant; and that the less holy any man is, the less is the covenant-promise accomplished to him. For the sanctification of sinners is the great design of that contrivance: it is that which the Father and the Son, looking therein to them, had chiefly in their view: and the promise thereof is the capital promise of the covenant, respecting them; being as it were written in great letters.

Now, at the time appointed for every one in the eternal council, this promise is accomplished. The sinner being justified by faith, and taken into a saving relation to God, being reconciled, adopted, and made an heir of God through Christ, is sanctified. The bar being removed, the gulf filled up as to him, his saving interest in, and relation to a holy God being established; the communication between heaven and the sinner is opened, and sanctifying influences flow amain, to the sanctifying of him throughout.

This is, by some divines, called the second regeneration, agreeable to the Scripture: Tit. ii. 5, "He saved us by the washing of regeneration, and renewing of the Holy Ghost;" compared with Eph. v.

26, "That he might sanctify and cleanse it with the washing of water." 2 Cor. v. 17, "If any man be in Christ, he is a new creature;" namely, being "created in Christ Jesus unto good works," as the apostle himself explains it, Eph. ii. 10. And as in regeneration taken strictly for the quickening of the dead soul, and called the first regeneration, new vital powers are given; so in regeneration taken largely for the forming of the new creature in all its parts and distinct members, which is called the second regeneration, there are new qualities and habits of grace infused: and it is the same with the second renewing, mentioned in our Shorter Catechism, on the head of sanctification, "whereby we are renewed in the whole man, after the image of God."

The matter lies here. The sinner being by faith united to Christ, through the communication of the quickening Spirit from Christ unto him, and thereupon justified, reconciled, adopted, and made an heir of God; there is a measure of every grace, even the seeds of all saving graces, derived from, and communicated out of all-fulness of grace in the man Christ the head, unto the sinner as a member of his, by the same Spirit dwelling in the head and members. Hereby the man is not only a spiritually living creature, but an all-new creature, sanctified wholly or throughout, renewed in the whole man, after the image of God. For the immediate effect of that communication of grace from Christ, must be the sealing of the person with the image of Christ; forasmuch as he receives grace for grace in Christ, as the wax doth point for point in the seal. So that the restored image of God is expressed on us immediately from Christ the second Adam, who is the image of the invisible God: even as Eve was made after God's image, being made after Adam's, according to Gen. ii. 18, "I will make him an help meet for him;" marg. as before him, that is, in his own likeness, as if he sat for a picture. Compare 1 Cor. xi. 7, "He," (to wit, the man) "is the image and glory of God: but the woman is the glory of the man." Ver. 8, "For the man is not of the woman: but the woman of the man." And 2 Cor. viii. 23, "Our brethren are the messengers of the churches, and the glory of Christ." And thus our uniting with Christ, through the Spirit, by faith, issues in our becoming one spirit, that is, of the same spiritual holy nature with him; as really as Eve was one flesh with Adam, being formed of him, of his flesh and of his bones, Gen. ii. 23; to which the apostle alludes, in the matter of the mystical union between Christ and believers, Eph. v. 30, "For we are members of his body, of his flesh, and of his bones."

This is the scripture-account of the matter: according to which, the sanctification of a sinner hath a special relation to Jesus Christ and his Spirit; depends withal on our relative state in the divine favour; and so is no less a mystery than our justification. As the depravation of human nature hath always been so manifest, that it could not escape observation in the world; so, in all ages, men have been aiming to discover and compass the cure thereof, in a right use they apprehend they could make of their rational faculties. The issue whereof hath always been, at best, but an outward show and semblance of sanctification, going under the name of moral virtue, having no special relation to Jesus Christ, and his indwelling Spirit; but such as it is, made the foundation of men's relative state in the fovour of God. And since the world by their wisdom knew not God; it is not at all strange, the produce of their wisdom, in the matter of sanctification, or assimiliation to his image, lies so wide of the true sanctification acceptable to him discovered in his word. Truly it is there only we can learn the mystery of the sanctification of a sinner. And there it is revealed, that that great work is wrought by the Spirit, on the souls of men in a state of union with Jesus Christ, and after believing, Eph. i. 13, "IN whom also AFTER that ye believed, ye were sealed with that holy SPIRIT of promise." It necessarily depends on our union with Christ, in that we are sanctified IN Christ Jesus, as members of his body, 1 Cor. i. 2, created IN Christ Jesus unto good works. And faith is the instrumental cause of our sanctification, being, We are sanctified by faith, Acts xxvi. 18: for thereby it is, that "of his fulness we receive grace for grace," (John i. 16.) the which is communicated to us by his Spirit, who glorifies him, by reforming us after his image, by means of that communication of grace from Christ unto us: John xvi. 14, "He shall glorify me: for he shall receive of mine, and shall shew it unto you." So "beholding as in a glass the glory of the Lord (Christ), we are changed into the same image, from glory to glory, even as by the Spirit of the Lord," 2 Cor. iii. 18. Thus one being in Christ is made a new creature; forasmuch as he is such a stock as changes the graft into its own nature; "Therefore if any man be in Christ he is a new creature, chap. v. 17, "For as many of you as have been baptized into Christ, have put on Christ," Gal. iii. 27. It dependeth also upon our justification, and reconciliation with God; inasmuch as the blood of Christ, with which we are sanctified, according to the scripture, (Rev. i. 5; 1 Pet. i. 2; 1 John i. 7,) is effective of our sanctification, as it is the meritorious cause thereof: and so the sanctifying virtue of that precious blood, proceeds from its atoning virtue; it sanctifies us, because it justifies and reconciles us to God; Heb. ix. 14, "How much more shall the blood of Christ, who, through the eternal Spirit, offered himself without spot to God, purge your conscience from dead works to serve the living God?" Wherefore, saith the apostle, 1 Thess. v. 23, "And the very God of PEACE sanctify you." In like manner, it pre-supposeth our adoption; inasmuch as it is upon our being adopted into the family of God, that we receive the Spirit of his Son, conforming us to his image as our elder brother, which is the very thing wherein our sanctification doth consist: "For whom he did foreknow, he also did predestinate to be conformed to the image of his Son, that he might be the first-born among many brethren," Rom. viii. 29. "And because ye are sons, God hath sent forth the Spirit of his Son into your hearts, crying, Abba, Father," Gal. iv. 6, "We are changed into the same image, even as by the Spirit of the Lord," 2 Cor. iii. 18. And it stands in the same relation to God's becoming our God, Ezek. xvi. 8, "I sware unto thee, and entered into a covenant with thee, saith the Lord God, and thou becamest mine." Ver. 9, "Then washed I thee with water: yea, I thoroughly washed away thy blood from thee, and anointed thee with oil."

But although in this work of sanctification, there is communicated out of the all-fulness of grace in Christ, a measure, and that a predominant measure of every grace: yet it is not a full measure of any grace. Hence it comes to pass, that howbeit we are thereby renewed in the whole man, yet we are still unrenewed in the whole man too; to wit, in respect of two general parts, thence called the renewed part, and the unrenewed part. For this communication of grace, being of grace for grace in Christ, we are thereby renewed in every particular part indeed: but the measure of none of these graces being full in any soul while here, we are not wholly renewed in any such part; but there are remains of corruption still indwelling in every such part, in the mind, will, and affections, and in the body by way of communication with the unrenewed part. Thus two contrary principles, to wit, grace and corruption, are in the sanctified; being together in such sort, that in every particular part where the one is, the other is there also by it: even as in the twilight, light and darkness are in every part of the hemisphere. All which the scripture doth abundantly declare. For what we have of this gracious work upon us, while here, is but in part; it is not perfect, 1 Cor. xiii. 9, 10. Though there is a new man put on, there is an old man to be put off, Eph. iv. 22, 24. There is flesh as well as spirit in the best, Gal. v. 17; who therefore do look forth but as the morning, Cant. vi. 10; or as the word properly signifies, as the dawning: yet, as the dawning differs from dark night, they differ thereby from the unsanctified, in whom there is no light, Isa.

viii. 20. (Heb. no dawning.) See Rom. vii. 14—24. Phil. iii. 21.

Howbeit, forasmuch as it is a predominant measure of every grace that is thus communicated: this work of sanctification doth issue in a state of death unto sin, and a state of life unto righteousness.

1. It issueth in a state of death unto sin, or in mortification. For by means of that communication of grace from Christ the head, though it is not full, the OLD man of sin gets his deadly wound. The reigning power of the whole body of sins is destroyed: inasmuch as a reigning principle of grace is thereby set up in the believer; and that " his seed remaineth in him; and he cannot sin, because he is born of God," 1 John iii. 9. " Sin shall not have dominion over you: for ye are not under the law, but under grace." And total pollution, or defilement, through sin, is by the same means purged off; inasmuch as the restored image of God makes one really and personally pure and clean in the sight of God, as far as it goes: Tit. iii. 5, " He saved us by the washing of regeneration, and renewing of the Holy Ghost." Compare Col. iii. 10, " And have put on the new man, which is renewed in knowledge, after the image of him that created him." And thus one is put into a state of death, in respect of his unrenewed part, Col. iii. 3, " For ye are dead; Rom. vi. 11, " dead indeed unto sin." The which state of death is such as a crucified man is in, who being nailed to the cross, shall never come down till he have breathed out his last; Gal. vi. 14, " The world is crucified unto me, and I unto the world." Rom. vi. 6, " Our old man is crucified with him."

2. It issueth also in a state of life unto righteousness, or in vivification. For by means of the same communication of grace from Christ the head, one is endued with infused habits of grace, the immediate principles of gracious actions: the law is written in his heart; and his heart is circumcised to love the Lord. And thus he is put into a state of life unto righteousness, in respect of his renewed part; being " dead indeed unto sin, but alive unto God, through Jesus Christ our Lord," Rom. vi. 11. So saith the apostle of himself: Gal. ii. 20, " I am crucified with Christ: Nevertheless I live." And this state of life is such, as a man is in for the common actions of life, who is not only quickened, but risen and come forth of the grave; Col. ii. 12, " Ye are risen with him, through the faith of the operation of God." Rom. vi. 4, " That like as Christ was raised up by the glory of the Father, even so we also should walk in newness of life." And it is an eternal life; for the grace communicated from Christ to the believer, for that effect, " shall be in him a well of water springing up into everlasting life," John iv. 14.

Now, this death unto sin, and life unto righteousness, spring from our communion with Christ in his death and resurrection. These last have in them a power and virtue to render his mystical members conformable to him in them. They have a power and virtue, to cause in them a dying unto sin, as Christ died for sin, a violent death, lingering, and painful, yet voluntary; and a rising from sin to a new manner of life, continued during their abode in this world, and perfected in glory; even as he rose from the dead to a new manner of life, continued till his ascension: Philip. iii. 10. "That I may know him, and the power of his resurrection, and the fellowship of his sufferings, being made conformable unto his death." Rom. vi. 4, "Therefore we are buried with him by baptism into death: that like as Christ was raised up by the glory of the Father, even so we also should walk in newness of life." Ver. 5, "For if we have been planted together in the likeness of his death: we shall be also in the likeness of his resurrection." Since there is in Adam's sin and death, a malignant virtue, conforming his natural offspring unto him therein, to their defilement; why should it be thought strange, that there should be such a benign virtue in the death, and resurrection of Christ the second Adam, conforming his mystical members unto him therein, to their sanctification? for "as in Adam all die, even so in Christ shall all be made alive," 1 Cor. xv. 22. The death and resurrection of Christ have this virtue, inasmuch as he died and rose again as a public person, and merited this conformation of his mystical members to his image, Rom. vi. 4.—12, Eph. iii. 5. 6. And they have this effect, as they are applied to us by the Spirit. For the case of our justification and sanctification, is much like that of the delivering one who is a prisoner for debt. When the surety's payment of the debt is legally applied to the prisoner, by the judge sustaining it as clearing his debt; in the moment of that application, the prisoner is legally free; he is no more a prisoner in point of right, though still in the prison, until that one sent by the judge, apply it to him really by opening the prison-doors to him, and setting him at liberty. Even so the death of Christ, and his resurrection, considered as the evidence of his complete satisfaction, being legally applied by God the Judge, to a sinner, upon his believing; they have an immediate effect on him, constituting him in a happy relative state, in justification, and new relation to God as his Friend, Father, and God; so that he is thereby free, even from the dominion and pollution of sin, in point of right, as well as he is in fact freed from the guilt of it: he is by that application legally dead unto sin, and alive unto God: Rom. vi. 10, "For in that he" (to wit, Christ) "died, he died unto sin once: but in that he liveth, he liveth unto God." Ver. 11, "Likewise reckon ye also yourselves to be dead indeed unto sin ; but alive unto God through Jesus Christ our Lord." Now, the curse which stood as a legal bar to sanctifying influences, in respect whereof the strength of sin is the law, 1 Cor. xv. 56, being thus quite removed by the legal application, of the death and resurrection of Christ to the believer; the Spirit doth really apply the same death and resurrection to him, conforming him personally thereto, through the communication of grace to him, out of the fulness of grace in Christ the head; without which there cannot be any such conformation, according to the stated method of grace revealed in the scripture. And thus they have a mediate effect on him, constituting him really and personally holy, in sanctification : Rom. viii. 2, "For the law of the Spirit of life, in Christ Jesus, hath made me free from the law of sin and death." Col. ii. 12, "Buried with him in baptism, wherein also ye are risen with him." 1 Cor. xii. 13, "For by one Spirit are we all baptized into one body." John xv. 4, "As the branch cannot bear fruit of itself, except it abide in the vine : no more can ye, except ye abide in me." There was a double sprinkling of the blood of the sacrifices, called the blood of the covenant, Exod. xxiv. First, it was sprinkled on the altar, for atonement and reconciliation with God for Israel, ver. 6. And next, it was sprinkled on the people, for their purification, ver. 8; its purifying virtue flowing from its atoning virtue. Accordingly there is a double application or sprinkling of the blood of Christ, thereby signified : one for our justification and reconciliation with God; mentioned Heb. xii. 22, "Ye are come"—Ver. 24,—"to the blood of sprinkling, that speaketh better things than that of Abel," namely, in that it speaks for mercy and pardon, whereas Abel's spoke for vengeance : and then another, for our sanctification; mentioned, 1 Pet. i. 2, "Through sanctification of the Spirit unto obedience, and sprinkling of the blood of Jesus Christ." And this is the only true sanctification of a sinner, having a special relation to Jesus Christ and his Spirit.

Now, the branches of the promise of sanctification are manifold : for it spreads as wide as the commandments of the holy law, which, in the station it hath in the gospel-covenant, are all turned into promises. Thus whereas the command is, "Know the Lord;" the promise is, "They shall all know me, saith the Lord," Jer. xxxi. 34. The command is, "Come unto me," Matt. xi. 28; and it is promised, "They shall come," Psalm xxii. 31. The command is, "Love the Lord," Psalm xxxi. 23; it is promised, "The Lord will circumcise thine heart to love the Lord," Deut. xxx. 6. It is the command, "Fear God," 1 Pet. ii. 17; and it is promised, "I will put my fear in their hearts," Jer. xxxii. 40. We are commanded to be meek, humble, and lowly, Matt. xi. 29; and it is promised, Isa. xi. 6, "The wolf shall dwell with the lamb,—and a little child shall lead them." And thus it is in all other cases, the whole commandments of the law in this station being inlaid with the gospel-promises, as appears from Heb. viii. 10, "I will put my laws into their mind, and write them in their hearts: and I will be to them a God, and they shall be to me a people."

But the chief branches are these two; to wit, the promise of repentance, and the promise of actual grace and strength for all holy obedience.

1. One chief branch of the promise of sanctification, is the promise of repentance. Not that legal repentance, which goes before saving faith, being common to the elect and reprobate; but that evangelical repentance, which is described in our catechisms, the seeds of which are said, in the Larger Catechism, to be put into the heart in sanctification; and so follows saving faith and justification, in the order of nature: Ezek. xxxvi. 31, "Then shall ye remember your own evil ways, and your doings that were not good, and shall loathe yourselves in your own sight, for your iniquities." Psalm xxii. 27, "All the ends of the world shall remember and turn unto the Lord." Zech. xii. 10, "They shall look upon me whom they have pierced, and they shall mourn for him." The whole spiritual seed were, by means of the breach of the first covenant, lost sheep, even as others. Adam left them as so many waifs and strays, wandering on the mountains of vanity, ready to become a prey to the roaring lion, who goes about there, seeking whom he may devour: Isa. liii. 6, "All we like sheep have gone astray: we have turned every one to his own way." All of them had lost the way, and none of them could find it again. They had gone away from God, and could not return. They had turned to him the back, and not the face, and had become so inflexible, they could not turn about to him, and to their duty. They had lost their eyes, and could not discern the way to return: "to do good they had no knowledge," Jer. iv. 22. They had lost the power of their limbs, and could no more return, though they had known the way, than "the Ethiopian can change his skin, or the leopard his spots," chap. xiii. 23. And they had withal lost heart to return: God being to them an unatoned God, his face set against them, they could not bear to approach him. So they never would have turned, although they had been able; but each of them would have said, "There is no hope. No, "for I have loved strangers, and after them will I go," Jer. ii. 25. Wherefore, had not the Mediator interposed, they had wandered endlessly: had not Jesus Christ taken the desperate case

in hand, there had never been a returning sinner of Adam's family, a true penitent, a heart kindly softened in sorrow for sin, nor turned in hatred against sin as sin, more than there is among the fallen angels. But upon consideration of the second Adam's walking with God, the whole way of obedience to the law, which they went off from; having withal laid on him the iniquities of them all; there was made a promise of giving them repentance, that "he should gather together in one, the children of God that were scattered abroad," John xi. 52. In performance of which promise, after his ascension into heaven, it was found, that God had also to the Gentiles granted repentance unto life, Acts xi. 18.

Now, when one is justified by faith, and new-related to God, as his Friend, Father, and God, he is sanctified, and brought to true and evangelical repentance, according to this promise. Being come to Christ by faith, he comes back unto God by him in repentance, Heb. vii. 25. Whence it is called repentance toward God, which is the end whereunto faith toward our Lord Jesus Christ is the means, Acts xx. 21. Then, and not till then, it is, that the heart is set a-going in true gospel-repentance, pleasing to God, and acceptable in his sight; according to the Scripture: Ezek. xvi. 62, "And I will establish my covenant with thee." Ver. 63, "That thou mayest remember and be confounded, and never open thy mouth any more because of thy shame, when I am pacified toward thee." Chap. xx. 42, "And ye shall know that I am the Lord, when I shall bring you into the land of Israel." Ver. 43, "And there shall ye remember your ways,—and ye shall loathe yourselves." Chap. xxxvi. 25, "Then will I sprinkle clean water upon you, and ye shall be clean." —Ver. 26, "A new heart also will I give you."—Ver. 28,—"And ye shall be my people, and I will be your God." Ver. 31, "Then shall ye remember your own evil ways,—and shall loathe yourselves." For then it is, that the love of God to the soul, which lay hid before, doth shine forth more or less clear; and being discerned by faith accordingly, warms the heart of the sinner with love to God again, according to that, 1 John iv. 19, "We love him, because he first loved us." And that love melts it into repentance for sin, as in the woman who, being forgiven much, loved much: and shewed her love, by her washing our Saviour's feet with tears, Luke vii. 37, 38, 47. The hard heart is then laid on the soft bed of the love and free grace of God in Christ; and the word of the law, inlaid with the gospel, falls on it, saying, "Break, for the Lord is gracious;" Joel ii. 13, "Rend your heart,—and turn unto the Lord your God: for he is gracious and merciful,—and of great kindness." And this, like a hammer, breaketh the rock in pieces. The party being, as is before declared, renewed in the whole man, put into a state of death unto sin, and life unto righteousness, the new nature vents itself in an ingenuous and thorough turning from sin unto God, in heart and life. By believing the sinner returns unto God as a portion, wherein to rest: in repenting he returns unto God as a Lord and Master, whom he is to obey. He turns from sin unto God, coming back as a runaway servant to his master, returning to his place and duty in the family. And he returns with blushing and tears. He is filled with sorrow and shame for offending a good and gracious God. His heart is turned against sin, in hatred of it: he hates it not only as a hurtful thing, that would ruin him: but as a filthy and loathsome thing, that defiles him. He loathes it, as the abominable thing that God hates; as the deformity of the soul, the very reverse of the glorious holiness of God expressed in his law. He loathes himself for it; calls himself fool and beast, for his entertaining it; smites on his breast, as if he would bruise that breast it was bred in; and smites on his thigh, as if he would break the legs that carried him in the way of it, Luke xv. 20, 21, and xviii. 13; Jer. xxxi. 18, 19. And he returns with full purpose of, and endeavours after new obedience; with a heart inclined to keep God's statutes always, even unto the end, Psalm cxix. 33; and filled with carefulness in that point, vehement desire of it, and zeal for it, 2 Cor. vii. 11.

The other chief branch of the promise of sanctification, is, the promise of actual grace and strength for all holy obedience; whereby one may be enabled acceptably to perform obedience, in all and every act of mortification or dying unto sin, and of living unto righteousness; to do every duty that is required of him, and to bear whatsoever affliction is laid upon him: Psalm xxii. 30, "A seed shall serve him." Zech. x. 12, "And I will strengthen them in the Lord, and they shall walk up and down in his name." Hos. xiv. 9, "The ways of the Lord are right, and the just shall walk in them." Ezek. xxxvi. 27, "And I will cause you to walk in my statutes, and ye shall keep my judgments, and do them." And, Deut. xxx., the root-promise of sanctification, in circumcising the heart to love the Lord, is in the first place proposed, ver. 6; and then follow both the branches thereof together, to wit, the promise of repentance, and of actual grace for new obedience, ver. 8, "And thou shalt return and obey the voice of the Lord, and do all his commandments." God planted Adam a noble vine, made him as a green tree full of sap, for bringing forth all fruits of holiness; but breaking the first covenant, he and all mankind in him withered and died, under the curse; upon which ensued an absolute barrenness, that no fruit of holiness could be expected from them more. But the second Adam having engaged to satisfy the law, by bearing the curse; there was thereupon made a promise of raising them up again to walk in newness of life. And it is performed in their habitual sanctification, wrought in them immediately upon their union with Christ: for though sanctification doth in the order of nature follow justification, and the new relation to God as a Friend, Father, and God; yet in respect of time, it is together and at once with them: in the same moment that a sinner is justified, he is also sanctified. But even when we are habitually sanctified, through the habits of grace infused into us by the Spirit; we are not of ourselves, that is to say, merely upon that stock, without new communications of actual grace by the same Spirit, able to bring forth any fruit of holiness: even of our gracious selves we can do nothing, as our Saviour teacheth, John xv. 4, 5. And the apostle professeth, in his own name, and in the name of all other gracious persons, 2 Cor. iii. 4, "And such trust have we through Christ to Godward." Ver. 5, "Not that we are sufficient of ourselves to think any thing as of ourselves; but our sufficiency is of God. For," saith he, Philip. ii. 13, "it is God which worketh in you, both to will and to do." And this is no more strange in the dispensation of grace, than that, in nature, fresh seed sown in good ground, yet cannot spring up, and bring forth fruit, without warming and moistening influences from the heavens; or, that we have a power of natural motion, and yet cannot actually move a finger, without a common providential influence of the Spirit of God, in, or by, whom we live and move, Acts xvii. 28. Wherefore the promise is extended, as we have said, unto actual grace and strength for the acts of holy obedience; and is so made forthcoming to believers in their actual and progressive sanctification.

And thus such a sufficient provision and allowance of grace is made in the covenant for believers, as that it is possible for them, even in this life, to perform obedience to the law of Christ, the ten commandments, the eternal rule of righteousness, in all the parts thereof, acceptably: so that there is no corruption so strong, but one may get it acceptably mortified; nor does the Lord require any duty so difficult, but one may get it acceptably done; nor is there any trial or affliction so heavy, but one may get it acceptably borne. If it had not been so, our Lord would not have made doing whatsoever he commands, the distinguishing mark of his friends, John xv. 14. The apostle doth indeed deny, that we are sufficient of ourselves; but withal he teacheth, that there is a sufficiency for us of God, 2 Cor. iii. 5. So the Lord himself taught him, in his own case, chap. xii. 9, "My grace is sufficient for thee." Without it were so, Christ's yoke could not be easy, nor his burden light, Matt. xi. 30. Nay, they would be like the yoke and burden of the law as a covenant of works, grievous to be borne, chap. xxiii. 4. But his commandments are not grievous, 1 John v. 3. It was no vain boasting the apostle used, when he said, "I can do all things through Christ which strengtheneth me," Philip. iv. 13. Nor was Epaphras out, in supposing that the Colossian believers might "stand complete in all the will of God," Col. iv. 12. David had God's own testimony, as to fact in that matter, Acts xiii. 22, "I have found David, a man after mine own heart, which shall fulfil all my will."

This bears no prejudice to the doctrine of the imperfection of the obedience of the saints in this life, maintained by orthodox divines against the papists and other perfectionists; which, as it is abundantly evident from the Holy Scriptures, hath also a concurring testimony to the truth thereof, in the breasts of all the serious godly, to whom it is given by the Spirit to discern the holiness of God, the spirituality of the law, and the corruption of their own nature. But I am persuaded, that, through the sleight of Satan, that doctrine is, as several other precious truths are, a stone of stumbling to many, through their not adverting to the provision and allowance of grace made in this promise of the covenant; and that by this means many a poor sinner is snared and ruined, and the hands of many saints weakened in the practice of holiness; to the great disadvantage of the cause of holiness in the world.

To break that snare, and set this matter in a clear light, there are three things carefully to be distinguished.

1. Distinguish between performing obedience, in all the parts thereof, and in all the degrees of these parts. The latter indeed no man can, at any rate, do in this life, James iii. 2; Eccl. vii. 20. But the former every true believer may do, yea, and actually doth, so far as these parts are known to him, as appears from the texts above alleged. In confounding of these there lies a snare. "The best of men," say crafty sinners, "do in many things come short of the obedience required of them: and but so do we." Now, that the saints do come short of the degrees of every part of obedience required of them, is very true: but that they come short of any of the parts themselves known to them, which is the case of the crafty sinner seeking shelter for his sin here, is false. And herein the former do really distinguish themselves from the latter; as David showed himself of another make than Saul, by his fulfilling all God's will, in the several parts thereof, which Saul did not, Acts xiii. 22. It is here as in the case of a family, consisting of pliable children, and refractory servants. The master of the family pre-

scribes several pieces of work to be done by them all: and his grown children, who have perfect skill of their business, to do them all exactly according to his mind; and thus glorified saints obey: the younger children who are learning to work, do, out of regard to their father's command, indeed put hand to every one of them, but they can do none of them exactly; even so it is with the saints on earth; but the refractory servants put hand to some of them, but quite neglect others of them, and this is the manner of the wicked and slothful servant, who seeks shelter here for his sloth, and his partiality in obedience.

2. Distinguish between performing obedience perfectly, and performing it acceptably. No man can perform obedience perfectly in this life, Philip. iii. 12; but every true believer performs obedience acceptably: Acts x. 35, "He that feareth him, and worketh righteousness is accepted with him." In confounding these there is a snare. The crafty sinner saith, "There is none that performs obedience perfectly: and I am sure I do many things, though indeed not all." Now, that true believers do not perform obedience perfectly, is very true; but that they do not perform it acceptably, which is the case of the crafty sinner, as not universal, and therefore not sincere, in his obedience, is altogether false. They who are masters know very well how to make this distinction, in their domestic affairs. If a child, or pliable servant, shew a real good-will to obey their orders, they will accept of their work, though it is not done, in every point, as they would have it; so, if there be first a willing mind, discovered in sincere endeavours, it is accepted of God for the sake of Christ, according to that a man hath, 2 Cor. viii. 12. But if a servant shall quite neglect to put hand to a thing which he is peremptorily ordered to do, because he cannot do it every way so as the master would have it done; this is construed to be a contempt of the master's authority. And what other account can men imagine will be made in heaven of their conduct, in instances of plain and unquestionable duty, which they quite neglect; and of sin, that they indulge themselves in?

3. Distinguish between ability in ourselves for performing obedience in all the parts thereof acceptably, and ability for it in Christ to be fetched in by faith. Neither saints nor sinners have the former, 2 Cor. iii. 5; but all true believers have the latter: they have such ability in Christ their head, Col. ii. 10, "Ye are complete in him," Philip iv. 13, "I can do all things through Christ which strengtheneth me." And it is in the gospel offered to all, so that whosoever will, may have it: Matth. xi. 28, "Come unto me, all ye that labour and are heavy laden, and I will give you rest." Ver.

29, "Take my yoke upon you." If a discreet master command his servant to go and do a particular piece of work, it will not excuse the servant's neglect, that he wanted instruments necessary for it; because he will reckon, that his bidding him do the work, did suppose his allowing him instruments, without which it could not be done; and that the servant ought to have called for them. But here lies a ruining snare to many. "We can do nothing of ourselves," say they: and hereupon the sluggard puts his hand in his bosom, and does nothing; but, having laid his head on this soft pillow, he sleeps to death on the bed of sloth and carnal ease. O that men would open their eyes, and see through this piece of ruining deceit! No man shall be able to excuse himself hereby, from the performance of holy obedience in all the parts thereof. Nay, this his conduct will bring him under a double guilt; one, of neglecting what it was his duty to do; another, of despising the grace offered him, to enable him thereto: and so he will be condemned, not because he could not obey, but because he would not. God hath never been a hard master to mankind, reaping where he did not sow; but hath always made a suitable allowance of grace and strength to them for his work. In the covenant of works, only perfect obedience could be accepted at the hands of the covenant-people; and there was a conformable allowance of grace and strength conform, made to them in it. God made man upright, able to obey the law in perfection. And the law justly insists for perfection of obedience still, upon the ground of that provision which was made for it, though it is now lost; being that it was lost by man's own fault. In the covenant of grace, which is adapted to our fallen state, sincere obedience may be accepted, notwithstanding of imperfections attending it. And accordingly, in it there is made a provision and allowance of such a sufficiency of grace and strength, as thereby every piece of obedience required of the covenant-people may be done, even in this life; though not as it should be done, yet so as it may be accepted: accepted, I say, not for its own sake indeed, nor for the worker's sake neither; but for Christ's sake, in whose name it is required to be done and offered to God, as a spiritual sacrifice, acceptable to God by Jesus Christ, 1 Pet. ii. 5. This is evident from the forecited passages, 2 Cor. iii. 5, and xii. 9; Philip. iv. 13. But withal, this sufficiency of grace and strength for that effect, is not lodged in the covenant-people themselves; but in Christ their head, in whom they have it, as the branches have a sufficiency of sap and juice in the vine, for their bringing forth fruit in the season: Isa. xlv. 24. "Surely, shall one say, in the Lord have I righteousness and strength." 2 Tim. ii. 1, "Thou therefore, my son, be strong in the grace that is in Christ Jesus." And it is fetched into the soul by faith, believing the promise: Jer. xvii. 7, "Blessed is the man that trusteth in the Lord." Ver. 8, "For he shall be as a tree planted by the waters." Psalm xxviii. 7, "My heart trusted in him, and I am helped." And so every command of Christ in this covenant, supposeth an allowance of grace and strength, sufficient for the performing of it in an acceptable manner. Accordingly, the declaration of grace stands on the front of the ten commandments, Exod. xx. 2, "I am the Lord thy God." Ver. 3, "Thou shalt have no other gods before me," &c. If the law came to us without the gospel, we might have some excuse for not doing what we are commanded; yet not so strong, but that it would be overthrown, as in the case of pagans, Rom. ii. 12. But since, with the commands of the law requiring obedience, the gospel also comes to us, shewing how we may be enabled to obey them acceptably, and offering us that ability in Christ Jesus; we are inexcusable in that matter: the plea of the wicked and slothful servant is rejected; and he is condemned, not only for not giving obedience, but for refusing grace and strength offered him, to enable him thereto.

Wherefore, let us firmly believe this promise of the gospel-covenant, that we may give obedience to the commands of the law: for where there is no hope of performing acceptably what is required, there can be no suitable endeavours after it. If the heart is hopeless in that matter, the hands will certainly hang down: and the issue must needs be, either a ceasing from the duty altogether, or else a very faint promise thereof, unacceptable to God. But the faith of this promise will remove the cover of sloth, animate to every good work, and bring in grace and strength for all holy obedience; "Having therefore these promises, dearly beloved, let us cleanse ourselves from all filthiness of the flesh and spirit, perfecting holiness in the fear of God," 2 Cor. vii. 1.

Since God hath not given to the church the command of sanctification to be obeyed, without the promise of sanctification to be believed; but he that hath said, "Wash ye, make ye clean," hath said also, "I will sprinkle clean water upon you, and ye shall be clean;" no man hath ground to imagine, that he doth so much as endeavour to comply with the true design of the command of sanctification, who doth not first believe and embrace the promise of sanctification; but falls to work with the nitre and soap of his own faithful endeavours, to wash himself clean. Such a one mistakes the true intent and import of the command of sanctification, as it stands in the Bible; and that as far as the command of a discreet master would be mistaken by a foolish servant, who being bid to go and dig a parcel of ground, should thereupon fall a digging it with his nails, never looking after a spade, mattock, or any other instrument proper to dig with.

Now, the promise of sanctification, which its several branches, is grafted upon the promise of a resurrection made to Christ. For the condition of the covenant being fulfilled, he as the head was, according to the promise, brought again from the dead, and lives unto God, death having no more dominion over him: and in virtue hereof again, his members are brought to repentance from dead works, and unto newness of life. Hence we are said to be begotten again, by the resurrection of Jesus Christ from the dead, 1 Pet. i. 3; forasmuch as we are raised with him (Col. iii. 1.) unto newness of life, (Rom. vi. 4, 5.), according to the promise, Is. xxvi. 19, " Thy dead men shall live, together with my dead body shall they arise :— The earth shall cast out the dead ;"namely, in the first place, the head Christ Jesus, the first-born from the dead, Col. i. 18, and then his mystical members after him in their order. Compare Hos. vi. 2, " In the third day he will raise us up, and we shall live in his sight."

Thus far of the promise of sanctification. Follows :—

IV. The promise of perseverance in grace.

The promise of eternal life doth in like manner comprehend the the perseverance in grace to be conferred on all the covenant-people, being justified, new-related to God, and sanctified; so that, being once brought into the state of grace, they shall never fall away from it totally nor finally. This promise we have, Jer. xxxii. 40, " And I will make an everlasting covenant, with them, that I will not turn away from them, to do them good; but I will put my fear in their hearts, that they shall not depart from me." Here they are secured on both sides; that God will never cast them off, and that they shall never desert him. And that this benefit is included in the promise of eternal life, is clear from the apostle's adducing this last to prove it, Heb. x. 38, " Now the just shall live by faith." Such is the malice of Satan, and the advantage he had against the saints in this life; so manifold are the snares for them in the present evil world; such a tender bud of heaven is the implanted grace of God in them, and so corrupt, fickle, and inconstant are the hearts of the best, while here; that, if their perseverance had not been secured by promise in the covenant, but made the condition of the covenant, and left to the management of their own free-will, they would have had but a sorry restoration of it into the state of grace; as much as if they had got a spark of fire to keep alive in the midst of an ocean. At that rate they might all have perished; and Jesus

Christ, notwithstanding of the shedding of his blood for them, might have eternally remained a head without members, a king without subjects. But the glory of Christ, and his salvation of his redeemed, were not left at such uncertainty. That perseverance which the first Adam failed of, and was made the condition of the second covenant, the second Adam did undertake in their name: and thereupon was made the promise of their perseverance. And he having accordingly persevered unto the end, in obedience to the law for them, being obedient even to the death, it was purchased for them. Thus Christ's perseverance in obedience to the law, till the condition of the covenant was perfectly fulfilled, is the ground in law upon which the perseverance of the saints is infallibly secured, in virtue of the faithfulness of God in the promise.

Now, this promise begins to be performed to them, as soon as they are united unto Christ; and it goes on all along, until their death, when they enter into glory: yea, strictly speaking, death is not the last, but a middle term of their perseverance; after which it proceeds far more illustriously than before. Upon their union with the second Adam, being savingly interested in his obedience which he persevered in unto the end, they are confirmed, that they can no more fall away: even as the first Adam's natural seed would have been confirmed, upon his having completed the course of his probationary obedience, and fulfilling the condition of the covenant of works. The mystical members of Christ do then obtain the former, as the reward of his continued obedience; as in the other supposed event, Adam's natural seed would have obtained the latter, as the reward of his continued obedience.

The promise of the perseverance of the saints, seems to be grafted upon the promise of assistance made to Christ in his work. The Father promised to him, that he would uphold him, so as he should not fail, Isa. xlii. 1, 4. The which promise being made to him as a public person, carries along with it the preservation and support of his members, in all their temptations, trials, and dangers of perishing; ensuring the safe conduct, as of the head, so of the mystical members through this world, till they be out of the reach of danger.

Now, of the promise of perseverance there are two chief branches.

1. A promise of continued influences of grace, to be from time to time conferred on them, being once brought into a state of grace: Isa. xxvii. 3, " I will water it every moment." Their stock of inherent grace would soon fail, if they were left to live upon it, without supply coming in from another hand: of itself it would wither away and die out, if it were not fed, Luke xxii. 32; John xv. 6. Innocent Adam had a larger stock of inherent grace than any of the saints in

this life, and yet he lost it. But the grace of God in believers cannot be so lost: for, in virtue of the promise, there are continued influences secured for them; namely, preserving influences, whereby grace given, is kept from dying out, that as they are sanctified by God the Father so they are preserved in Jesus Christ, Jude 1, exciting influences, whereby the grace preserved beginning to languishing, or being brought low by the prevailing of corruption, and temptation is stirred up and put in exercise again; and strengthening influences, whereby the grace excited, is increased, and gathers more strength, to the overtopping of corruption, and repelling of temptation: Hos. xiv. 7, "They shall revive as the corn, and grow as the vine." Accordingly, their faith is never suffered to fail totally, but is preserved, excited, and strengthened; and all the graces with it, and by it. And this is brought to pass, through the communication of new supplies of grace to them, by the Spirit, from Christ their head, from which all the body having nourishment ministered, (namely, through the supply of the Spirit, Phil. i. 19), increaseth with the increase of God," Col. ii. 19.

2. The other chief branch of this promise, is a promise of pardon, continued pardon for the sins of their daily walk; whereby emergent differences betwixt God and them, come to be done away from time to time, so that a total rupture is prevented: Jer. xxxiii. 8, "I will pardon all their iniquities." Howbeit the justified have, as to their state, no need of a new formal pardon, but only of a manifestation of their former pardon; since the pardon given in justification, is never revoked, though by means of their after-sins they may lose sight of it: yet as to their daily walk, they have great need of a formal pardon; forasmuch as they are daily contracting new guilt: John xiii. 10, "He that is washed, needeth not, save to wash his feet." For howbeit no sins of the justified can bring any more under the guilt of eternal wrath; nevertheless they do bring them under the guilt of fatherly anger, Psalm lxxxix. 30—32. And therefore they need to pray every day, "Our Father, forgive us our debts."

This pardon is given them, upon their renewed actings of faith in Jesus Christ, and of repentance towards God; yet not for their believing and repenting, but for Christ's sake, even as the first pardon is given, 1 John ii. 1, 2, and i. 7. Applying the blood of Christ afresh to their souls, they are anew moved to repentance, turning from their sins with hatred of them, sorrow, shame, and self-lothing for them. Looking by faith on him whom they have pierced, they mourn in renewed repentance; and so receive this pardon. For although repentance doth not go before, but follows after the pardon of sin in justification; yet not only faith, but repentance also, goes before the pardons given to those already justified: 1 John i. 7, "If we walk in the light, as he is in the light, we have fellowship one with another, and the blood of Jesus Christ his Son cleanseth us from all sin." Vers. 9, "If we confess our sins, he is faithful, and just to forgive us our sins, and to cleanse us." Therefore we are ordered to pray thus, "Our Father, forgive us our debts, as we forgive our debtors," Matth. vi. 9, 12.; to teach all the children of God, that if they would have their Father's forgiveness, they must in the first place forgive others: which is yet more clearly intimated, Luke xi. 4, "And forgive us our sins; for we also forgive every one that is indebted to us." But the matter is not so stated, with respect to the pardon of sin in justification; but that pardon is the spring of our forgiving others, Matth. xviii. 32, 33. For our hearty and acceptable forgiving of others, proceeds from true Christian love to our neighbour; and that flows from love to God; the which is kindled in our hearts by God's pardoning grace to us, Luke vii. 47; Eph. iv. 32. The reason of the difference lies here, the unjustified sinner is under the guilt of revenging wrath, which seeks not the amendment, but the destruction of the guilty: wherefore till once it is removed, there can be no true evangelical repentance, no acceptable amendment, in the sinner; these being really a restoration of him to life, incompatible with a legal destination of him to destruction. But the justified saint is only under the guilt of fatherly anger, which seeks not the destruction, but the recovery and amendment of the guilty: and therefore it is not removed until he repent, turning from his sin unto God in an acceptable manner; and that is the very amendment God seeketh in shewing his anger against him, as in the case of David, and of Peter.

And thus are the saints caused to persevere in grace, both real and relative. The promise of continued influences secures not only the preservation, but the renewed exercise of their grace, particularly of their faith and repentance: and the promise of continued pardon to them believing and repenting, secures the removal of the guilt of fatherly anger. The Spirit of Christ ever dwells in them, and so continues an inviolable bond of their union with him; and dwelling in them, he recovers them when they are fallen, stirs up the holy fire of grace lying hid with ashes of corruption. Then the withered hand of faith is again stretched out; and the man believes the promise of the pardon of guilt of eternal wrath, as to all his sins; this melts his heart in kindly repentance; and so he believes the promise of continued pardon, as to fatherly anger, with respect to the sins the causes of God's present controversy with him, and obtains pardon accordingly. By these means, matters are always kept from coming to a total rupture.

V. THE PROMISE OF TEMPORAL BENEFITS.

In the fifth and last place, the promise of eternal life to the elect, considered in this period, comprehends a promise of temporal benefits to be conferred on them, and every one of them, being united to Christ; and that in such measure, as God sees meet for his own glory and their good. This promise stands imbodied with the spiritual promises in the covenant, Ezek. xxxvi. 29, "I will also save you from all your uncleannesses, and I will call for the corn, and I will increase it." Hos. ii. 22, "The earth shall hear the corn, and the wine, and the oil, and they shall hear Jezreel." Indeed this is not the principal thing contained in the promissory part of the covenant: but it is a necessary addition thereto; as the present state of the saints, while in this world, doth require, Matth. vi. 33. And thus godliness, as the apostle observes, 1 Tim. iv. 8, hath promise of the life that now is, and of that which is to come.

When God took man into the first covenant, he made provision in it for his temporal as well as for his spiritual and eternal welfare. He gave him a right to, and dominion over the creatures in the earth, sea, and air; giving and granting upon him full power, soberly to use them, and to dispose of them, for God's glory and his own comfort: and this lordship to be holden of him as sovereign lord of all, firm and irreversible, by the tenor of that covenant, as long as he should continue in his obedience; but to be forfeited to all intents and purposes, in case he should by transgression break the covenant, Gen. i. 28, and ii. 16, 17. But man continued not in this honour: he brake God's covenant, and so fell from that his right to, and dominion over the creatures. By his transgression he forfeited life itself; and consequently lost his covenant-right to all the means and comforts of life. And in this condition are all natural men, with respect to these things. They have no covenant-right to the means and comforts of life, whatever portion of them they are possessed of. All the right that they have to them, is a mere providential, precarious right; such as a condemned man hath to his food, during the time his execution is delayed at the pleasure of the prince. This is a most uncertain and uncomfortable holding: nevertheless it so far avails, that they are not, properly speaking, violent possessors of temporal benefits; having just the same right to them as to their forfeited life, while it is left them by the disposal of providence. Wherefore the worst of men may lawfully eat and drink, and take the benefit of other necessaries of life, whatever Satan may suggest to the contrary in the hour of temptation; yea, they ought to do it, and they sin against God egregiously if they do it not; because he hath said, " thou shalt not kill."

But the second Adam having undertaken to bear the curse, and to give perfect obedience to the law, in the name of his spiritual seed; there was thereupon made a promise of restoring to them the forfeited life, with all the means thereof; and particularly, a promise of the good things requisite for the support and comfort of their temporal life in this world, till at death they be carried home to heaven. And the performance of this promise to them, is begun immediately upon their uniting with Christ: then their covenant relation to the first Adam is found to be lawfully dissolved; the forfeiture is taken off; and a new covenant right to the creatures is given them: 1 Cor. iii. 22, 23, "All are yours; and ye are Christ's." And it goes on, all along till death; so much of this their stock being from time to time put into their hands, as the great administrator sees needful for them. And whether that be little or much, they do from that moment possess it by a new title: it is theirs by covenant.

Now, this promise is grafted upon the promise made to Christ of his inheriting all things. For they that are his, are joint heirs with him, Rom. viii. 17, to inherit all things too through him, Rev. xxi. 7. The estate and honour which the first Adam lost for himself and family, by his disobedience in breaking of the first covenant, was, in the second covenant, made over by promise to Christ the second Adam, for him and his, upon the condition of his obedience. The which obedience being performed the whole ancient estate of the family was recovered, together with the honours thereunto belonging. The ancient dominion was restored, in the person of Christ as second Adam: and all his mystical members partake thereof in him. This the Psalmist teacheth, Psalm viii. 4, " What is man, that thou art mindful of him? and the son of man that thou visitest him?" Ver. 5, " For thou hast made him a little lower than the angels, and hast crowned him with glory and honour." Ver. 6, "Thou madest him to have dominion over the works of thy hands; thou hast put all things under his feet." Ver. 7, " All sheep and oxen, yea, and the beasts of the field." Ver. 8, " The fowl of the air, and the fish of the sea, and whatsoever passeth through the paths of the seas." Though there is here a manifest view to the first Adam and all mankind in him, as they were happily and honourably stated at their creation; yet we are infallibly assured by the apostle, that this passage is meant of Christ the second Adam. Heb. ii. 6, 7, 8, 9, and his mystical members in him, ver. 6. Accordingly, Abraham had the promise, that he should be the heir of the world; and he had it through the righteousness of faith, *i.e.* the righteousness which faith apprehends, Rom. iv. 13. Now, Abraham was a type of Christ, and the father of the faithful, who are all blessed as he was. Therefore this promise was primarily to Christ, through the righteousness by him wrought; secondarily to his members, through the same righteousness apprehended by faith.

This promise of temporal benefits, carries believers' possession of the same, as far as their need in that kind doth go, Phil. iv. 19. Of which need, not they themselves, but their Father, is the fit judge, Matt. vi. 32. Accordingly, there are two chief branches of the promise, namely, a promise of provision, and a promise of protection.

1. A promise of provision of good things necessary for this life; upon which they may confidently trust God for them, whatever straits they are at any time reduced to: Psalm xxxiv. 10, "The young lions do lack, and suffer hunger: but they that seek the Lord, shall not want any good thing." Their meat and drink are secured for them in the covenant; the which being perceived by faith, cannot miss to give them a peculiar relish, however mean their fare be, as to quantity or quality: Isa. xxxiii. 16, "Bread shall be given him, his water shall be sure." They shall be fed, though they be not feasted: Psalm xxxvii. 3, "Verily thou shalt be fed." They shall have enough, they shall be satisfied, Joel ii. 26. And even days of famine shall not mar that, their satisfaction: Psalm xxxvii. 19, "In the days of famine they shall be satisfied." And as sleep for their refreshment is necessary too, the promise bears it also: Prov. iii. 24, "Thou shalt lie down, and thy sleep shall be sweet." They need clothing; and provision is made as to it: Matt. vi. 30, "If God so clothe the grass of the field—shall he not much more clothe you, O ye of little faith?" Having made them, by covenant, a new grant of life, and of a body, which are more than meat and clothing, he will not refuse them these lesser things necessary for the support of the greater. Ver. 25, "Is not the life more than meat, and the body than raiment?" Thus our fallen first parents, having believed and embraced the promise of life, had, with the new grant of life, food and raiment provided for them, as is particularly taken notice of, Gen. iii. 15, 18, 21. A blessing also on their labours is promised, and success in their lawful callings and affairs, Isa. lxv. 21, 22, 23. In a word, the covenant bears, that God will withhold no good thing from them that live uprightly, Psalm lxxxiv. 11.

2. There is also a promise of protection from the evil things that concern this life: Psalm xci. 10, "There shall no evil befal thee."

Ver. 11, "For he shall give his angels charge over thee, to keep thee in all thy ways." Together with the bread and the water provided by the covenant for them to live on, the munitions of rocks are secured to them for a place of defence, where they may safely enjoy them, Isa. xxxiii. 16. The same Lord who is a sun to nourish them, will be a shield to protect them, Psalm lxxxiv. 11. He will be a wall of fire round about them, to cherish them, and to keep off, scare, and fright away all their enemies, Zech. ii. 5. The covenant yields a broad covert for the safety of believers; Psalm xci. 4, "He shall cover thee with his feathers." The covert of the covenant is stretched out over their bodies; over their health, to preserve it, while it is necessary for God's honour and their own good, Prov. iii. 7, "Fear the Lord, and depart from evil;" ver. 8, "It shall be health to thy navel, and marrow to thy bones;" over their lives, as long as God has any service for them in this world: so in sickness they are carefully seen to, Psalm xli. 3, "Thou wilt make all his bed in his sickness;" their diseases healed, and they recovered, Psalm ciii. 3, 4. And they are delivered from enemies that seek their life, Psalm xli. 2. Yea, when death rides in triumph, having made havoc on all sides of them, as by sword or pestilence, they are found safe under the covert of the covenant, Psalm xci. 6, 7. This covert is stretched over their names, credit, and reputation: Job v. 21, "Thou shalt be hid from the scourge of the tongue:" either the tongues of virulent men shall not reach them; or they shall not be able to make the dirt to stick on them: or else if they shall be permitted to make it stick for a while, the covert of the covenant shall wipe all off at length, and their righteousness shall be brought forth as the light, and their judgment as the noon-day, Psalm xxxvii. 6. It is stretched over their houses and dwelling-places: Psalm xci. 10, "Neither shall any plague come nigh thy dwelling." It goes round about their substance, making a hedge about all that they have, Job i. 10. Yea, and there is a lap of it to cast over their widows and children, when they are dead and gone: Jer. xlix. 11, "Leave thy fatherless children, I will preserve them alive, and let thy widows trust in me."

Thus far of the promise of eternal life, considered in the second period, to wit, from union with Christ, until death.

PERIOD III.

FROM DEATH, THROUGH ETERNITY.

It remains that we consider the promise of eternal life to the elect, as it is accomplished to, and hath its effect upon them, from their death, all along through eternity. And so the great lines of it are two; to wit, a promise of victory over death, and a promise of everlasting life in heaven. And these things I shall touch more briefly, having handled them at large elsewhere.

II. THE PROMISE OF VICTORY OVER DEATH.

The promise of eternal life comprehends a promise of victory over death, to be conferred on all and every one of the spiritual seed, in the encounter with that last enemy: Isa. xxv. 8, "He will swallow up death in victory, and the Lord God will wipe away tears from off all faces." After the wearisome march, and the reiterated fights of faith they have in their passage through the wilderness of this world, they have to pass the Jordan of death, and to fight the last battle with that enemy. But the victory is secured on their side by promise; of which there are two chief branches, to wit, a promise of disarming death, and a promise of destroying it.

1. There is a promise of disarming death to the dying believer; so that it shall at no rate be able to reach him a ruining stroke: Hos. xiii. 14, "O death, I will be thy plagues;" namely, by taking the sting quite away, 1 Cor. xv. 55. When sin entered the world, death followed; and sin furnished death with an envenomed sting, wherewith to kill the sinner, both soul and body at once; the holy law, with its curse, fixed this sting in death's hand; having first so pointed it, that it could not miss of doing execution. But Christ, the second Adam, having undertaken to bear the curse, and to die in the room and stead of his people; there was thereupon made a promise of disarming death to them: since the Surety suffering the pains of death armed with its sting, the principal behoved to be liberate from suffering the same thing over again. And thus the covenant secures believers from death's harm. Yea, it so alters the nature thereof, that it makes it a quite new thing to them from what it was originally. Hence death is found in the inventory of the saints' treasure, 1 Cor. iii. 22, "Whether life, or death, or things present, or things to come; all is yours." Not only is life theirs by the covenant, but death is theirs too by the same tenor. And indeed as it is new-framed by the covenant, it is of excellent use to them, bringing them into a state of perfection, and everlasting rest, Heb. xii. 23; Rev. xiv. 13.

This promise is grafted upon the promise of victory made to Christ, as appears from the forecited, Isa. xxv. 8. He encountered death, armed with its sting, on purpose to disarm it to his people:

he received the sting thereof into his own soul and body, that they might be delivered from it. Wherefore the promise of victory over death made to him, secures the disarming of it to them. And as the promise makes them safe, in the encounter with that last enemy: so the lively faith of it may in this case deliver from fear.

2. There is a promise of destroying death to the dead believer, by a glorious resurrection at the last day; Hos. xiii. 14, "O grave, I will be thy destruction." When death entered into the world by sin, then came the grave, as death's attendant, to keep fast his prisoners for him, till the general judgment: and thus the grave serves death, in the case of all who die in a state of enmity with God. But Christ, the second Adam, having in the second covenant engaged to go, in the room and stead of his people, death's prisoner, into the grave, and there to lie till their debt should be fully paid; there was made thereupon a promise of a glorious resurrection to his members, whereby they shall be put out of the reach of death for good and all, at the last day: for "then shall be brought to pass the saying that is written, death is swallowed up in victory," 1 Cor. xv. 54; and then shall they triumphantly sing, "O death, where is thy sting? O grave, where is thy victory?" ver. 55. And thus the covenant secures the forming anew of their dissolved bodies, the return of their departed souls into them, and their coming forth of their graves glorious, immortal, and incorruptible. In the faith of which, the saints may with comfort consider the grave as but a retiring place, from whence after a while they shall come forth with unspeakable joy.

This promise is grafted upon the promise of a resurrection made to Christ, Isa. xxvi. 19, "Thy dead men shall live, together with my dead body shall they arise." The promise of a resurrection being made to him as a public person, it must take place also on his mystical members, whose federal head he was. Hence the Psalmist says, his flesh should rest in hope, namely, in the grave, in hope of a glorious resurrection, because the holy one Jesus was not to see corruption, Psalm xvi. 2, 10, with Acts xiii. 35; thereby teaching, that Christ's resurrection would insure his glorious resurrection, as a member of the mystical body by faith. And indeed there is such a connection between Christ's resurrection and the happy resurrection of the saints, that they stand and fall together: 1 Cor. xv. 16, "For if the dead rise not, then is not Christ raised."

II. THE PROMISE OF EVERLASTING LIFE IN HEAVEN.

The promise of eternal life doth, in the last place, comprehend a promise of everlasting life in heaven, to be conferred on all and every one of the spiritual seed after death: Dan. xii. 2, "And many of them that sleep in the dust of the earth shall awake, some to everlasting life." This was more sparingly revealed under the Old Testament, than under the New, 2 Tim. i. 10. Yet was it, even then, so clearly revealed, that all the holy patriarchs lived and died in the faith of it, Heb. xi. 13—16. The fathers before Abraham saw it in the promise of the seed of the woman, which was to bruise the serpent's head: and from Abraham, they saw it in the promise of Canaan. But now by the gospel, this life and immortality are set in a full light. By the breach of the first covenant that life was forfeited, the heavenly paradise lost to Adam and all mankind; in token whereof, he was turned out of the earthly paradise. But the second Adam, having in the second covenant, undertaken the redemption of the forfeited inheritance, there was a new promise of it made in favour of his seed: and they are invested with an indefeasible right thereto, in the first moment of their union with Christ by faith; howbeit they are not instantly put in possession thereof. And when they do come to the possession, it is not given them all at once, but at two different periods, in different measures; according to the two chief branches of the promise thereof, namely, a promise of transporting their souls into heaven at death, and a promise of transporting them soul and body thither at the last day.

1. There is a promise of transporting their souls separate from their bodies, into heaven, there to behold and enjoy the face of God. And it is accomplished to them immediately after their death. It was most plainly declared and applied by our Saviour to the penitent thief on the cross, Luke xxiii. 43, "To-day shalt thou be with me in paradise." But it was in the faith of it, that the covenant was to David, even in the face of death, all his salvation, and all his desire, 2 Sam. xxiii. 5; and that Paul had a desire to depart, knowing that he was to be with Christ upon his departure, Philip. i. 23. And it is in the faith of the same, that the whole church militant doth groan earnestly, desiring to be clothed upon with the house which is from heaven, that is, the heavenly glory, 2 Cor. v. 2. Indeed the curse of the first covenant did, upon the breaking of that covenant, fall to their lot, as well as to the rest of mankind; and that curse would natively have issued in cutting them asunder, as covenant-breakers, and appointing them their portion with the hypocrites; but that being executed to the full on Christ their head, to the parting asunder of his holy soul and body, it can operate no more on them. Wherefore, howbeit others die in virtue of the curse, separating their souls and bodies, the one to the place

of torment, the other to the grave, till the last day; yet they do not so die. Being redeemed from the curse, Gal. iii. 13, they shall never see such death, John viii. 51. But they die in conformity to Christ their head, being predestinate to be conformed to his image, (Rom. viii. 29), who is the first-born from the dead, Col. i. 18. and the first fruits of them that sleep, which every man is to follow in his own order, 1 Cor. xv. 20, 23. That, as in the case of the head, so in the case of the members, as death came on by sin, sin may go off by death. In virtue of their communion with Christ in his death, the union betwixt their souls and mortal bodies is dissolved; their souls dismissed in peace into the heavenly glory, there to remain till such time as their bodies, laid down in the grave, come, in virtue of their communion with Christ in his resurrection, to put on incorruption and immortality.

This promise is grafted upon the promise of acceptance made to Christ, when he should make his soul an offering for sin. In confidence of which acceptance, dying on the cross he commended his spirit, or soul, into the hands of his Father, Luke xxii. 46; and told the penitent thief, he was to be that very day in paradise, though then it was towards the evening of it, ver. 43. The words in which he commended his soul to his Father, were David's, Psalm xxxi. 5, "Into thine hand I commit my spirit;" thereby intimating, that the reception of the souls of his dying people into the hands of the Father, depends on the reception of his soul into them. For his soul was, in virtue of the covenant, so received, as a public soul, representing the souls of the whole seed; whence David speaking of Christ, saith, "Thou wilt not leave my soul in hell," Psalm. xvi. 10, with Acts ii. 31. Wherefore in the promise of receiving Christ's soul, was comprehended a promise of receiving the souls of all his mystical members.

2. There is a promise of transporting them, soul and body, into heaven, there to be ever with the Lord; which is to be accomplished unto them at the last day: Dan. xii. 2, "And many of them that sleep in the dust of the earth shall awake, some to everlasting life, and some to shame and everlasting contempt." Ver. 3, "And they that be wise, shall shine as the brightness of the firmament; and they that turn many to righteousness," (or rather, they that do righteously, of the many), "as the stars for ever and ever." Whereas the many mentioned, ver. 2, and comprehending all, are there divided into two sorts, in respect of their future state, in the event of the resurrection: the happy part, being the first sort of them, is designed ver. 3, from their present state in this life, the wise, and they that do righteously; that is, in New Testament lan-

guage, the righteous, Matt. xiii. 43, and they that have done good, John v. 29, in opposition to the foolish, and they that have done evil. Those having come forth, unto the resurrection of life, John v. 29, shall shine as the brightness of the firmament, and as the stars for ever and ever: yea, they shall shine forth as the sun, in the kingdom of their Father, Matt. xiii. 43. This is the highest pinnacle of the saints' hopes; wherein they, in their whole man, shall have the whole of eternal life in its perfection. Man had a conditional promise hereof, in the covenant of works; but the condition being broken, the benefit promised was lost; heaven's gates were shut against Adam, and all his natural seed. Howbeit Christ the second Adam, having undertaken to fulfil the condition of the second covenant, which was stated from an exact consideration of the demands that the broken first covenant had on his spiritual seed; there was a new promise of it made in their favour; and it absolute. And to his fulfilling of that condition, both the making and performing of this promise are owing allenarly. None other's works but his could ever have availed to reduce the forfeiture, and purchase a new right: and his works do it so effectually, that they secure the putting all his seed in actual possession of the purchased inheritance; so that they shall reign in life by one, Jesus Christ, Rom. v. 17.

This is the promise of the covenant, which is the last of all in performing; as being the consummation of all the rest, not to be accomplished until the mystery of God be finished. The Old Testament saints died in the faith of it; and it is not as yet performed to them: nay, the New Testament saints have died, and still must die, in the faith of it; not having it performed to them neither, till it be at once accomplished to the whole seed together, at the end of the world. Thus this promise remains to be an unseen object of faith to the church militant; and to the church triumphant too, whose flesh must rest in hope till that day, Psalm xvi. 9. But because the term prefixed for performing thereof, is, in the depth of sovereign wisdom, for reasons becoming the divine perfections, set at such a distance; there have been some signal pledges given of it, to confirm the church's faith in the case. Such was the translating of Enoch, soul and body, into heaven, in the patriarchal period; Elias, in the time of the law; and our blessed Saviour, in the time of the gospel.

This promise is grafted upon the promise of a glorious exaltation made to Christ; by which was secured to him his ascension, in soul and body, into heaven, and entering into his glory: Luke xxiv. 26, "Ought not Christ to have suffered these things, and to enter into his glory?" Both these were necessary in respect of the covenant: his suffering was necessary, in respect of the condition thereof, which behoved to be fulfilled by him; and his entering into his glory was necessary, in respect of the promise thereof, which behoved to be fulfilled unto him. Now, Christ ascended and entered into glory, as a public person, as a forerunner entering for us, Heb. vi. 20. And therefore the promise, in virtue of which he ascended and entered into it, comprehends the ascension and glory of all his mystical members, who are therefore said to sit together in heavenly places, in Christ Jesus, Eph. ii. 6. And then, and not till then, will the promise be perfectly fulfilled to him, when all the mystical members are personally there, together with their head; when the whole seed, perfectly recovered from death, shall reign there, together with him, in life, for evermore.

And this shall suffice to have been said here of the promise of eternal life, in the last period thereof.

INFERENCE FROM THE PROMISE OF ETERNAL LIFE.

Thus we have opened the promise of eternal life to the elect, with the effects thereof on them, in its several periods; to wit, before their union with Christ: and then, from their union with Christ until death; and finally, from their death, through eternity: the whole springing out of the promises peculiar to Christ himself. For as these last were fulfilled, in preserving the root of Jesse, notwithstanding of the various changes that family did undergo, in which it was often in hazard of extinction, until such time as Christ sprang out of it, as a root out of a dry ground, Isa. xi. 1, 10; and liii. 2; and then, in carrying him up, and carrying him through in his work notwithstanding of the load of imputed sin that lay upon him, and the opposition he met with in the world, and the powers of hell, engaged against him, Isa. xlix. 8; and l, 7, 8, 9; and finally, in raising him from the dead, taking him up into heaven, and glorifying him there for ever and ever, 1 Tim. iii. 16. Even so the promise of eternal life to the elect, included therein, is fulfilled, in preserving them in their unconverted state, till such time as they are united to Christ by faith: and then, in carrying them up, and carrying them through, in favour and communion with God, during the whole time of their continuance in this world, notwithstanding of all the opposition from the devil the world and the flesh: and lastly, in raising them up at the last day, and receiving them soul and body, into heaven, there to be ever with the Lord.

And now, from the whole of what hath been said on that point, we deduce the following inference, that all the benefits of the covenant of grace bestowed, or to be bestowed on sinners, are the sure mercies of David, Isa. lv. 3. This may be taken up in these three things following:—

1. They are all of them mercies, pure mercies, without respect to any worthiness in the receivers. They all are free grace gifts; for the covenant is to us a covenant of grace, from the first to the last: Eph. ii. 7, "That in the ages to come, he might show the exceeding riches of his grace, in his kindness towards us, through Christ Jesus." Ver. 8, "For by grace are ye saved, through faith: and that not of yourselves: it is the gift of God." The receiving of believers into glory, is, after all their working, as much of free grace, as is the quickening of them, when being dead in sin, they could do no good work at all. They have their faith and their works, their grace and their glory, their temporal and their eternal good things, all of them equally of free grace: for they are all secured to them in, and flow from the promise of the covenant made before the world began; and are founded on a ground which they had no manner of hand in the laying of.

2. They all are the mercies of David, that is, of Jesus Christ the Son of David. His obedience and death are the alone channel wherein the free grace of the covenant runs, bringing along with it all those mercies, Eph. ii. 7. It is to the holiness of his nature, the righteousness of his life, and the satisfaction made by his death, they are all owing: for upon these alone, and upon nothing in us, whether before or after conversion, is the promise of eternal life founded. Our believing through grace, while others continue in unbelief; our seeing God in glory, while others are cast into outer darnness; the bread we eat, and the water we drink, in this life, together with the hidden manna we shall eat of, and the rivers of pleasures we shall drink of, in heaven; are all equally the purchase of our Redeemer's blood.

3. *Lastly*, They are all of them sure mercies. What of them the saints have already got, they could not have missed of; and what of them they have not as yet received, is as sure as if they had it in hand, 2 Sam. xxiii. 5, "David perceived that the Lord had confirmed him king over Israel;" and that upon this ground, "for his kingdom was lift up on high," 1 Chron. xiv. 2. Now, Saul's kingdom was lift up on high too; and yet he lost it. But David had his kingdom by the covenant; Saul, not so: hence the former seeing the promise begin to be accomplished, rightly concluded, that it would hold on till it was fully performed; notwithstanding that the latter fell from his excellency. Uncovenanted mercies are totering

mercies; but the covenant-mercies are sure. The former may flow plentifully for a while, and yet at length be quite dried up for ever; but the spring of the latter being once opened, will flow for evermore without interruption. The promise is infallibly sure, and cannot miscarry: it is sure from the nature of God who made it; even from his infallible truth, and from his justice too in respect of Christ, 2 Thess. i. 6, 7.

Thus far of the second part of the covenant, namely, the promissory part.

NO PROPER PENALTY OF THE COVENANT OF GRACE.

A penalty is no essential part of a proper covenant. It is but accidental only, arising not from the nature of a covenant, but from the nature of the covenanters, who being fallible, may break either the condition, or the promise: in which case a penalty is annexed, to secure the performance of the condition on the one side, and of the promise on the other. Wherefore, since the party contracting on man's side, on whom it lay to perform the condition of this covenant, was infallible; as was the party contracting on heaven's side, on whom it lay to perform the promise of it: there was no place at all for a penalty thereof, properly so called; as there was none in the first covenant, but upon one side. In the second covenant, the Father and the Son absolutely trusted each the other. Upon the credit of the Son, the Father received all the Old Testament saints into heaven, before the price of their redemption was paid; and upon the credit of the Father, the Son, nearly seventeen hundred years ago, paid the full price of the redemption of the elect, while vast multitudes of them were not as yet born into the world, and many of them are not even to this day.

It is true, the parties contracted for are fallible: but then the performing of the condition of this covenant, as such, doth in no case lie upon them; Christ having taken it entirely on himself, and accordingly performed it already. While they continue in their natural state, without Christ, they are personally in the covenant of works, not in the covenant of grace. And being once become believers in Christ, the promise of the covenant of grace stands always entire to them, notwithstanding of all their failures; and must needs stand so, in virtue of the condition of the covenant already performed, and judicially sustained, as performed by Jesus Christ for them. And though they are fallible in respect of their actions, as long as they are in this world; yet from the moment of their union with Christ by faith, they are not fallible in respect of their state: they can no more fall from their state of grace, than the saints in heaven can. Hence, even in their case, there is no place for the curse, or eternal wrath, the only penalty by which they should lose their right to the promise of the covenant. They are indeed liable to God's fatherly anger and chastisements for their sins: but forasmuch as by these there is no intercision of their right to the promise; and that they are not vindictive, but medicinal; they cannot be accounted a proper penalty of the covenant of grace, however they may be improperly so called; but do really belong to the promissory part, and administration of the covenant, Psalm lxxxix. 30, 31, 32, 33, 34; Isa. xxvii. 9; Heb. xii. 5, 6, 7. Where the condition of a covenant is fully performed, and legally sustained as such, in favour of the party who is to receive the benefit promised, it is evident there can be no more place for a proper penalty of the covenant on that side: and so it is here in the case of believers.

And thus we have dispatched the third head, namely, the parts of the covenant.

HEAD IV.

THE ADMINISTRATION OF THE COVENANT OF GRACE.

It remains now to consider the administration of the covenant. And since the salvation of sinners doth entirely depend on this covenant; and that all the dispensations of God toward them, for carrying on and completing that gracious design, are regulated according to it: and since withal it is in itself the deepest secret, being a compact entered into betwixt the Father and the Son, before the world began: it is altogether necessary, that there be an administration of it, whereby it may be rendered effectual to the end for which it was made. And hereof we will have a view, by considering, 1. The party on whom the administration of the covenant is devolved; 2. The object of the administration; 3. The ends of it; and, 4. The nature of it. Of all which in order.

I. CHRIST THE ADMINISTRATOR OF THE COVENANT.

Such is the nature of the thing, the weight and importance of this administration, that none who was not fit to be a party-contractor in the covenant, could be meet to be intrusted therewith. Wherefore the administration of the covenant was devolved upon no mere man nor angel, but on the Lord Jesus Christ, the second Adam: and he hath it by the covenant itself, as a reward of his work. It was therein made over to him by promise; particularly, by the promise of a glorious exaltation, to be the Father's honorary servant, prime minister of heaven, mentioned before, and now to be more fully and distinctly unfolded. It was for this cause the last Adam was made a quickening spirit, as saith the text, 1 Cor. xv. 45, with which we shall compare the promise,

Isa. xlix. 8, "I will—give thee for a covenant of the people."

These are the Father's words to Christ the second Adam, the great surety-servant, chosen to make reparation of the injury done to the honour of God by the spiritual Israel, ver. 3; the light of the Gentiles, ver. 6, which is none other but he, Luke ii. 32; Acts xiii. 47; whose appearing in the world made the acceptable time, the day of salvation, as in the preceding part of this 8th verse, compared with 2 Cor. vi. 2. And they are a promise made to him of a reward of his work, in fulfilling the condition of the covenant by his obedience and death: for they are immediately subjoined to the promise of assistance therein; I will preserve thee, (namely, in the course of thy obedience, doing and dying, so that thou shalt not be utterly swallowed up of death, but swim through these deepest waters safe ashore,) and give thee for a covenant of the people; or simply, of people. Not that Christ was never given for a covenant of the people till he rose from the dead; nay, he was so given immediately after the fall, Gen. iii. 15: but that it was always upon the view, and in consideration of his obedience and death he was so given; and that he was at his resurrection and ascension solemnly invested with that office.

This giving, according to the scripture-phraseology, imports a divine constitution or settlement. So it is said, ver. 6, "I will give thee for a light to the Gentiles, that thou mayst be my salvation unto the end of the earth;" *i. e.* I will constitute or set thee for a light: even as God set (Heb. gave) the sun and moon in the firmament of the heaven, to give light upon the earth, Gen. i. 17. Thus the people making or appointing a captain, are said to give a head or captain, Numb. xiv. 4; Neh. ix. 17. Wherefore, to give Christ for a covenant of the people, is to constitute or make him the covenant; whereby the people, any people, Jews or Gentiles, may become God's people, and receive all the benefits of that covenant-relation to God. This then speaks Jesus Christ to be the ordinance of God for the reconciliation of sinners to God, and their partaking of all the benefits of the covenant: even as the sun is the ordinance of heaven for light to the world, unto whose light all have free access; though in the meantime it doth not enlighten the blind, nor those who will needs live in darkness, because they hate the light. This honour was secured to him in the promissory part of the covenant, in consideration of his fulfilling the conditionary part thereof.

Now, that Christ is by the authority of heaven constituted or made the covenant, imports these two things. (1.) He is constituted administrator of the covenant: as he had the burden of purchasing the promised benefits, so he hath the honour of distributing and conferring them on sinners. This meaning of the phrase appears from the following words, declaring the end of this constitution; to "establish the earth, to cause to inherit the desolate heritages;" ver. 9, "That thou mayest say to the prisoners, Go forth." See chap. xlii. 6, 7. (2.) The whole of the covenant is in him: so that he that hath Christ, hath the covenant, the whole of the covenant; he that hath not Christ, hath no saving part or lot in it. This is the native import of this unusual phrase, occurring only here and chap. xlii. 6, and is confirmed by the following words, to establish the earth. A covenant is an establishing thing. When the first covenant was broken, the foundations of the earth were, so to speak, loosened, that it could no more stand firm, until Christ was given for a covenant, to establish it again: he bore up the pillars thereof, in virtue of the new covenant in himself. And if his administration of the covenant were once at an end on the earth, the earth will stand no longer, but be reduced to ashes. The saying concerning the sacramental cup, "This cup is the new testament in my blood," 1 Cor. xi. 25, is somewhat akin to the expression in the text, and serves to confirm the sense given of it. For it surely bears, (1.) That the sacramental cup is the ministration of the New Testament to believing receivers; so that receiving the one in faith they receive the other too. (2.) That the New Testament is in Christ's blood; so that their communion of the benefits of the testament, is by their communion of the blood of Christ, 1 Cor. x. 16.

Now, from these texts compared, it appears, That the administration of the covenant of grace is devolved on Jesus Christ the second Adam, for that end made a quickening spirit, having the whole of the covenant in him.

This constitution, lodging the administration of the covenant in the Mediator Christ Jesus, is at once suited to the glory of God, the case of sinners, and the honour of Christ himself.

1. It is suited to the glory of God the offended party. In the face of Jesus the administrator, shines forth the glory of the God of the covenant, 2 Cor. iv. 7. His spotless holiness, and tremendous jus-

tice, appear there; together with his matchless love, freest grace, and tenderest mercy. God is in Christ reconciling the world to himself, with the safety of his glory; giving forth his peace and pardons freely, without any merit of the receivers, and yet not without sufficient satisfaction to his justice, and compensation of his injured honour; as from a throne of grace, stablished upon justice satisfied, and judgment fully executed, the firm bases thereof.

2. It is suited to the case of sinners, the offending party. In Christ the administrator of the covenant, they have to do with a God, whose rays of majesty, that the guilty are not able to behold, are vailed with the robe of a spotless humanity. An inviting sweetness appears in the face of the administrator, "full of grace and truth," John i. 14. In him they may see their salvation so dear to the God that made them, that he himself would put on their nature, to establish, by his own blood, a covenant of peace between heaven and them. He is true man, of the same family of Adam with themselves; unto whom they may confidently draw near, joining themselves to him as the head of the covenant: and withal, he is the true God, undoubtedly able to make the covenant effectual for their salvation, notwithstanding all their unworthiness.

3. It is suited to the honour of Christ himself, the peace-maker, who hath it as the reward of his work. Joseph, being sold for a bond-servant, behaved himself with all meekness, patience, faithfulness in that low character; the which was afterwards, by all-ruling providence, abundantly rewarded with honour, in his being advanced to be the prime minister of the kingdom of Egypt, having the administration of the whole kingdom committed to him, Psalm cv. 17—22. Herein he was a type of Christ. The Lord Jesus did voluntarily submit himself to the lowest step of reproach and disgrace, taking upon him the form of a bond-servant, and humbling himself in that form, even unto the death of the cross; and that to perform the condition of the covenant, for the glory of God, and the salvation of his people: and therefore he was exalted to the highest pinnacle of honour, being advanced to the prime ministry of heaven, having the administration of the covenant put into his hand, ruling over all under his Father; whereby is given him a name which is above every name, whether of men or angels, "all things being put under his feet," Philip. ii. 7, 8, 9; Eph. i. 20—23. In respect hereof, he is often called the Father's servant, namely, his honorary servant: and his honour in that character is often promised to be made very great, Isa. xlix. 6, and lii. 13, 14, 15; Zech. iii. 8, with vi. 12, 13.

And forasmuch as the everlasting covenant will continue to be the ground and rule of God's dispensations towards his people for evermore; by the constitution lodging the administration of the covenant in the person of Christ, he is to enjoy that honour and dignity for ever and ever. For "unto the Son he saith, thy throne, O God, is for ever and ever," Heb. i. 8. Even of his kingdom which is given him, that is, his mediatory kingdom and administration there shall be no end, Luke i. 32, 33. The time comes indeed, wherein he will "deliver up the kingdom to God even the Father; presenting to him at the last day, the whole church, and every member thereof, brought by his administration, according to his commission, into a state of perfection. And then cometh the end, 1 Cor. xv. 24, namely, the end of the world, but not the end of his administration: for being constituted administrator of the covenant, "there was given him dominion and glory, and a kingdom; and his dominion is an everlasting dominion, which shall not pass away," (as the world shall, 1 Cor. vii. 31), "and his kingdom that which shall not be destroyed," (as all the four monarchies have been), Dan. vii. 14.

And thus we have seen Christ to be the party on whom the administration of the covenant is devolved.

II. SINNERS OF MANKIND THE OBJECT OF THE ADMINISTRATION OF THE COVENANT.

The object of the administration of the covenant, is, sinners of mankind indefinitely: that is to say, Christ is empowered, by commission from his Father, to administrate the covenant of grace to any of all mankind, the sinners of the family of Adam without exception: he is authorized to receive them into the covenant, and to confer on them all the benefits thereof, to their eternal salvation; according to the settled order of the covenant. The election of particular persons is a secret, not to be discovered in the administration of the covenant, according to the established order thereof, till such time as the sinner have received the covenant, by coming personally into it. And the extent of the administration is not founded on election, but on the sufficiency of Christ's obedience and death for the salvation of all; neither is it regulated thereby, but by the fulness of power in heaven and earth given to Jesus Christ, as a reward of his becoming obedient even unto death.

For confirming this truth, let the following things be considered.

1. The grant which the Father hath made of Christ crucified, as his ordinance for the salvation of lost sinners of mankind. In the

case of the Israelites in the wilderness, bitten by fiery serpents, God instituted an ordinance for their cure, namely, a brazen serpent lifted up on a pole; and made a grant thereof to whosoever would use it for that purpose, by looking to it. No body whosoever that needed healing, was excepted: the grant was conceived in the most ample terms, Numb. xxi. 8, "It shall come to pass, that every one that is bitten, when he looketh upon it, shall live." So all mankind being bitten by the old serpent, the devil, and sin, as his deadly poison, left in them; God hath appointed Jesus Christ the ordinance of heaven for their salvation. There is a word of divine appointment passed upon a crucified Christ, making and constituting him the ordinance of God for salvation of sinners; and God hath made a grant of him as such, to whomsoever of Adam's lost race will make use of him for that purpose, by believing on him; in the which grant none of the world of mankind is excepted. All this is clear from John iii. 14, 15, 16, "And as Moses lifted up the serpent in the wilderness, even so must the Son of man be lifted up: that whosoever believeth in him, should not perish, but have eternal life. "For God so loved the world, that he gave his only begotten Son, that whosoever believeth in him, should not perish, but have everlasting life." Now, the administration of the covenant being settled in pursuance of this grant therein made for a reward of the Mediator's obedience, the object of the former can be no less extensive than that of the latter.

2. The Mediator's commission for the administration, is conceived in the most ample terms; and he is clothed with most ample powers with relation to that business. It carries his administering the covenant, not only to the meek, the poor, the broken-hearted; but to the captives, blind, bruised, prisoners, bond-men and broken men, who have sold their inheritance and themselves, and can have no hope of relief but by a jubilee, Luke iv. 18, 19; with Isa. lxi. 1, 2. What sort of sinners of mankind can one imagine, that will not fall in under some of these denominations? Christ is indeed given for a covenant of people; not of this or that people, but of people indefinitely. "All power is given him in heaven and in earth," Matth. xxviii. 18. So there are none on earth excepted from his administering the covenant to them. He is empowered to save the guilty law-condemned world, by administering it to them; "For God sent not his Son into the world to condemn the world; but that the world through him might be saved," John iii. 17; forasmuch as he is the ordinance of God for taking away the sin of the world, chap. i. 29; though many to whom he offers the covenant, do refuse it, and so are not saved eventually. Accordingly, from this fulness of

power he issues forth the general offer of the gospel; wherein all without exception are declared welcome to come and suck of the full breasts of the divine consolations in the covenant: Matth. xi. 27, "All things are delivered unto me of my Father." Ver. 28, "Come unto me, all ye that labour and are heavy laden, and I will give you rest." Chap. xxviii. 18, "All power is given unto me in heaven and in earth." Ver. 19, "Go ye therefore and teach all nations." Mark xvi. 15, "Preach the gospel to every creature."

3. He executes his commission in an unhampered manner, administering the covenant to any sinner of mankind: Prov. viii. 4, "Unto you, O men, I call, and my voice is to the sons of man." The object of his administration is not this or that party of mankind, under this or the other denomination; but men, any men, sons of men indefinitely. So the gospel, in which he administers the covenant, is good tidings to all people, Luke ii. 10, a feast made unto all people, Isa. xxv. 6, though many, not relishing the tidings, never taste of the feast. Accordingly, he commissioned his apostles for that effect, in terms than which none can imagine more extensive, Mark xvi. 15, "Go ye into all the world, and preach the gospel to every creature." The Jews called man the creature, as being God's creature by way of eminence: so by every creature is meant every man. There are in the world, some men, who, by reason of their monstrous wickedness, are like devils; there are other men, who, by reason of their savageness seem to differ but little from brutes: but our Lord saith here in effect, "Be what they will, if ye can but know them to be men, ask no questions about them on this head, what sort of men they are: being men, preach the gospel to them, offer them the covenant; and if they receive it, give them the seals thereof: my Father made them, I will save them."

4. If we inquire, who they are to whom Christ stands related as a Saviour? or, whose Saviour he is, according to the scripture? we find, that considered as an actual Saviour, saving actually and eventually, he is indeed only Saviour of the body, Eph. v. 23; but considered as an official Saviour, a Saviour by office, he is the Saviour of the world, 1 John iv. 14; John iv. 42. Thus one having a commission to be the physician of a society, is the physician of the whole society, by office; and so stands related to every man of them, as his physician: howbeit, he is not actually a healer to any of them, but such as employ him. Though some of that society should not employ him at all, but on every occasion call another physician; yet he is still their physician by office: though they should die of their disease, being averse from calling him; yet still it is true, that he was their physician, they might have called him, and had his reme-

dies; and it was purely their own fault, that they were not healed by him. Even so our Lord Jesus Christ hath Heaven's patent, constituting him the Saviour of the world; by the authority of his Father he is invested with that office: and wheresoever the gospel comes, his patent for that effect is intimated, 1 John iv. 14, "And we have seen and do testify, that the Father sent the Son to be the Saviour of the world." Wherefore, none of us shall perish for want of a Saviour. Jesus Christ is the Saviour of the world; he is your Saviour, and my Saviour, be our case what it will: and God, in and by him, is the Saviour of all men, specially of those that believe, 1 Tim. iv. 10. Hence Christ's salvation is the common salvation, Jude 3.: and the gospel is the grace of God that bringeth salvation to all men, Tit. ii. 11, marg. Christ then stands related as a Saviour by office to the world of mankind; he is their Saviour: and he is so related to every one of them, as sinners, lost sinners of that society, 1 Tim. i. 15, "Christ Jesus came into the world to save sinners." Luke xix. 10, "The Son of man is come to seek and to save that which is lost." Let no man say, "Alas! I have nothing to do with Christ, nor he with me; for I am a sinner, a lost sinner." Nay, upon that very ground there is a relation between him and you. Since you are a sinner of mankind, Christ is your Saviour: for he is by office Saviour of the family whereof you are a branch. If you will employ another than him, or pine away in your disease, rather than put yourself in his hand, ye do it upon your peril: but know assuredly, that you have a Saviour of your own, chosen of God for you, whether you employ him or not. He is by his Father's appointment the physician of souls: ye are the sick; and the less sensible ye are, the more dangerously sick; there is a valuable relation then betwixt Christ and you, as such, Matth. ix. 11, 12. He is the great burden-bearer, that gives rest to them that labour and are heavy laden, Matth. xi. 28; Psalm li. 22. Ye labour, spending your labour for that which satisfied not: and are laden with iniquity, even heavy laden; and nothing the less so, that ye are not duly sensible thereof: there is a relation then betwixt Christ and you, on that very score. Now, if Christ stands related to the world of mankind-sinners, as their Saviour, then they are the object of his administration of the covenant.

5. Lastly, If it were not so, then there would be some excepted persons of the world of mankind-sinners, for whom there is no warrant, more than for devils, to take hold of the covenant, by believing in Christ: contrary to the constant voice of the gospel, John iii. 16; Mark xvi. 15. For surely they have no warrant to take hold of the covenant, to whom the Administrator is not empowered to give it.

Which of the world of mankind-sinners can these excepted persons be? Not pagans, and other infidels, who hear not the gospel: for howbeit, in the depth of sovereign wisdom, that warrant is not intimated to them; yet it doth really extend to them; as included under that general term, whosoever, John iii. 16. And if it did not extend to them, the covenant could not lawfully be preached and offered to them by ministers of the gospel; more than a crier could lawfully go and proclaim and offer the king's indemnity to those who have no concern in it, but are excepted out of it. The ministerial gospel-offer is undoubtedly null and void, as far as it exceeds the bounds of the object of Christ's administration of the covenant; as being, in so far, from one or more having no power to make it. Neither are any who hear the gospel excepted: for the not taking hold of the covenant by faith in Christ, is the great sin and condemnation of all who, having the gospel, do so entertain it, Prov. viii. 36; John iii. 19; Mark xvi. 16. But it could not be the sin of such persons; because it can never be one's sin, not to do a thing which he hath no warrant from God to do. Much less are the non-elect excepted: for at that rate, not only should their unbelief be none of their sin; but the elect themselves could never believe, till such time as their election were, in the first place, revealed to them, which is contrary to the stated method of grace: for none can believe in Christ, till once they see their warrant; forasmuch as that warrant is the ground of faith.

Wherefore we conclude, that sinners of mankind indefinitely are the object of Christ's administration of the covenant; that he is empowered to administer it to you, and every one of you, whatever you are, or have been; and that you must either take hold of the covenant for life and salvation, or perish as despisers of it, since ye have heard the gospel.

III. The ends of the administration of the covenant.

The ends of the administration of the covenant, which make the business of the Administrator as such, are these three: to wit, (1.) the bringing of sinners into the covenant; (2.) the management of them therein, according to it, in this world; and, (3.) the completing of their happiness, according to it, in the other world.

1. The bringing of sinners personally and savingly into the covenant, Isa. xlix. 5, " And now, saith the Lord that formed me from the womb, to be his servant, to bring Jacob again unto him, though Israel be not gathered, yet shall I be glorious in the eyes of the Lord." Though the covenant was concluded from eternity, when we could neither consent nor dissent; yet, by the constitution thereof, it is

provided, that, even to the end of time, any sinner of the race of Adam, who shall believe, his receiving and embracing the covenant by faith, shall be as good and valid to enter him into it, as if he had personally subscribed it at the making thereof, John iii. 16. Thus it is left open to mankind-sinners, that they may come into it, taking place therein under Christ the head; and so become personally confederate with Heaven, to their eternal salvation. And there is room enough within the compass of the infinite name of the second Adam, for all of us to subscribe our little names. Wherefore, notwithstanding of all that have already subscribed, in that name, saying, "I am the Lord's," *i.e.* the Lord Christ's, Isa. xliv. 5, since Eve first set down her name there, by believing the promise first, whereby she then commenced, and actually was the mother of all living, Gen. iii. 20; yet the voice of the gospel still is, and will be even to the end, "And yet there is room," Luke xiv. 22. For typifying which Noah's ark was, by the appointment of Heaven, made all little rooms, Gen. vi. 14, called in the margin there, nests. Now, the Mediator is authorised to treat with sinners, rebels to God, and subjects of Satan's kingdom, to bring them over to Heaven's side again; and for that effect to administer the covenant unto them, to propose it to them, and gather them into the bond thereof. Wherefore, having gone forth on that errand, he testifies his earnestness in the work, Matth. xxiii. 37, "How often would I have gathered thy children!" and declares himself the door of the sheep, John x. 7, 9.

2. The management of them in the covenant, according to it, during their continuance in this world. When sinners are, by the Mediator's administration, brought within the bond of the covenant, they are not thenceforth trusted with the management of themselves and their stock: but their stock being lodged with him, they are put under his hand as their sole manager, the chief Shepherd and Bishop of souls, unto whose oversight the strays once returned are committed, 1 Pet. ii. 25. Whatever they need, they must receive from him: he is to dispense all the benefits of the covenant, of whatever kind, unto them. Are they to be justified? he is to pass the sentence, "Thy sins be forgiven thee," Matt. ix. 2, 6. Are they to be brought into a new saving relation to God? he is to give them power to become the sons of God, John i. 12. Are they to be sanctified? he is to wash, sanctify, and cleanse them, John xiii. 8; Eph. v. 26; and to give them repentance, as well as forgiveness of sins, Acts v. 31. Are they to be caused to persevere? he is to keep them, and to account for each one of them to his Father, John xvii. 12. Are they to be seen to in all their temporal concerns? the

care of them all lies upon him, 1 Pet. v. 7. He is our Joseph, who hath all the stores of the covenant in his hand: and of him God hath said, as Pharaoh said to his famishing people crying unto him for bread, "Go to Joseph," Gen. xli. 55. Moreover, they must receive all their orders from him, touching their duty in all points. They must receive the law at his mouth; since it is by him God speaks unto them, according to the constitution of the covenant: for which cause God hath given a solemn charge to all the covenant-people, saying, "This is my beloved Son, in whom I am well pleased: hear ye him," Matt. xvii. 5.

3. And *lastly*, The completing of their happiness, according to the covenant, in the other world: Eph. v. 27, "That he might present it to himself a glorious church, not having spot or wrinkle, or any such thing." It is the comfort of believers, that Jesus Christ administers the covenant in this world; so that whatever part thereof they may be driven to, they can never be driven to any part unto which his administration doth not extend. Howbeit, the most glorious part of his administration takes its place in the other world: for it is in heaven, that the promises of the covenant have their perfect accomplishment: the which makes heaven home to believers. "O! but the passage betwixt the two worlds is a dark, dangerous, and gloomy one! Who can without horror think of the Jordan of death, and the darksome region of the grave!" But withal, God's covenant-people should remember, that their Lord hath business in that passage, as well as on either side of it. The line of the covenant is drawn through it, making a path by which the redeemed safely pass. So there also is the scene of Christ's administration of the covenant; he hath the keys of hell and of death, Rev. i. 18. It is great weakness, to think that he doth only, as it were, stand on the other side of the river, directing the believer in his passage, and ready to receive him when he comes ashore: nay, it lies on him, as administrator of the covenant, even to go into the water with the passenger, to take him by the arm, and going between him and the stream, to break the force thereof unto him, and to bring him safe ashore: Psalm xxiii. 4, "Though I walk through the valley of the shadow of death, I will fear no evil; for thou art with me." In the Israelites passing over to Canaan, the ark went first into Jordan, and was last in coming out, being there till all the people were passed clean over, Josh. chap. iii. iv. The ark being a type of Christ, as Canaan was of heaven, this teacheth us, that our Lord Jesus will have business in the passage between the two worlds, as long as there is one of his people to pass that way; and that his administration there will never be at an end, until the last man

within the bond of the covenant is safely landed on the other side. This done, he is to administer the covenant to them there also, completing their happiness by a perfect accomplishment of all the promises thereof unto them. As Jesus is the author, so he is the finisher of our faith, Heb. xii. 2. In which texts there is an allusion to the races famous among the ancient Greeks, wherein there was one that opened the race, ran it, and went on the head of all the rest; another who was set on a throne at the end of the race, and gave the prize to such as won it. In the spiritual race, Christ acts both these parts. As performer of the condition of the covenant, in the course of his obedience, wherein he endured the cross, despising the shame, he is the author of our faith, or the chief leader, expressly called the forerunner, chap. vi. 20, in bringing many sons unto glory, going on their head as captain or chief leader, chap. ii. 10. Then, as administrator of the covenant, he is the finisher of our faith, or the perfecter that gives the crown to the runners, and is set down at the right hand of the throne of God. And thus it is his business to put the crown of glory on the heads of those whom by his grace he hath made conquerors. From his hand Paul expected it, 2 Tim. iv. 8, "Henceforth there is laid up for me a crown of righteousness, which the Lord, the righteous Judge," to wit, Christ, the judge of the world, "shall give me at that day." To him it belongs to grant to the overcomers to sit with him in his throne, Rev. iii. 21. And therefore I cannot help thinking, that the text, Matt. xx. 23, may safely be read without the supplement, "To sit on my right hand, and on my left, is not mine to give, but for whom it is prepared of my Father." So the particle but is used exceptively, 2 Cor. ii. 5, for save, Mark ix. 8. The fulness of power given to the Mediator, comprehends all power in heaven, as well as in earth: accordingly he prepares the place for his several people in his Father's house, having the whole at his disposal as administrator of the covenant. And he is to administer the covenant to them, not only at their first entrance into the regions of bliss, but all along through the ages of eternity, being to remain the eternal bond of union and mean of communication betwixt God and the saints for ever, Heb. vii. 25; Rev. vi. 17.

And these are the ends of the administration of the covenant. Follows,

IV. THE NATURE OF THE ADMINISTRATION OF THE COVENANT.

The nature of this administration offers itself to our view, in the relations Christ hath to the covenant as he is administrator thereof.

We have already seen, how that Christ became the Mediator of the covenant, both substantial and official; and have observed, that his official mediation runs through the whole of the covenant; and we have taken notice of a threefold relation of his unto it, namely, his being 1. The Kinsman-redeemer in it; 2. The Surety of it; and, 3. The Priest, the sacrificing priest, of it; the which parts of his mediation, respecting the condition of the covenant, do belong to the making of it. We shall now consider his other relations thereto, bearing those parts of his mediation, which, respecting the promises of the covenant, do belong to the administration of it. And they are these five. 1. He is the Trustee of the covenant; 2. The Testator of the covenant: 3. The Prophet of the covenant; 4. The King of the covenant; and 5. The Intercessor of the covenant: each of which is a syllable of the name above every name, given him of the Father, as the reward of his work. And in viewing these in order, the nature of the administration of the covenant will plainly appear.

I. CHRIST THE TRUSTEE OF THE COVENANT.

Our Lord Jesus as administrator, is, in the first place, the Trustee of the covenant; having the covenant, and all the benefits thereof, committed to his trust: Col. i. 19, "For it pleased the Father, that in him should all fulness dwell." This greatest of all trusts, too great for any mere man or angel, our blessed Redeemer was perfectly qualified for; and so was set over the house of God, the most precious things thereof being put under his hand. What is sealed up from the highest angel, he hath access to; he is trusted to loose the seals, for he is worthy, Rev. v. 2—5. A holy jealous God put no trust in his servants, and his angels he charged with folly: for they were fallible; there was a possibility of their betraying their trust, Job iv. 18. But it pleased him to trust the blessed Jesus, that in him, as an infallible administrator, all fulness should dwell.

This high trust was a necessary prerequisite of the administration: and therefore, upon his engagement to fulfil the condition of the covenant, reputed in heaven as sure as if it had been actually performed, all the benefits of the covenant were not only made over to him in point of right, but were delivered over into his hand in actual possession, that he might dispense them to sinners, according to the method therein stated and agreed upon: John iii. 35, "The Father loveth the Son, and hath given all things into his hand." Matth. xi. 27, "All things are delivered unto me of my Father." Ver. 28, "Come unto me, all ye that labour, and are heavy laden, and I will give you rest." Hence it was that he entered upon the administration of the covenant, long before his incarnation; even as soon as there was any place for the administering thereof, which was in paradise after the fall: though the solemnity of his investiture and taking possession, was reserved unto his ascension into heaven, when the man Christ was set at God's right hand, Gen. iii. 8, 15; with Psalm lxviii. 18; Eph. i. 20—22.

Thus the fulness of the covenant is in him: and this trust makes the unsearchable riches of Christ, not to be particularly inventoried by us, since they are unsearchable. But, agreeable to what hath been said before, we shall, for opening thereof, mark the following things:—

1. The unseen guard of the covenant is under his hand. There is given unto him all power over natural and spiritual things, to manage the same for the preservation, protection, and restraint of those sometime to be brought into the covenant; while yet they are strangers from it, and neither perceive the guard about them, nor the commander thereof: John v. 22, "The Father—hath committed all judgment unto the Son." Hos. xi. 3, "I taught Ephraim also to go, taking them by their arms, but they knew not that I healed them." Sometimes they are, during their state of blindness, in eminent hazard of their lives, and narrowly escape, before the stream of strong temptations threatening to carry them quite away; and yet the force of these is broken one way or other, and they brought back from the very brink of ruin; and they never truly know, whose debtors they are for these things, nor see the love-design in them, until converting grace has reached them; and then they hear the captain of that guard saying to them, as he said to Cyrus, Isa. xlv. 5, "I girded thee, though thou hast not known me." So the mountain was full of horses and chariots of fire, for the defence of Elisha and his servant; while yet the servant saw none for them, but against them, until the Lord opened his eyes, 2 Kings vi. 17.

2. The quickening Spirit of the covenant is in him, whereby to quicken dead sinners, and cause them to live. The Spirit of life behoved to be purchased for sinners, otherwise there was no life for them. Now, the fulness thereof is purchased, and actually lodged in the Mediator, according to the covenant. Hence Christ proposeth himself to dead Sardis, as having the seven spirits of God, Rev. iii. 1; and saith to the Jews, John v. 25, "The dead shall hear the voice of the Son of God;" that is, dead souls shall be quickened, and being quickened, shall believe. The first Adam being made a living soul, was capable to communicate natural life; but not being made a quickening spirit, he could not restore life once lost: but

the last Adam was made a quickening spirit, to restore spiritual life to sinners dead in trespasses and sins. So, in Christ as the Trustee of the covenant, is the fountain of life. Adam's sin put out the lights of the whole world; and his natural offspring were all left by him as so many blind candles: but the second Adam is made, and set up, a flaming lamp to light them again; and as many of them as it toucheth, do instantly flame too: and could they all but touch it, and none are forbidden, they should all be lighted again, and shine with the light of spiritual life, partaking of the Spirit of life in Christ Jesus.

3. The righteousness of the covenant is in him, whereby to justify the ungodly that have no righteousness of their own. Hence his name is, "The Lord our righteousness," Jer. xxiii. 6. Righteousness of man before the Lord was quite worn out: there was nothing of that kind left upon any of Adam's children, "as it is written, there is none righteous, no not one," Rom. iii. 10. But Jesus Christ having, in his birth, life, and death, wrought out the righteousness of the new covenant, brought it in, and presented it unto his Father, Dan. ix. 24, with Lev. xvi. 15. And it was sustained and accepted as the new-covenant righteousness, for justifying all that believe; and was lodged with the worker thereof, intrusted with it as Administrator of the covenant. Hence he is said to be made unto us righteousness, 1 Cor. i. 30, namely, by a divine constitution, even as he was made the covenant. And intimation hereof is made unto sinners in the gospel, for a ground of faith, Isa. xlv. 24, "Surely, shall one say, in the Lord have I righteousness," Heb. Only in the Lord (concerning me he hath said) is righteousness. They are the words of the Lord Jesus Christ, narrating the divine constitution concerning himself. Compare ver. 23; with Rom. xlv. 10, 11. Wherefore, the gospel is called the ministration of righteousness, 2 Cor. iii. 9; and his ministers, ministers of righteousness, chap. xi. 15; he being intrusted with the new covenant righteousness, for to administer it to sinners, unto justification of life, as the phrase is, Rom. v. 18.

4. The new covenant right to God is in his person as Mediator: and he is actually possessed of the fulness of the Godhead, as he is administrator of the covenant, to communicate of that fulness to all that shall believe, Col. ii. 9, "For in him dwelleth all the fulness of the Godhead bodily." Ver. 10, "And ye are complete in him, which is the head." Our Lord Jesus, as the eternal Son of God, had a natural indefeasible right to the fulness of the Godhead: but as the second Adam, he took out a new right thereto, purchasing the same by his obedience and death; and as such, it is now lodged

with him, to be communicated by him. And thus the peace of the covenant, peace with God, is in him, Eph. ii. 14; the sonship of the covenant, the adoption into the family of God, is in him as the first-born among many brethren, Psalm lxxxix. 27; with John i. 12; the covenant interest in God as one's own God, is in him, John xx. 17. And to obtain all these in one, let the sinner but receive Christ by faith, and he hath them; for they are all under his hand as trustee of the covenant, yea, in him as the storehouse of the covenant.

5. The covenant fulness of the Spirit of sanctification is in him, whereby to make sinners holy: Col. i. 19, "It pleased the Father, that in him should all fulness dwell." John i. 16, "And of his fulness have all we received, and grace for grace." Having purchased the same with his own blood, it is lodged in him as administrator of the covenant, in respect of which he is said to be made unto us sanctification, 1 Cor. i. 30. Therefore out of his pierced side came there forth blood and water; blood to remove the guilt of sin, water to wash away the defilement thereof. So he is the fountain opened for sin and for uncleanness: not a vessel of that water of purification, which, how full soever, would lack as much as it should communicate; but a fountain, a living spring of it, to supply the needs of the unclean, without any lack in itself: "For God giveth not the Spirit by measure unto him," John iii. 34. Wherefore there is in him such a fulness of the Spirit of holiness, as is, by the infinite efficacy thereof sufficient to sanctify the whole family of Adam, and even the worst of them. There is a fulness of all grace in him, to be communicated for the repairing of the lost image of God in us. There is grace enough in him to melt the hardest heart into evangelical repentance, Acts v. 31, to mortify the strongest lusts, Gal. v. 24, and to quicken, and to strengthen unto holy obedience, 2 Tim. ii. 1.

6. The establishing grace of the covenant is in him, whereby to cause the most fickle and inconstant, once in him, to persevere unto the end: Jude, ver. 1, "Them that are sanctified by God the Father, and preserved in Jesus Christ." He is constituted the head of influences for all his mystical members, which are to have their nourishment ministered from him, Col. ii. 19. The giving out of continued pardons, necessary for them in this their state of imperfection, is also in his hand, as the Trustee of the covenant, "exalted to be a Prince and a Saviour, to give repentance unto Israel, and forgiveness of sins," Acts v. 31. Thus he is fully furnished for preserving them in a state of grace, having a fulness of grace in himself to communicate unto them, suitable to all their exigencies, whether in respect of the power, or of the guilt of their sin.

7. The temporal things of the covenant are all in his hand, whereby to provide for, and afford protection to his people, during their continuance in this world. In the covenant there was made to him a promise of his inheriting all things, as the first-born of the family of Heaven; and in his person as the last Adam, the ancient dominion over the creatures was restored, as we heard before. Now, as he is the Trustee of the covenant, the heritage of the world, and all things therein, is actually delivered over into his hand: so that he is not only Lord of the world in point of right, but in fact; having the power of all therein, from the smallest rag for covering of nakedness, even to the crowns and sceptres. This he himself witnesseth, Matt. xxviii. 18, "All power is given unto me in heaven and in earth." Chap. xi. 27, "All things are delivered unto me of my Father." Hence to encourage his impoverished people in their building of the second temple, he saith, Hag. ii. 8, "The silver is mine, and the gold is mine," namely, to give them to whom I will. And that these are Christ's words, appears from ver. 6, compared with Heb. xii. 26. Accordingly, from Psalm xxiv. 1, "The earth is the Lord's, and the fulness thereof," the apostle clears believers' right to the creatures, 1 Cor. x. 25, 26. And thus he is fully furnished for affording all manner of provision to his people, in temporal things: and all protection from whatever dangers they can be in while here. The sun, moon, and stars, the earth, sea, and air, with all that in them is, are under his hand as the Trustee of the covenant; and he can dispose of them all for the ends of the covenant, as the glory of God and the welfare of his people do require.

8. The covenant-fulness of power over death and the grave is in his hand, whereby to disarm death of its sting, and bring about a glorious resurrection. "I," saith he, "have the keys of hell and of death," Rev. i. 18. Death goes through the world as a mighty conqueror, whom none is able to resist; the grave follows, and none can keep back its prey, nor cause it to give it up again. But the Mediator hath an effectual check upon them both. They are not absolute potentates, as mighty as they are: there is one above them, to whose orders they must precisely stick. Death may indeed enter in within the boundaries of the covenant, and carry off the covenant-people as well as others: but at the border it must drop its sting, and enter without it; for the power of death is now in Christ's hand, and he will not suffer it to enter there with it. And the time cometh wherein he will say to the grave, Give up: and then the bars thereof will be broken asunder, the gates thereof fly open, and it will deliver up to him its lodgers; for he is intrusted as administrator of the covenant, with full power over death and the grave.

9. *Lastly*, The eternal consummate happiness of the covenant is in his hand, whereby to render the souls of his people happy immediately after death, and then soul and body together happy at the last day: for all power in heaven is given him. The Father hath made him the great repository of eternal life, the fountain from whence it shall stream forth to all the heirs of life; and the dispensing of it is intrusted to him: 1 John v. 11, "God hath given to us eternal life: and this life is in his Son." John xvii. 2, "As thou hast given him power over all flesh, that he should give eternal life to as many as thou hast given him." Wherefore his dying people do in faith commit their souls to him, as Stephen, Acts vii. 59, "Saying, Lord Jesus, receive my spirit." And at the last day he pronounceth the sentence, and solemnly receives them into the kingdom of heaven, Matth. xxv. 34.

And thus Christ is the Trustee of the covenant.

II. CHRIST THE TESTATOR OF THE COVENANT.

In the next place, our Lord Jesus is the Testator of the covenant, as the apostle teacheth, Heb. ix. 15—17. By the conditionary part of the covenant, God had a compensation of the wrong done to his glory by sinners: and by the promissory part, Christ had unsearchable riches to communicate unto them, whereby they might be made happy, and being to die in the cause, according to his covenant, he timely made his testament, as a deed of conveyance thereof unto them; turning the promissory part of the covenant respecting lost sinners, into a testament in their favour, 1 Cor. xi. 25, "This cup is the new testament in my blood."

Hence it appears, that this belongs to the administration of the covenant, committed unto him, for making sinners partakers of the covenant-benefits; yea, and that it is the first and fundamental act of that his administration, laid as a foundation of all the other acts thereof, which are but so many means of executing the testament. Upon the Mediator's undertaking to fulfil the condition of the covenant, the Father made to him a disposition of the covenant-benefits contained in the promissory part: and the benefits so disponed, were actually delivered over into his hand, as the appointed trustee of the covenant, as we have already seen. Now, he having them all thus in his hand, hath made a disposition of them to poor sinners, by way of testament, Luke xxii. 29, "And I appoint unto you a kingdom, as my Father hath appointed unto me." Or, "and I dispone to you, as my Father disponed to me, a kingdom." The word here used, signifies to dispone; and hath in it the notion of a federal or covenant disposition, and a testamentary disposition too. Of the former sort was the disposition made by the Father to Christ, namely, a federal disposition; as being made on a most onerous cause, a condition properly so called, to wit, his making his soul an offering for sin: and it can by no means be a testamentary disposition, since "where a testament is, there must also of necessity be the death of the testator," Heb. ix. 16; the which, it is evident, could have no place in the case of the Father. Of the latter sort is the disposition made by Jesus Christ to sinners, namely, a testamentary disposition, which, of its own nature, is a deed or conveyance of grace and liberality, without conditions properly so called: and forasmuch as sinners were under an utter disability to perform conditions properly so called, it was therefore necessary for their behoof, to make it a testamentary disposition or testament.

For clearing of the nature of this testament, which is of so great importance for all to know, who have any concern for their salvation, we shall consider, 1. The making thereof; 2. The legatees; 3. The executor; and, 4. The legacies.

First, As to the making of Christ's testament, it is first of all to be observed, that though the covenant was indeed from eternity, the testament was not so. For Christ made his testament as administrator of the covenant; which administration he did not enter upon but in time. He was from eternity the trustee of the covenant, which grand trust was a necessary prerequisite of his administration: yet forasmuch as his commencing testator of the covenant was an act of his administration thereof, there could be no place for it until there was place for administering the covenant, which there was not, till once the covenant of works was broken. And hereto best agreeth the nature of a testament, which is not simply a will, but a will declared, testified, and signified by word or writ, or some one or other external sign pleadable by the legatees, in order to their obtaining of the legacies bequeathed.

Christ's testament, which for substance is but one, is yet twofold, in respect of different circumstances wherewith it hath been vested; namely, the old or first testament, and the new testament, 2 Cor. iii. 14; Heb. ix. 15.

Christ's old testament is the declaration of the last will of our dying Saviour, touching his unsearchable riches, confirmed by slain sacrifices of divine institution, sealed with the seals of circumcision and the passover, and enduring in the church till the fulness of time, and the manifestation of himself to Israel in the flesh, Heb. ix. 20; Rom. iv. 11; 1 Cor. v. 7; Luke xvi. 16. This his testament was originally made by word of mouth; which kind of testament is called a nuncupative testament: but it was afterwards committed to writing; so that there was not only a word of the testament to be heard, but a book of the testament to be read, by the legatees, Heb. ix. 19, 20. And so we have it a written testament, in that part of the holy scripture called by the name of the Old Testament.

Christ's new testament is the declaration of the same last will of our dying Saviour, touching his unsearchable riches, confirmed by his own death on the cross, sealed with the seals of baptism and the Lord's supper, and to continue for evermore, 1 Cor. xi. 23, 24, 25; Matth. xxviii. 19; Heb. vii. 12, 16, 17. This also was originally made by word of mouth, in the time of his public ministry, wherein he declared his will anent the great salvation, which, as the apostle observes, at first began to be spoken by the Lord, Heb. ii. 3. And it was in like manner afterwards committed to writing: and we have it too a written testament, in that part of the holy scripture called by the name of the New Testament.

If we look for the original date of Christ's old or first testament, we find his testament to be of a date as early as the nature of the thing could bear, being made in paradise, on the day of Adam's fall, in the cool of the day, Gen. iii. 8, otherwise called the time between the two evenings, Exod. xii. 6, that is between three and six o'clock in the afternoon. At the which time, our Lord Jesus did, in the promise of the seed of the woman to bruse the head of the serpent, which should bruise his heel, Gen. iii. 15, signify his death, and declare his will for the benefits of his purchase their accruing to sinners thereby. And that day I judge to have been the sixth day of the creation, the same day wherein man was created; reckoning that the scripture teacheth, that Adam lodged not one night in honour, as some do, agreeable to the original, read Psalm xlix. 12. They who cannot think that the events recorded from Gen. iii. 7, to the end of the third chapter, were crowded within the compass of one day, may weigh therewith the events relating to the death of Christ, which are recorded Luke xxii. 66, to the end chap. xxiii. 1.—33; John xix. 1; Matth. xxvii. 27, 28; John xix. 2, 5, 9—15; Matth. xxvii. 24. All which things were done in the space of half a day: for Christ was crucified about twelve of the clock, Luke xxxiii. 44—46.

Some, through an unwillingness to think of their death, do put off the making of their testaments unto a death-bed: but so very willing was Christ, the second Adam, to die for us, that he set his house in order, and so prepared himself for death, that very day wherein the first Adam fell. The business of the great King, and the business of the ruined world of mankind, required haste. The whole fabric of the world was by Adam's fall so unhinged, that it was hastening to a total dissolution, and mankind about to perish in the ruins; till the second Adam went in, and bore up the pillars thereof, in virtue of his death to establish the earth again, Is. xlix. 8. Wherefore in paradise he made his testament in a few words, containing a disposition of the benefits of the covenant, in favour of poor sinners, Gen. iii. 15, and typically went in under that weight of wrath, which was pressing down all: and so he established the earth again. In this form it was, that they of the first ages of the world had the testament. But it was repeated and renewed to Abraham, to whom the promises were made, Gal. iii. 16, comprehended under the name of the covenants or testaments of promise, Eph. ii. 12. As also to Israel in the wilderness, whom Moses sprinkled with blood, "saying, This is the blood of the testament," Heb. ix. 19, 20. And this was Christ's old testament, upon which all that believed, from Adam to Christ, built their faith, and hope of obtaining the legacies left therein; though it was upwards of four thousand years, from the first making of the testament, unto the death of the Testator, by which the new testament was confirmed.

Now, the apostle saith that, "a testament is of force after men are dead: otherwise it is of no strength at all whilst the testator liveth," Heb. ix. 7. Was Christ's testament then of no force all that time? Yea, it was of force; and that by means of a pre-confirmation, being confirmed before, Gal. iii. 17. The confirmation of a testament, in the sense of the holy scripture, is by the death of testator; as the apostle, in the forecited text, teacheth the Hebrews. And in scripture-reckoning, there was a twofold death of the Testator here: one typical, another real. In respect of the former of these Christ was the Lamb slain from the foundation of the world, Rev. xiii. 8, having died typically in the sacrifices then offered, Gen. iii. 21, and thereafter all along under the Old Testament. And by that death of the Testator was the pre-confirmation of the testament: so that from the day it was first made, it was of force, for the legatees obtaining the legacies therein bequeathed; forasmuch as it was then also confirmed. Wherefore the apostle observes, that, in full consistency with that known maxim anent testaments, Heb. ix. 17, above-cited, "Neither the first testament was dedicated without blood," ver. 18. What the apostle means by the dedication of the testament, will be plain, if it is considered that what our version of the Bible calls dedication, is, in the scripture-use of words so rendered therein, nothing else but an entering on, or a first, or new using of a person or thing, to what they were designed for: insomuch that the very dedication of the temple was no more but that, as appears by comparing 2 Chron. v. 13; chap. vi. and vii. 1, with 4. 5. Wherefore by the dedication of the testament, must be meant the legatees beginning to claim and obtain their legacies, upon the testament. And this, the apostle saith, was not done without the testament's being confirmed by blood, or death: the which, though really the blood or death of beasts sacrificed; yet, according to the apostle's reasoning, were reckoned the blood or death of the Testator, they being sacrificed as types of him.

And hence it appears, that whatever have been the different circumstances wherewith the testament in different periods hath been vested; the Old and New Testament, nuncupative and written, are for substance but the one testament of Jesus Christ the same yesterday, and to-day, and for ever, Heb. xiii. 8, having the same force and effect for full remission of sin and eternal salvation, legacies claimed and obtained by faith, in virtue of the testament, Acts xv. 11; Rom. iv. 13: only, what was first declared by word of mouth, the same was thereafter written. The legacies at first bequeathed in general comprehensive terms, were afterward particularly nominated: and in the New Testament they are more clearly expressed than in the Old. The former was a copy of the testament, fitted for the times before the testator really died: the latter, fitted for all times thereafter, to the end of the world; and therefore no other copy is to be accepted after it.

Secondly, It is to be inquired, Who are the legatees, the parties in whose favour the testament was made, and who may, in the method of the testament, claim and obtain the legacies therein bequeathed? Christ's making his testament, being the fundamental act of his administration of the covenant, as we have already seen; the legatees in the testament must needs be the same as the objects of his administration of the covenant, that is to say, sinners of mankind indefinitely: for if Christ is authorized by the Father to administer the covenant to sinners indefinitely, and hath accordingly made his testament for that effect; surely none can be excepted out of the testament, that are not excepted out of his administration. Therefore the apostle lays down, for the foundation of faith, to those who had even imbrued their hands in the blood of the Lord of glory, their interest in the promise, Acts ii. 39, "For the promise is unto you, and to your children, and to all that are afar off, even as many as the Lord our God shall call." To whomsoever then the gospel comes, we may warrantably say the promise is to you, and to you, and every one of you; even the promise of the testament: and ye have access to claim it by faith, as your own legacy, your own mercy, Jon. ii. 8. And all the arguments adduced on the head of the object of Christ's administration, which need not to be repeated here, do prove this.

And it is most agreeable to the nature of the thing. In Christ's testament, the legatees are not expressed by their names, as in testaments where the testator hath his children and friends about him, to whom he leaves his legacies: but it is here as in the case, wherein some of the children or friends of the testator are not come into the world at the time of the making of the testament; who must therefore have their legacies left to them under some general designation. Multitudes, multitudes of Christ's legatees were not born when he died; and multitudes of them have not to this day seen the sun: nay, when Christ first made his testament, there were but two persons in the world. Therefore the legatees have been expressed in it under a general designation, as those of such a family. Now, this general designation of the legatees in Christ's testament, is not actual believers, that is, such as have already believed: for actual believing is the legatees' claiming of the legacies left them; whereby they are put in possession thereof; the which claim must of necessity have a foundation in the testament prior unto it. And indeed the testament is the ground of faith. Therefore it was made before there was one actual believer in the world, being made in paradise, and there recited in the hearing of our guilty first parents, who, upon the hearing of it, Gen. iii. 15, believed, and so were put in possession of their legacies. And thus will it be to the end of the world: faith will come by hearing of the testament, Rom. x. 17; Gal. iii. 2. Neither is it the elect: for howbeit in them only is the testament effectual, yet it is not to them only the legacies are left; they are not the only persons in whose favour the testament was made. For election being a secret not to be known by us, until once we believe, cannot be the ground and warrant of believing, or embracing the testament, and claiming the legacies. Besides, at that rate, unbelievers continuing so to the end, could not be justly reckoned refusers and slighters of Christ's testament, as having no portion nor concern in it, more than fallen angels. But the general designation of the legatees in Christ's testament, is mankind sinners indefinitely: to those of the family of Adam are the legacies left, to be claimed and possessed of them by faith: Prov. viii. 4, "Unto you, O men, I call, and my voice is to the sons of man." Rev. xxii. 17, "Whosoever will, let him take the water of life freely." John vi. 37, "Him that cometh to me, I will in no wise cast out."

Put the case, that a rich man should, for the love and favour he bears to a particular family, leave his substance to them by testament, to be divided among them: in this case, it is evident, that however numerous that family be, all and every one of them are this man's legatees, howbeit their names are not particularly expressed in the testament; and they need no more to clear their claim, each to his share of the legacy, but that they are of that family. And upon the executors' making lawful intimation to that family, that, such a testament being made in favour of them, they come, claim, and get their legacies, in the method of the testament: it is manifest, that all of them, who accordingly come and make their claim, as members of that family, will obtain a share of the legacy: but in case there be any of them, who will not come and make any claim thereto, they will justly lose the benefit thereof, and may die of want for all the legacy that was left them in that testament. Our Lord Jesus Christ has made such a testament: the lost family of Adam, is the family constituted his legatees: and the gospel is the lawful intimation made to them, to come to the executor and receive their legacies. All that believe get the legacy; all unbelievers lose it, and perish under the want thereof; and they perish without all excuse. They cannot pretend, that there was nothing left them by the testator; which is the case of the fallen angels: nor yet, that it was not intimated unto them; which is the case of those that never heard the gospel. But they perish, because, howbeit there was a rich legacy left them, yet they undervalued the testator's kindness, and would never come and claim it by faith. Hence the benefits of the covenant of grace, even in respect of unbelievers, are called their own, namely, in virtue of the right they have to them by the tenor of Christ's testament: Jon. ii. 8, "They that observe lying vanities, forsake their own mercy." Accordingly, to the elder brother in the parable, Luke xv. the father saith, ver. 31, "Son, all that I have is thine." So chap. xvi. 12, "If ye have not been faithful in that which is another man's, who shall give you that which is your own?" that is, "the true riches," ver. 11. And their ruin is lodged at the door of their unbelief, in not coming to Christ to receive them, John v. 40, "And ye will not come to me, that ye might have life." Christ's promises in his testament are to mankind-sinners, as the promise of Canaan was to the Israelites in Egypt, indefinitely, those not excepted whose carcases fell in the wilderness, Exod. vi. 6, "Say unto the children of Israel, I am the Lord."—ver. 8, "And I will bring you in unto the land concerning the which I did swear." Thus was there a promise left them of entering into the rest of Canaan: and those who believed it, got the possession accordingly; those who believed not, did lose it. And they fell short of it, not because it was not left to them; but because, though it was left to them, as well as to those that entered, yet they believed it not. So says the apostle, "They could not enter in because of unbelief," Heb. iii. 19. And this was no imputation on the faithfulness of God: for even in promises, as well as in covenants, there is a necessity of a mutual consent unto the same thing; the party to whom the promise is made, his acceptance thereof being necessary to complete the obligation on the promiser to make it effectual: because none making a promise of a benefit to another, can in reason be thought either to bind himself thereby to obtrude his benefit on the other against his will; or yet to give up with it, as a thing to be abandoned by him at any rate. Now, to this very purpose the apostle makes use of that case of the Israelites having the promise of Canaan left them, and yet coming short of it through unbelief, Heb. iv. 1, "Let us therefore fear, lest a promise being left us of entering into his rest, any of you should seem to come short of it." Ver. 2, "For unto us was the gospel preached, as well as unto them: but the word preached did not profit them, not being mixed with faith in them that heard it." Compare Exod. vi. 9, "And Moses spake so unto the children of Israel: but they hearkened not."

Thirdly, It is to be inquired, who is the executor of the testament? In testaments among men, the testator and the executor are always different persons: and it must needs be so, because the testator dying cannot live again to see his will executed; therefore one or more, who live when he is gone, must be nominated for that purpose. But here that reason ceaseth. Jesus Christ could well be the executor of his own testament, and needed not to appoint any other to see to that matter. He was the Lord of life and death; and it was not possible he should be holden of death, Acts ii. 24. Though he was really to die, to confirm his testament; yet he was quickly to rise again, for the effectual execution thereof: accordingly the apostle observes, that he was delivered for our offences, and was raised again for our justification," Rom. iv. 25. And he lives for evermore. Even when he was in the grave, he was capable of executing his testament, being God as well as man, having a life which could not be lost, no not for a moment; namely, the divine life. And the executing of it then, when the human nature was in the state of death, was much the same as his executing of it before he had actually assumed the human nature at all.

And that Jesus Christ really is the executor of his own testament, appears from his being constituted by the Father Administrator of the covenant, to dispense the benefits thereof as great Steward of the house of heaven; and from the acts of his administration, both in this life, and in that which is to come: for he it is that hath in his hand the conferring of grace, both real and relative, on sinners; and the conferring of glory on saints: the which are the executing of his testament, as well as the administering of the covenant: the former being subordinated to the latter. Meanwhile it cannot be refused, that he executes it by his Spirit, and employs gospel-ministers in the matter. Wherefore, whosoever would have any saving benefit by Christ's testament, or would partake of the legacies therein bequeathed, must come to himself to receive them; since he is the Executor of his own testament. And therefore the constant call of the gospel to perishing sinners, is to come to Christ for life and salvation; and the complaint on those who forsake their own mercy, is, that they will not come to him, John v. 40. And the whole life of believers must be a coming to him, 1 Pet. ii. 4, that is, a living by faith in him, Gal. ii. 20, whereby they may be daily receiving of the legacies, according to their exigencies.

Fourthly, In the last place, it is to be inquired, What are the legacies left in Christ's testament, to poor sinners of mankind, his only legatees? In the general, there is left to them therein what is sufficient to make them happy for time and eternity; even all the benefits of the covenant to be received by faith. These are Christ himself, and all things in and with him, Rom. viii. 32. And the general clause of the testament is, "According to your faith be it unto you," Matt. ix. 29. It being beyond our reach fully to reckon up the particulars, it shall suffice to point at a few things, as the comprehensive legacies, left by Jesus Christ in his testament, to sinners of mankind indefinitely.

Legacy 1. His own complete righteousness, to cover us before the Lord; hence called the gift of righteousness, Rom. v. 17, as being made over to us in his testament, to be received by faith; in which sense it is said to be revealed unto faith, that is, to be believed or trusted on, and so received and put on, chap. i. 17. Dying persons are wont to leave suits of mourning to their poor friends: but our dying Saviour left to all his legatees, the garments of salvation, the robe of righteousness, Isa. lxi. 10; beautiful garments, chap. lii. 1; white raiment, Rev. iii. 18, as a suit of rejoicing: for that, though he was dead, he is alive, and lives for evermore. Our father Adam left us naked, to our shame: yet need we not go naked, nor our shame be seen. For, by the second Adam's testament, sufficient clothing is left to our father's broken family; even the robe of his own righteousness: and nothing remains, but that we receive it as his legacy to us, and put it on. A holy God cannot admit us into his presence in our spiritual nakedness: the law requires us to appear before him in unspotted holiness of nature, and perfect righteousness of life, as the condition of life; and withal, with a satisfaction to justice, by suffering, because we have sinned. But how can we make such an appearance before him? We can by no means put ourselves in such a condition, by any thing we can do or suffer. Yet is our case not hopeless. We have a good friend, the Lord Jesus Christ, who hath left us by testament the holiness of his nature, wherewith he was born; the righteousness of his life, even all the good works he wrought in obedience to the ten commandments, during his life on earth; and the satisfaction made by his death, and sufferings from the womb to the grave: he hath made all these one undivided gift of righteousness, and bequeathed the same to us in his testament, to be received by faith. By means hereof, the most wretched sinner of us all may be beautified in the sight of a holy God, have wherewith to answer all the demands of the law for life, and obtain a full pardon and acceptance with God as righteous in his sight. How shall we escape, if, never claiming this legacy, we trample on the Testator's kindness?

Legacy 2. His new-covenant interest in God, whereby to render us happy: Heb. viii. 10, "I will be to them a God." Our father Adam left his whole family without God in the world, Eph. ii. 12. This was an unspeakable loss, a ruining loss: all misery in time and eternity was wrapt up in it. It was a loss that could never have been compensed: and to us it was irrecoverable. But Jesus Christ hath recovered for us the lost covenant-interest in God, and bequeathed it to us in his testament. This is a legacy full beyond our comprehension. Who can conceive fully what is in that, "I will be your God?" Surely all blessedness is in it, for time and eternity: Psalm cxliv. 15, "Happy is the people whose God is the Lord." Herein is left you peace, and reconciliation with God, John xiv. 27; adoption into the family of God, 2 Cor. vi. 16, 17, 18; yea, that ye shall have God for your own God, your own heritage, in a joint-heirship with Christ, Rom. viii. 17: all the persons of the Godhead to be yours; the Father to be your Father, the Son your Saviour, the Holy Ghost your Sanctifier: and all the attributes of God to be employed for your happiness. Nothing on Christ's part, nothing on God's part, stands between you and all this: nothing can make you come short of it but unbelief. That new-covenant interest in God is purchased by the blood of the everlasting covenant; it is given over unto Jesus as Administrator of the covenant; and he again hath made it over to you by testament. And what remains, but that ye come to the Executor, and receive your legacy, by faith? Alas! that any should be found who have no heart to it,

Legacy 3. His Spirit of grace, we so much need. Hear the words of the testament, Prov. i. 23, "Turn you at my reproof: behold, I will pour out my Spirit unto you." Christ hath the seven spirits of God, even a fulness of the Spirit in himself, to communicate; and hath made over the same, by his testament, to sinners of Adam's race: withal, as Executor of the testament, he hath made intimation thereof, declaring himself ready to give the Spirit unto all that come to him accordingly: John vii. 37, "Jesus stood and cried, saying, If any man thirst, let him come unto me, and drink." Ver. 38, "He that believeth on me, as the scripture hath said, out of his belly shall flow rivers of living water." Ver. 39, "But this spake he of the Spirit, which they that believe on him, should receive." O suitable legacy for Adam's children! Here is life for us, life for our dead souls: for his Spirit is the Spirit of life, loosing the bands of sin and death, Rom. viii. 2. How shall dead souls live? Our Lord himself answers that question at large, John vi.; shewing himself to be the life-giving bread, that giveth life unto the world, ver. 33; that it is by eating this bread souls shall live, ver. 57; that the quickening Spirit is in it, ver. 63; and that it is to be eaten by faith, ver. 35, 63, 64. Whither then should the soul go for life, but to Christ as executor of his own testament? ver. 68. For as we derived death from the first Adam, so we must derive life from the second Adam, else we cannot have it, ver. 53. Here is regenerating and sanctifying grace for us, whereby our natures may be changed, Ezek. xxxvi. 26, the image of God repaired in us, through grace received, answering to the grace in the man Christ, as the wax to the seal, John i. 16; for all this worketh the Spirit of Christ in those who believe, Eph. i. 13. Here is made over to us grace whereby we may be enabled to true evangelical repentance, Zech. xii. 10; Ezek. xxxvi. 31, to walk in newness of life, ver. 27, and to mortify the deeds of the body, Rom. viii. 13. Here is bequeathed unto us enlightening grace, whereby we may discern our duty: for the Spirit is the Spirit of light and direction, John xvi. 13; exciting and strengthening grace, which comes by the supply of the Spirit, Phil. i. 19; Eph. iii. 16; comforting grace, in all trials and afflictions, for he is the Comforter abiding for ever where once he comes, John xiv. 16; and establishing grace, whereby the sinner once in Christ, is for ever kept from falling away, either totally or finally, ver. 17, 1 John ii. 27. In a word, Christ having left us the Spirit of grace in his testament, all grace suitable to our needs lies open to us. Wherefore none that hear the gospel remain destitute of grace, but because they will not come to Christ for it.

Legacy 4. A suitable portion of the good things of this life, as infinite wisdom sees needful: Psalm xxxvii. 3, "Thou shalt dwell in the land, and verily thou shalt be fed." Christ in his testament has disponed to sinners a kingdom, even the kingdom of God, and added those things thereunto, Matt. vi. 33. His testament is suited to all our needs, even in temporal things; he hath seen to our provision and protection, according to the promises made thereanent in the covenant. These promises primarily made to himself in the eternal covenant, he hath by his testament, as it were, indorsed to us, to be made forthcoming to all who by faith embrace it, and claim them upon it. Wherefore believers may go to Christ for their daily bread, as well as for spiritual benefits; pleading the testament for the one, as for the other. And to receive the bread and the water in virtue of Christ's testament, will be more satisfying to a Christian in the exercise of faith, than all the fulness of worldly men can be; forasmuch as at that rate they have them as the purchase of the precious blood of the Testator, and his Father's blessing therewith.

Legacy 5. An unstinged death: John viii. 51, "If a man keep my saying, he shall never see death." Men in their testaments make provision for the comfortable life of their legatees; but they can leave them nothing to make death safe and comfortable to them. But in Christ's testament there is special provision for his legatees in death, as well as in life: and in the faith thereof, the saints have welcomed the grim messenger, dying comfortably in the faith of the sealed testament, Heb. xi. 13. Our Lord Jesus being to encounter death armed with its sting, and that in its full strength given it by the broken law, was perfectly sure of the victory: so making his testament, he left it as a part of his last will, that sinners of Adam's race should be free from the sting of death, through faith in him. A precious legacy which he could well bequeath, because purchased by his own death; and which he can and will make effectual, since the fulness of power over death and the grave is in his hand, and he is executor of his own testament. How lamentable is it, that men knowing they must die, should slight the testament, and the kindness of their best friend, appearing here, where none else are capable to help!

Legacy 6. And last. Everlasting life on the other side of death: John vi. 58, "He that eateth of this bread, shall live for ever." Christ's testament looks not only to this, but the other world: in it is provision made not only for time, but for eternity: he hath disponed in it a kingdom, the kingdom of heaven, as an everlasting inheritance for the legatees, Luke xxii. 29. This comprehends the happiness of the soul in its separate state; the glorious resurrection of the body at the last day; and the complete happiness of soul and body together, from thenceforth, and for evermore. The importance thereof who can express? But whatever is in it, it is in the testament made over to sinners of mankind: and whosoever of them come to Christ for it, shall, upon the ground of his faithfulness, without all peradventure obtain it.

These are the comprehensive legacies of Christ's testament. To enter more particularly into the detail of them, there would be no end. Ye have the book of the testament, both old and new, among your hands: read it diligently; and that as Christ's testament, as indeed it is: and in every page ye will perceive of the unsearchable riches. Withal remember that it nearly concerns you, and every one of you, as parties legatees in whose favour it was made: since ye are men, sons of men, Prov. viii. 4. The testament is lawfully intimated to you, both by the preaching of the word, and by putting a copy of it, a Bible, in your hands. And ye are called to come to Christ, as executor of it, by faith in him, to receive your legacies. Happy will you be, if ye answer the call. But if ye do not, it will be "more tolerable for Tyre and Sidon at the day of judgment than for you:" for it will aggravate your condemnation, that not only were all these legacies left you in Christ's testament, but the same was intimated unto you, and ye were called to come to the executor to receive them, but ye believed not, ye would not.

Thus far of Christ the Testator of the covenant.

III. CHRIST THE PROPHET OF THE COVENANT.

The covenant being an eternal transaction, which no creature had access to be witness unto; the being thereof was an absolute secret to the whole creation: and, in that it was a mystery of the manifold wisdom of God, Eph. iii. 10, no creature was sufficient to unfold the nature thereof. Upon the which accounts, the apostle calls it the wisdom of God in a mystery, even the hidden wisdom, which God ordained before the world, 1 Cor. ii. 7. And thence appears a necessity of constituting a prophet of this covenant: and that none but a divine person was fit to be the original prophet thereof; and this so much the more, that, by reason of the spiritual blindness of the parties unto whom it was to be revealed, a mere objective revelation could not be sufficient in the case: for "the natural man receiveth not the things of the Spirit of God; for they are foolishness to him; neither can he know them, because they are spiritually discerned," ver. 14. Wherefore Jesus Christ was, as administrator of the covenant, constituted the Prophet thereof; being he of whom, by the apostle's testimony, "Moses truly said unto the fathers, A Prophet shall the Lord your God raise up unto you, of your brethren, like unto me, Acts iii. 22. And whosoever else were at any time prophets thereof, he alone was the original prophet of it, John i. 18, "No man hath seen God at any time; the only begotten Son, which is in the bosom of the Father, he hath declared him."

And in this character Christ was constituted, (1.) The Messenger, (2.) The Witness, and (3.) The Interpreter of the covenant.

1. In the capacity of Prophet, he was constituted the Messenger of the covenant, Mal. iii. 1, to bring the good tidings of that treaty of peace into the world; and not only so, but, by the authority of heaven, to proclaim the treaty to sinners, to offer them the benefit thereof, and to deal with them to accept, by coming into it personally. A covenant surely of unparalleled weight and importance, that had such a messenger thereof.

2. In the same capacity he was constituted the witness of the covenant, Isa. iv. 4, "Behold, I have given him for a witness of the people." God knew the world to be a guilty world, whose consciences witnessed the demerit of death; and that therefore they would be very slow to believe the good news from heaven, touching the covenant of peace: and for this cause he would give them one competent to witness the truth thereof; and pitched upon Jesus Christ for that effect. He was a son of Adam; so the more fit to attest it unto men: he was the eternal Son of God; and therefore not liable to error or mistake in his testimony: he was an eye-witness to the eternal transaction; and so he could speak on the matter that which he had seen with his Father, John viii. 38. He came down from heaven where the covenant was made, unto earth, in favour of which it was made: wherefore he could witness in the earth what he had seen in heaven about it, chap. iii. 31, "He that cometh from heaven, is above all." Ver. 32, "And what he hath seen and heard, that he testifieth." In him we have a twofold witness, which is full evidence in law, He is the amen, the faithful and true witness, Rev. iii. 14. In him we have the witness of man; in respect whereof he is the faithful witness: and the witness of God; in respect whereof he is the true witness, even truth itself. Compare John viii. 18, "I am one that bears witness of myself;" where Christ being a divine witness, in respect of his Godhead, is said to bear witness of himself, as a man appearing in the world, revealing the covenant. And in respect of both these, he is the Amen, whose witness conffrms and determines the truth of the law.

3. He is in the same capacity constituted the interpreter of the covenant, Job xxxiii. 23, to teach it unto men. We are not only

slow to believe the covenant, but it is hard for us to understand it. It lies so far beyond the reach of our natural understanding, that we cannot understand it in a saving manner, unless the Son of God hath given us an understanding, (a supernatural one), that we may know him that is true, 1 John v. 20. And whosoever shall so understand it, must be all taught of God, John vi. 45, that is, of Jesus Christ, ver 46. So he is by the Father constituted interpreter, and great teacher of the mystery of the covenant: and all the children of the covenant must be his disciples, and learn of him.

Now Christ's administration of the covenant, as the prophet thereof, may be taken up in these three things following.

1. His intimating and offering the covenant to sinners, by his word, for bringing them personally into it. This he did from the time of Adam's fall, is now doing, and will do even unto the end of time, that the mystery of God shall be finished. He began the Old Testament dispensation thereof, in person. Appearing in human shape, with his own mouth he gave the first notice of the covenant that ever there was in the world, and made the first offer of it in paradise, Gen. iii. 8, 15. He carried it on by prophets and ordinary teachers, whom he commissioned for that effect, and furnished with gifts for the work. The former of these he employed to write in his name, as well as to speak therein, in that matter: and by both he spoke to sinners, intimating and offering the covenant unto them, by their means; whether through the word written or spoken. And thus he managed that work, to the salvation of those who believed, in the patriarchal ages before and after the flood; and all along the time of the Jewish church, from Moses to the end of that dispensation. Then he also began the New Testament dispensation in his own person. Having by his incarnation become man, he applied himself to this work. Though he was born "king of the Jews," Matt. ii. 2, and many of them would have had him to have mounted their throne, John vi. 15; yet he choosed rather to appear in the character of a prophet, and betake himself unto the work of the ministry, for to preach the gospel, and intimate and offer the covenant to perishing sinners; and so he was a minister of the circumcision, Rom. xv. 8. Of him in this capacity particularly, Solomon, that king-preacher, was a type, Eccl. i. 1. And this also he did, and still doth carry on mediately and by proxy, especially after his ascension into heaven; and that partly by his apostles and other extraordinary officers, whom he employed to write, as well as to speak, in his name; and partly by ordinary ministers of the gospel, to be continued in the church to the end of the world, Eph. iv. 11, 12, 13. Thus he is now administering the covenant unto us, by

putting his written word of the Old and New Testament in our hands, and sending men in his name to preach the gospel unto us. By these means he speaks to sinners, intimating and offering them the covenant: and so he carries on the work, to the salvation of those that believe, and rendering unbelievers inexcusable, 2 Cor. v. 20; Rev. iii. 22; Luke x. 16. Wherefore the offer of the covenant made to us in the gospel, is his offer: and though the word is sent to us by men, they are but his voice in the matter, he is the speaker. Then "see that ye refuse not him that speaketh," Heb. xii. 25.

2. His making the intimation and offer of the covenant effectual to the elect, by the Spirit, 1 Pet. i. 12, "By them that have preached the gospel unto you, with the Holy Ghost sent down from heaven." The great Prophet of the covenant can effectually teach the most unteachable sinners of mankind; causing light not only to break forth in a dark world, by his word, but in dark hearts, by his Spirit: for the fulness of the Spirit of light is in him, and he hath eye-salve for the spiritually blind, Rev. iii. 18. He knoweth who are his, in whose name he contracted with the Father, and received the promise of the Spirit: and, sooner or latter, he so enlightens them, that he rescues them from under the power of their spiritual darkness, and renders the administration of the covenant effectual to them, however ineffectual it be to others, Col. i. 13. And this he doth, by bringing his word to them with power, through the efficacy of his Spirit opening their eyes. In the first place, by his Spirit acting upon them, as a Spirit of bondage, he sets home on their consciences, the holy law in the commands and curse thereof, as of divine authority, and binding on them in particular. Hereby they are convinced of their sin and misery, seeing their sin as henious in the sight of God, and his wrath due to them for their sin: they are filled with remorse, terror, and anxiety; are made to pant for relief, feel an absolute need of Christ and his righteousness, and despair of relief by any other way, Acts ii. 37, and xvi. 29, 30. And then, by the same Spirit acting within them as a Spirit of life, and communicated unto them from himself, in the word of the gospel, he sets home on their hearts and consciences, the glorious gospel in its free promise of life and salvation to sinners through Jesus Christ, as it stands in the holy scriptures; clearing and demonstrating the same unto them, to be the infallible word of the eternal God, and his word to them in particular: 1 Thess. ii. 13, "Ye received it not as the word of men, but (as it is in truth) the word of God." Chap. i. 5, "For our gospel came not unto you in word only, but also in power, and in the Holy Ghost, and in much assurance." This demonstration of the Spirit is that which immediately cleareth to them the ground of their

believing in particular; as saith the apostle, 1 Cor. ii. 4, 5, "My preaching was—in demonstration of the Spirit, and of power: that your faith should not stand in the wisdom of men, but in the power of God." And it is an internal attestation of the word of the gospel unto them, distinct from the clearest external or ministerial attestation of it; according to the saying of our Saviour, John xv. 26, "The Spirit of truth, which proceedeth from the Father, he shall testify of me." Ver. 27, "And ye also shall bear witness." By the power hereof, getting, by way of spiritual sight, John vi. 40, a knowledge of Christ in his transcendent glory and excellency, exhibited to them in the free promise of the gospel, they are infallibly brought to believe. The Spirit thus applying the word of the gospel to them, they greedily embrace it, and apply it to themselves by faith; as may be seen in these converts, Acts ii. 38, "Then Peter said unto them, repent, and be baptized every one of you in the name of Jesus Christ, for the remission of sins." Ver. 39, "For the promise is unto you." Ver. 41, "Then they that gladly received his word, were baptized."

3. *Lastly*, His teaching and instructing them by his word and Spirit, from thenceforth, as children, of the covenant, his own disciples. The whole plan of salvation is laid down in the covenant, being a mystery of the manifold wisdom of God, whereof there is still more and more to be learned: and Christ is the great Prophet to teach it. And "the secret of the Lord is with them that fear him; and he will shew them his covenant," Psalm xxv. 14. The saints, by reason of the remains of darkness in their minds while here, are apt to lose sight of the parties in the covenant: but the great prophet is to shew them the Father, and to manifest himself unto them, by the Spirit. The condition of the covenant, the Mediator's own righteousness, the sole ground of all their hopes, cannot be kept in view, but by means of the light of life from himself. And in his light only can they have a believing view of the promises and privileges of the covenant. The duties of the covenant, whereof the exceeding broad law of the ten commands is the rule, are many; and though they be clear in themselves, yet are they often so dark and perplexed to us, that we cannot distinguish between sin and duty: but the children of the covenant have an infallible teacher, whom they may consult in all cases, and of whom they may learn how to steer their course in every point; and "the meek will he guide in judgment, the meek will he teach his way," Psalm xxv. 9.

The darkness brought on mankind by sin, nothing but the grace of the new covenant can effectually dispel. The true light is a benefit of that covenant, purchased by the blood of Christ, and lodged with him among the rest of the benefits of his great trust: and he hath the dispensing of it, as the great Prophet of the covenant. To him then must we have our recourse for light in all cases, whether we be under the midnight darkness of a natural state, or under the twilight-darkness of the present imperfection of a state of grace: yea, in the mid-day light of glory, the Lamb is the light of the heavenly city, Rev. xxi. 23.

And thus Christ is the Prophet of the covenant.

IV. CHRIST THE KING OF THE COVENANT.

The covenant of grace is a matter of so vast importance, both to the honour of God, and the good of souls; and of such a diffusive and general concern to mankind, that the administration thereof required one invested with kingly power and authority for that effect. And the disposition of the parties, objects of the administration, together with the nature of the thing itself, which concerns the inner man chiefly, and the disposal of the choicest of Heaven's favours, at once laid aside the greatest of men, and the highest of angels, as no more fit to bear that office, than to produce another world out of nothing. Wherefore the Father's choice in that matter natively fell on his own Son, the Second Adam: and he was made King of the covenant.

God as Creator of the world, is King of the same, by an original, underived right: and so he hath the supreme power over it, of which he can no more divest himself, than of his being. This is the essential kingdom, common to the three persons in the glorious Godhead, the Father, the Son, and the Holy Ghost.

But the kingdom of the covenant, whereof we speak, is a derived, delegated one, which the Mediator Christ holds of his Father, by the tenor of the covenant, for the administration thereof; as is declared, Psalm. ii. 6, "Yet have I set my King upon my holy hill of Zion." Now, the great design of that administration, is to gather together sinners of mankind into one body, under the bond of the covenant; and to make them happy, in the enjoyment of the privileges thereof, in grace and glory, the which body, the church, is the kingdom of the covenant, a kingdom that was to be won, and raised out of the rebel-world of mankind, lying in wickedness; and whereof Christ was, by his Father, constituted the alone King and Head.

In subserviency to this kingdom, the kingdom of providence throughout the world was also committed to him, being made the head over all things to the church, which is his body, Eph, i. 22, 23, he was appointed to rule, not only over his willing subjects, but in the midst of his enemies, Psalm cx. 2. The management of the wheel of providence, throughout the whole world, was put into the hand of Zion's King. Into the same hand that the Father hath committed the government of the church, he hath also committed the government of the world : for there is no exception. "The Father hath committed all judgment unto the Son," John v. 22, "all power in heaven and in earth," Matth. xxviii. 18. So he is "Lord of lords, and King of kings," Rev. xvii. 14, and "by him kings reign—princes rule, and nobles, even all the judges of the earth," Prov. viii. 15, 16. This headship over the world was necessary to his administration of the covenant, as head of the church; necessary for compassing the ends thereof. Being vested therewith, he sets up and pulls down, in the world, as he sees meet for the great purposes of the covenant: and of what use this is, in the administration thereof, may be learned from Isa. xliii. 14, "For your sake" (namely, for the sake of the church) "I have sent to Babylon, and have brought down all their nobles, and the Chaldeans." Ver. 15, "I am—your King." Thus the King and Head of the church manageth all things by his providence, as well without as within the church; though in a very different manner, because in a very different relation, as to his own people, and to strangers. The which was typified in David, who for the benefit of his own kingdom, the kingdom of Israel, was made "the head of the Heathen," Psalm xviii. 43. For David smote the Philistines, and subdued them, 2 Sam. viii. 1, and the "Moabites." ver. 2, "and the Syrians," ver. 6, "and all they of Edom became David's servants," ver. 14, "And David reigned over all Israel, and David executed judgment and justice unto all his people," ver. 15.

Now, the chief acts of Christ's administration of the covenant, as he is King thereof, are these.

1. His appointing ordinances of his kingdom, both for bringing sinners personally into the covenant, and for confirming and strengthening the covenanted ; as also officers of his kingdom, to administer these ordinances in his name and authority. Both the one and the other were different, under the Old Testament, and under the New; which hath made two different forms of external administration of the covenant; the old, which is passed away, and the new, that will continue to the end of the world : but both were from the same authority, and for compassing the same great designs of the covenant, agreeable to the different times for which they were appointed; and are all of them to be found in the scriptures of the Old and New Testament, the book of the manner of the kingdom. It was the same Lord Jesus, the angel of the covenant which spake to

Moses in the mount Sinai, Acts vii. 38, who instituted the new testament church and ordinances, and "gave some apostles, and some prophets, and some evangelists, and some pastors and teachers; for the perfecting of the saints, for the work of the ministry," Eph. iv. 11. 12. The Saviour, King, and Lawgiver of the church, are one, Is. xxxiii. 22, "The Lord is our Lawgiver, the Lord is our King, he will save us."

Emitting his royal proclamations into the world, by the hand of his messengers, in the gospel; bearing, that whosoever will come unto him, and unite with him as the head of the covenant, by faith, shall be readily received into it, and have a right to all the privileges thereof, in him: Mark xvi. 15, "Go ye unto all the world, and preach the gospel to every creature." Ver. 16, "He that believeth and is baptized, shall be saved." Therein the covenant is published, and offered in his name to every sinner of mankind unto whose ears this voice reacheth: and they are called, commanded, and charged to come into it, and submit to his royal sceptre. His call and offer is their warrant to come: his command obligeth them, that they cannot refuse, but in rebellion and disobedience against his royal authority. The promises are set before them indefinitely, that whosoever will, may, by believing, apply them to themselves. The king's proclamation meddles not with the secrets of the eternal election, to reveal them. But the promises of the covenant, infallibly to be accomplised in some, are, in Christ's testament, as indorsed to sinners of mankind indefinitely, to be fulfilled unto all and every one who shall by faith embrace them: and the proclamation makes lawful intimation of the testament, This intimation is the appointed means of begetting faith, and of bringing sinners into the covenant thereby; for faith cometh by hearing, Rom. x. 17. And it is made effectual to some, by the Spirit, through the grace of the covenant secured by promise for them.

And hence it is, that the covenant being thus administered to all promiscuously, there is an use of conditional phrases in the administration thereof: though in the covenant itself there are no conditions, properly so called, but what were fulfilled by Jesus Christ in his own person. The word of the covenant coming with alike warrant to the elect and the non-elect; to them who certainly will believe, and to them who will continue in their unbelief; the administering of it equally to both in the gospel-proclamation, must needs be by proposing the promises indefinitely as to persons; the which must at length be resolved into conditional phrases. So it is proclaimed in the ears of all, "I will betrothe thee unto me," and "I will be to them a God." And one believes and applies the same; and he is thereupon united to Christ, and instated in the covenant to all saving purposes: another who hath as good a revealed warrant to believe as the former, yet believes not; and so comes short of the promise. Now, to speak alike to those who will thus differently entertain the words of the covenant, it follows of course, to resolve them into such expressions as these, "Believe on the Lord Jesus Christ, and thou shalt be saved:" and "He that believeth shall be saved, he that believeth not shall be damned." Meanwhile the covenant itself is a different thing from the form of the external administration of it.

3. Effectually subduing the elect to himself, through the power of his Spirit so managing the word, that it operates on them like a sword, piercing their souls, conquering their natural aversion and obstinacy, and making them willing to yield, and embrace the covenant. Rev. i. 16, "Out of his mouth went a sharp two-edged sword." What that sword is, and by what a strong arm it is wielded in this case, may be learned from the apostle calling it "the sword of the Spirit, which is the word of God," Eph. vi. 17; and what the effect of it is, being managed by that "arm of the Lord revealed," is declared by the Psalmist, Psalm cx. 3, "Thy people shall be willing in the day of thy power;" and by the prophet, Isa. xliv. 3, "I will pour my Spirit upon thy seed;"—Ver. 4, "And they shall spring up."—Ver. 5, "One shall say, I am the Lord's." Christ communicates to them, and every one of them, at the time appointed in the eternal counsel, the Spirit and grace of the covenant, therein secured for them by promise: and thereby they are quickened, enabled, and determined to believe. And whereas he finds them prisoners of hope, he opens the house of their bondage, breaking the yoke of sin, death, and the devil, from off their necks, by his Spirit applying to them his satisfaction. The which has that mighty effect, inasmuch as then the law hath full satisfaction as to them; and the law being satisfied, the strength of sin is broken, and the strength of sin being broken, the sting of death is taken away; and the sting of death being taken away, the devil loseth his power over them; and Satan's power over them being lost, the present evil world, which is his kingdom, can hold them no longer. Thus are they separated from the world lying in wickedness, and constituted members of the kingdom of Christ; delivered from the power of darkness, and translated into the kingdom of God's dear Son, Col. i. 13. And from thenceforth, though they be in the world, yet they are no more of it; but strangers and pilgrims in it, true and lively members of the invisible kingdom of Christ; a society to which the world is an im-

placable enemy, John xv. 19, "Ye are not of the world, but I have chosen you out of the world, therefore the world hateth you." And herein Christ doth, in a special manner, shew himself a King mighty in battle, by the power of his grace overcoming the most perverse and rebellious to a cordial submission, and rescuing them from the bondage and dominion of their enemies.

4. Gathering them and others with them together into a visible church-state, Gen. xlix. 10, "Unto him shall the gathering of the people be." Thus is erected the visible church or kingdom of Christ in the world; a society separate from the visible kingdom of the devil, and professing faith in, and obedience to Christ, outwardly bearing his badge, and the signs of his covenant. Among them is the ordinary seat of the administration of the covenant, the ordinary means of salvation, and offers of grace. In their land the voice of the turtle is heard, and the singing of birds, in the preaching of the glorious gospel; while there is a lasting winter over all the world besides. They have the Bible, and sabbaths, the ministry of the word, and the holy sacraments. Among them is to be found the communion of saints, and a church-government, instituted for controlling the unruly, suppressing sin and wickedness, and encouraging an orderly walk. And they have the privilege of heaven's protection; insomuch that the church shall be defended, and her enemies so restrained and conquered by her King, that she shall continue while the world stands, maugre all opposition that hell can make against her: Matt. xxviii. 20, "Lo I am with you alway even unto the end of the world."

5. *Lastly*, Ruling and governing his true and kindly subjects agreeably unto the covenant, by which his royal prerogative is stated, and their privileges are secured, Isa. ix. 6, "The government shall be upon his shoulder." Of this his government there are several acts, the chief of which are these following.

1*st*, He gives them the laws of the covenant; not only intimating the same unto them externally by his word; but teaching them internally by his Spirit, writing them upon the tables of their hearts, and leaving an indelible copy of them affixed there: Heb. viii. 10, "I will put my laws into their mind, and write them in their hearts." These laws of the covenant are no other but the laws of the ten commandments, originally given to Adam in his creation, and at his transportation into paradise and settlement there, vested with the form of the covenant of works; and now unto believers in Christ, standing without that form, in the covenant of grace as the eternal rule of righteousness, whereunto they are to be conformed by the grace of the covenant; the effectuating of which is committed by the

Father to Jesus Christ as administrator thereof. And accordingly he carries it on, by his word and Spirit, in a suitableness to their nature as rational agents, and to their state; making these laws known to them, as the rule of life, unto which they stand bound by the authority, and matchless love of God their Creator and Redeemer; and withal inclining their hearts unto the obedience of the same.

2dly, He gives them the rewards of the covenant in the course of their obedience: Psalm xix. 11, "In keeping of them there is great reward." He puts his people indeed to work and labour; but not to labour in the fire, and for vanity, as the servants of sin do: they are to work and labour, like the ox treading out the corn, which was not to be muzzled, but to have access at once to work and to eat. The service now done to Zion's King, hath a reward in this life, as well as a reward in the life to come. By the order of the covenant, there is privilege established to follow duty, as the reward thereof; the which order is observed by the King in his administration. Accordingly, he proposeth the privilege of comfort, to excite to the duty of mourning, Matt. v. 4, "Blessed are they that mourn for they shall be comforted:" the special tokens of heaven's favour, to excite unto a holy tender walk, John xiv. 21, "He that hath my commandments, and keepeth them,—shall be loved of my Father, and I will love him, and will manifest myself to him." In like manner to excite the same holy obedience, he proposeth the full reward in the life to come, 1 Cor. ix. 24, "So run that ye may obtain." Rev. iii. 21, "To him that overcometh will I grant to sit with me in my throne." And so certainly doth he accomplish the promise of the reward of both kinds, that his people may be assured "their labour is not in vain in the Lord," 1 Cor. xv. 51: for faithfulness is the girdle of his loins; and, in dispensing the privileges to his people upon the back of their duty, he doth but observe the stated order of the covenant. Not that the order of the covenant is in every particular first—duty, then privilege: nay, it is first, privilege; next, duty; then privilege again; and so forward, till privilege and duty come both to perfection in heaven, not to be distinguished more. Wo to us if it were otherwise! truly, if it were otherwise, we could neither be brought into the covenant, nor kept within it in life: for how shall one at first believe, till once he is privileged with the quickening Spirit? and how shall a fallen saint renew his faith and repentance, till once he is privileged with new influences of grace? John xv. 5, "Without me ye can do nothing." But here lies the matter, the leading privilege bringing in duty, there follows further privilege on the back of duty, according to the order of the covenant: and these further privileges are the rewards we speak of. And the scripture calls them rewards, even in respect of the saints: because they are given to a working saint, on the back of his work. Howbeit they are as far from the nature of a reward, strictly and properly so called, the which on the account of one's work is of debt to him, as the leading privileges are, that produce the working: but both the one and the other are equally the reward of Christ's work, in the most strict and proper notion of reward.

3dly, He ministers unto them the discipline of the covenant, in case of their disobedience. The discipline of the covenant is fatherly chastisement, which their state of imperfection in this life makes necessary to their welfare: and therefore it is secured for them in the covenant, Psalm lxxxix. 30, "If his children forsake my law:" ver. 32, "Then will I visit their transgression with the rod." Ver. 33, "Nevertheless"—ver. 34, "My covenant will I not break, nor alter the thing that is gone out of my lips." It belongs to the promissory part of the covenant, and particularly to the promise of sanctification: forasmuch as it is not vindictive, but medicinal; being an appointed means of advancing holiness in them. He chastens for our profit, that we might be partakers of his holiness, Heb. xii. 10. And thus it serves to purge iniquity, and to take away sin, Isa. xxvii. 9; namely, in that as a fire melting down the paint and varnish of the defiling objects in the world, in our sight, and as a looking-glass shewing us our pollution, it occasions and excites us unto washing in the only laver of the blood of Christ, by faith. Now, the administering of the discipline of the covenant is committed unto Zion's King, John v. 22, "The Father hath committed all judgment unto the Son." Rev. iii. 19, "As many as I love, I rebuke and chasten." And, as to the nature of it, it comprehends all manner of strokes upon their worldly substance, name, employments, and relations; all manner of bodily afflictions, diseases, and pains, incident to sinful flesh; even natural death itself, 1 Cor. xi. 30, 32; and generally, all outward strokes which any of the children of men are liable to, Eccl. ix. 2, "All things come alike to all." Moreover, it comprehends spiritual strokes, such as desertion, God's hiding his face from them, withdrawing the light of his countenance, their losing some measure of their graces and comforts, woundings of spirit, horrors of conscience, whereby they may be brought to the very brink of despair: so that, howbeit the casting them into hell is not within the compass of the discipline of the covenant, yet the casting a kind of hell into them, making them to roar by reason of disquietness of heart, Psalm xxxviii. 1, is within the compass of it. And, what is worse than any of all these, it comprehends their being harassed with horrid temptations, and set up as marks for Satan's fiery darts, Eph, vi. 16, the hardening of their hearts, Isa. lxiii. 17, and their being suffered to fall into one sin, and that a gross sin too, for the punishment of another, as in the case of David and Peter. All these things are within the compass of the discipline of the covenant; and believers are particularly and directly threatened with them, in case of their disobedience, to move them to beware of it: yea, and they are often inflicted by Zion's King on his beloved subjects, that, by these marks of his displeasure against their sin, he may correct them, make sin bitter to them, and stir them up to repentance and watchfulness. And the worst of them all, even the very hardening of their hearts, and the punishing of one sin with another, are, by the sovereign grace of the covenant, made effectual for these holy ends: the which grace opening the heart in renewed repentance, godly sorrow for sin breaks forth the more forcibly, as waters do which have been long dammed up. Thus these bitter waters, running in the channel of the covenant, become healing waters: these sharp swords are, by the covenant, beaten into ploughshares; and these piercing spears into pruning-hooks. Of this discipline of the covenant, all the subjects of Christ in this world do partake: and they must be under it, till they arrive at perfection in the other world, Heb. xii. 6—8.

4thly, He gives them the pardons of the covenant; the pardoning of crimes committed against the laws of God, being one of the royal prerogatives of Zion's King, whom " God hath exalted to be a Prince and a Saviour, for to give repentance to Israel, and forgiveness of sins," Acts v. 31. He gives them the first pardon, removing the guilt of revenging wrath, in their justification; and he gives them also the subsequent pardons, removing the guilt of fatherly anger, upon their renewing the actings of faith and repentance, as was observed before. The Father having committed all judgment unto the Son, he hath the dispensing of Heaven's favours, according to the method and order of the covenant; and they are not only conferred for his sake, but by his hand.

5thly, He affords them the defence of the covenant, while in this life they are amongst their enemies, Psalm lxxxix. 18, " For the Lord is our defence; and the holy One of Israel is our king." Satan is their enemy, a malicious, subtile, and powerful enemy: but Christ is their friend, and takes them under his protection. He loves them dearly, as the purchase of his own blood, the members of his own mystical body, and bearing his Father's image: he is infinitely wise, and can outshoot the devil in his own bow: and he is the stronger man, who can bind the strong man. The world joins issue with Satan in opposing them; but shall not prevail to ruin them, neither by force nor fraud: for greater is he, than the god of this world and all his dominion, 1 John iv. 4, "Ye are of God, and have overcome them: because greater is he that is in you, than he that is in the world." Their worst enemies are within them, namely, the remains of corruption, which, in the depth of sovereign wisdom, are not expelled during this life; but left for their exercise and trial, and for the discovery of the power of the grace of their King. And he manifests his power, in keeping alive in them the spunk of holy fire, in the midst of an ocean of corruption; and causing it to make head against the same, until it quite dry it up: Rom. vii. 24, "O wretched man that I am, who shall deliver me from the body of this death!" Ver. 25, "I thank God, through Jesus Christ our Lord." He has all their enemies in chains, that they can act no further against them than he sees meet to permit: and at his pleasure he restrains them, bounding them by his power, as to the kind, degree, and continuance of their attacks, Psalm lxxvi. 10, "The remainder of wrath shalt thou restrain."

Lastly, He authoritatively completes the happiness of the covenant in them. He purchased it for them as a Priest: he reveals it to them as a Prophet: but as a King, he doth, in the way of authority, put them in full possession thereof, Matth. xxv. 34, "Then shall the King say unto them on his right hand, Come, ye blessed of my Father, inherit the kingdom prepared for you from the foundation of the world." And by the same authority he will pass sentence against his and their enemies, having fully conquered them, ver. 41. And so he will complete for ever the peace of his covenant-subjects.

Thus far of Christ's administration of the covenant, as he is King thereof.

V. CHRIST THE INTERCESSOR OF THE COVENANT.

As for performing the condition of the covenant, Jesus Christ became the priest, namely, the sacrificing priest of it, as hath been said in the due place: so, for the administration of the covenant, he became the intercessor, namely, the interceding priest of it. Christ's intercession did not take its place in the making of the covenant. The love and grace of God made the motion for a new covenant freely: and the breach betwixt God and sinners was of another nature, than to be made up by a simple intercession; the which might have moved mercy, but could not have satisfied justice, that, requiring a sacrifice for sin, could not be satisfied by pleading, but by paying a ransom: Heb. ix. 22, "Without shedding of blood is no remission." Neither doth Christ's sacrificing take its place in the administration of the covenant: there is no need of any new sacrificing there; "For by one offering he hath perfected for ever them that are sanctified," chap. x. 14. But his sacrificing natively took its place in the making of the covenant, and fulfilling the condition thereof; and his intercession, in the administration of the covenant, and fulfilling the promises of it. Accordingly, for the administration of the covenant, he is the intercessor thereof: Rom. viii. 34, "It is Christ that died, yea rather, that is risen again, who is even at the right hand of God, who also maketh intercession for us."

And indeed there was need of an intercessor for that effect: since an infinitely holy God, and sinful creatures, could neither come together into a state of peace, nor continue in it, with the safety of God's honour, without an intercessor. Wherefore Jesus Christ being appointed thereto, is, in that character, "entered into heaven itself, now to appear in the presence of God for us," Heb. ix. 24, to manage the business of the covenant for our behoof; willing the merit of his sacrifice to be applied to all those in whose room and stead he died, and that for all the intents and purposes of the covenant in their favours, according to the method laid down and stated therein. And this his intercession is always effectual, as he himself testifieth, saying unto his Father, John xi. 42, "I knew that thou hearest me always. Whence it appears, that the object of it is not of equal latitude with the object of the administration of the covenant, and of his acting in the other relations belonging to that administration; but that it is restricted unto those whom he, as second Adam, represented in the eternal transaction. And this is very agreeable to the nature of the divine contrivance for the salvation of sinners; in which the eternal purpose hath made a difference of persons, according to sovereign will and pleasure: this being, as it were, one clause in the constitution of the administration, peculiarly in favour of the objects of electing love. So the intercessor himself teacheth us, John xvii. 9, "I pray not for the world, but for them which thou hast given me:" ver. 20, "For them which shall believe on me." Ver. 24, "Father, I will that they also whom thou hast given me, be with me where I am."

Now, Christ administers the covenant as intercessor thereof, these following ways chiefly.

1. Effectually procuring, by his interest in heaven, the actual inbringing of his elect, at the time appointed, into a covenant-state of union, communion, peace, and favour with God: John xvii. 20,

"Neither pray I for these alone, but for them also which shall believe on me through their word:" ver. 21, "That they all may be one, as thou, Father, art in me, and I in thee; that they also may be one in us." They are by nature in a state of enmity with God, even as others: but through Christ's intercession the peace is made between Heaven and them. He purchased it for them by the blood of his sacrifice; it was promised to him in the covenant on that score; and by his intercession he actually obtains it unto them. His intercession is the spring that puts all the wheels in motion, that are set a-going, in the time of loves, for bringing one out of the state of nature, into a state of grace. Providence manageth favourably towards the conversion of the man; the word powerfully affects him, while on others it falls like rain on a rock, running off as fast as it comes on; the business of eternal salvation is closely laid to heart with him; the law doth its office upon him, and so doth the gospel also in its turn: and these things cease not, until he is brought into a new state, and is become a new creature. Whence did all this take its rise! Why, the man had an unknown friend in the court of heaven, who spoke for him to the King: and all this is the fruit of that intercession made for him.

2. Appearing for them, and in their name taking possession of heaven, and all the other benefits of the covenant, which they have a right to, in virtue of their new covenant state: Eph. ii. 6, "And hath raised us up together, and made us sit together in heavenly places in Christ Jesus." Heb. vi. 20, "Whither the forerunner is for us entered." That moment wherein a sinner enters into the covenant by believing, he hath a right to all; for if children, then heirs, Rom. viii. 17. Howbeit, in the case of most of the children of God, the possession seems to be delayed long after that time. But it is to be considered, that possession may not only be taken by a man in his own person; but also in the person of another: thus one may by his attorney take possession of an estate which he never saw; and a minor, by his representative, may be possessed of what it is not as yet meet to give him into his own hand. So, howbeit, the believer's possession of all in his own person is indeed delayed: yet in this respect it is not delayed one moment after his believing in Jesus Christ: for his intercessor acts for him in the matter. What should hinder this manner of possession one moment after believing? For the covenant of promises is an undoubted right; the sinner, though on earth, doth by faith plead it before God in heaven; and Christ is there, as his representative and intercessor, to take possession in his name. Wherefore every believer shall justly reckon himself, though having nothing, yet possessing all things, 2 Cor. vi. 10, and complete in him, Col. ii. 10.

3. Maintaining the peace between God and them while they are here in this world. Having purchased their peace with heaven, by the sacrifice of himself, and by his intercession brought them into a state of peace, he doth not leave it to themselves to maintain it. If it were so, it would soon be at an end. There are so many failures on their part, while they are compassed with the body of sin, that their own consciences have whereof to accuse them every day; and the devil is an incessant accuser of the brethren: but Christ intercedes for them, to the preventing always a total rupture betwixt heaven and them; however they may for their sins fall under God's fatherly displeasure: upon the ground of his satisfaction for them, he answereth all accusations against them, and takes up all emerging differences between them and their covenanted God: 1 John ii. 1, "If any man sin, we have an advocate with the Father, Jesus Christ the righteous:" ver. 2, "And he is the propitiation for our sins." Hereupon the apostle triumphs over all their accusers, Rom. viii. 33, "Who shall lay any thing to the charge of God's elect? It is God that justifieth:" ver. 34, "Who is he that condemneth? It is Christ that died, who also maketh intercession for us." Wherefore their state of peace with God is inviolably maintained; though, for their correction, they may indeed lose the sight and sense of it for a time. Having once become their friend in Christ, he may indeed severely chastise them for their faults, but he never becomes their enemy again, even in the way of legal enmity, far less in the way of real enmity, Rom. viii. 1; Isa. liv. 9.

4. Procuring them access to God, and acceptance with him, notwithstanding of their imperfections, while in this life. Saints on earth never want business in the court of heaven. Yet being sinful, they are in themselves unfit to come into the presence of the King. But the Intercessor of the covenant introduceth them, procuring them access by his interest in the court; "For through him we have an access by one Spirit unto the Father," Eph. ii. 18. And by this means they are allowed access with boldness, chap. iii. 12. He makes their persons accepted, notwithstanding of the sinfulness cleaving to them: they are accepted in the beloved, chap. i. 6. And in him they have an altar that sanctifies their gifts, Heb. xiii. 10. So that their spiritual sacrifices, howbeit they want not their blemishes, yet are acceptable to God by Jesus Christ, 1 Pet. ii. 5. Their prayers made in faith, though smelling rank of the remains of the corruption of nature, yet being perfumed by the Intercessor with the incense of his merit, are accepted in heaven, and have gracious returns made them, Rev. viii. 4. Their doing service, and their suffering services, which howsoever costly, could not be ac-

cepted for their own worth, because imperfect, are through his intercession accepted, as being washed, and made white in the blood of the Lamb, chap. vii. 14.

5. *Lastly*, Obtaining their admittance into heaven, in the due time; and continuing their state of perfect happiness there for ever and ever: John xvii. 24, "Father, I will that they also whom thou hast given me, be with me where I am." Our Lord Jesus Christ was by his Father constituted a priest for ever, Psalm cx. 4. Nevertheless, after his having once offered himself a sacrifice on the cross, he offereth no more sacrifice. Therefore he must be, not a sacrificing Priest for ever, but an interceding Priest, as the apostle explains it, Heb. vii. 25, "He ever liveth to make intercession for them." Now, the spirits of just men being made perfect immediately after death, there is no more imperfections about their souls morally considered, Heb. xii. 23; and after the resurrection, there will be no more imperfection about their bodies neither, 1 Cor. xv. 53. The effect then of Christ's intercession for ever, must be the everlasting continuation of their happy state; their Intercessor externally willing the continuance of the same, on the ground of the eternal redemption obtained for them, by the sacrifice of himself. The infinite merit of his sacrifice will be eternally presented before God in the holy place, while he shall appear there in our nature continually: and this will be the everlasting security for the continuation of the saints' happiness. The which happiness issuing from the merit of his sacrifice as their Priest, will be communicated unto him as their Prophet and their King: for these his offices will never be laid aside. As he is a Priest for ever, so of his kingdom there shall be no end, Luke i. 33, and the Lamb will be the light of the heavenly city, Rev. xxi. 23; the saint's communion with God there, being still in and through the Mediator, in a manner agreeable to their state of perfection, chap. vii. 17.

And these are the chief acts of his administration of the covenant, as Intercessor thereof.

Thus far of the fourth head, namely, the administration of the covenant.

HEAD V.

THE TRIAL OF A SAVING PERSONAL INBEING IN THE COVENANT OF GRACE.

We have now opened the doctrine of the covenant of grace, in treating of the parties in it, the making of it, the parts of it, and the administration thereof: it remains to make some practical improvement of the whole, in this and the following head.

If one seriously considers the covenant of grace, as that on which the salvation of our soul depends, he can hardly miss to put the question to himself, What interest have I in that covenant? There is no question but you have a common interest in it, by which you are sufficiently warranted to come into it: but that you may have, and yet perish; for even "children of the kingdom shall be cast out into outer darkness," Matt. viii. 12. But the question is, Whether ye have a saving interest in it, being actually come into it, or not? The covenant is indeed brought unto you, in the ordinances of the gospel: but are you brought into the covenant, united with the head thereof, Christ Jesus? It hath been administered to you: but have you by faith taken hold of it? You have received the sacrament of baptism, the seal of the covenant, in the right of your parents; but have you personally embraced the covenant in sincerity? The two covenants, of works, and of grace, divide the whole world between them: every man is under one of the two; and no man can be under both at one and the same time, in respect of his state before the Lord, Rom. vi. 14. Under the first covenant stands a numerous party, in the first Adam, head of that broken covenant, deriving sin, death, and the curse from him: under the second covenant stands a party, in the second Adam, head of that fulfilled covenant, deriving life and salvation from him. These parties will be judged, each according to the covenant they are under: so the former will be condemned, in virtue of the curse of the covenant in which they are; and the latter will be eternally saved, in virtue of the promise of life, in the covenant wherein they are. In the meanwhile there is access for those of the first covenant to leave their party and covenant, and to join the party in the second covenant: but death will block up that access. Wherefore it is the interest of the one as well as of the other, to know which party and covenant they belong to. And for trial hereof, I offer the following marks, signs, or characters of those who are savingly and personally within the covenant of grace.

I. They are such as have fled for refuge from the covenant of works; that have come into the covenant of the second Adam, as refuges from the covenant of the first Adam. For that is the character of the heirs of promise, Heb. vi. 17, 18. Though time was when they lived at ease within the dominion of the covenant of the law; yet God hath set fire to their nest there, that they have found themselves unable to dwell any longer within the boundaries of that covenant. Mount Sinai hath been altogether on a smoke round about them; and the trumpet of the curse of the law hath waxed louder and louder, till it made them to hear it on the side of their righteousness and best works, where they were deafest; and it hath caused them exceedingly to fear and quake, as a curse denounced against them in particular: Rom. vii. 9, "When the commandment came, sin revived, and I died." It hath chased them from all the starting holes about that mountain, and left no place within the bounds of that covenant safe to them: not only has it chased them out of their profane courses, but also out of all confidence in their good works and duties of whatsoever kind; to flee for their life into the covenant of free grace, as the slayer into the city of refuge; what things were gain to them, counting these loss for Christ, Phil. iii. 7.

II. They are such as cordially approve of, and acquiesce in the plan of the covenant, as suited to the honour of God, and to their case in particular: looking upon it as well ordered in all things, 2 Sam. xxiii. 5. Whosoever duly considers the corruption brought into man's nature by the fall, will plainly perceive, that the method of salvation laid down in the covenant of grace, is the very reverse of the inclination of corrupt human nature: so that nothing less than the powerful efficacy of divine grace can bring a soul unto a cordial approbation of it, and acquiescence in it: wherefore our Lord pronounceth them blessed, whosoever shall not be offended in him, Matth. xi. 6. Natural men may indeed shape the covenant, in their own apprehensions, into such a form, as they may have a very good liking of it. They may apprehend it as a covenant designed to make men easy and happy; while in the meantime it allows them, at least in some instances, to be unholy: as a covenant wherein through Christ's means, they may obtain acceptance with God by their good works, notwithstanding of their ill works. But in all this they are in love with a creature of their own fancy, not with God's covenant of grace. Let the covenant be set before them in the light of the holy scripture, and viewed by them in that light; they will be sure to dislike it, and pick holes in it. Let the design of the covenant be fairly discovered, as being to exalt God's free grace on the ruins of all excellency left with man; to make Christ all, and man nothing in his own salvation; the proud heart cannot away with that, cannot submit to the righteousness of God, Rom. x. 3. The efficacy of it, in working out sin, separating between the soul and its dearest lusts, once fairly appearing; natural men flee from it, as if one cried unto them, There is death in the pot. Let them seriously enter into the thought, how it is suited to the honour of God, and the divine perfections; and how it is suited to their real safety before him: and they can not see how it is so. To the Jewish wisdom it is a stumbling-block, a device inconsistent with the divine perfections: the Grecian learning pronounceth it foolishness, a method of salvation unsafe to be trusted to: only the eye of faith discovers it to be the power of God, and the wisdom of God; safe for guilty creatures, and honourable for a holy God, 1 Cor. i. 23, 24.

III. Upon the discovery of the covenant to them, as made from eternity between God and the second Adam, and offered to them in the gospel; they will satisfy themselves in their covenanting, with heaven's draught of it, so far as they understand it; and they will not go about to add unto it, nor to diminish from it; but will stand to the terms of God and Christ's making, Acts ix. 6, "Lord, what wilt thou have me to do?" They will put a blank in the Lord's hand, for their part; as content if all within the compass of the covenant, without putting in their exceptions, or desiring amendments and alterations to be made in their favour. They are content of the laws of the covenant; as well as of the privileges of it; of the discipline of the covenant, as well as of the rewards of it; of the condition of the covenant as fulfilled by Christ alone, as well as of the promises of it to be fulfilled to them; and of the promise of santification, as well as of the promise of justification and glorification. Hence the covenant, as revealed in the gospel, is by the Holy Ghost called a hearing, Isa. liii. 1, marg. that is, a thing to be heard and received by faith, as a voice is received and heard by the ear, according to that, chap. lv. 5, "Hear, and your soul shall live." It is the natural disposition of mankind, to speak rather than to hear: for we are more ready to declare our own will by speaking, than to receive the will of another by hearing. Wherefore the gospel being the declaration of the will of God for our salvation, only to be heard and received by faith, and therefore called the hearing of faith, Gal. iii. 2, there is need of the power of grace, to subdue the heart to the hearing thereof, and to stop the mouth from making proposals of our own in that matter.

IV. The love of God in Christ is habitually predominant in them: Prov. viii. 17, "I love them that love me." Great was the love to them appearing in the covenant. The parties-contractors about them acted therein from a principle of free, and yet greatest love. From thence sprung the first motion for a covenant of life and salvation unto them: thence it was the Father was content to give his Son for them; the Son was well pleased to become man, and suffer death for them; the holy Spirit to take them for his habitation, to quicken, sanctify, and perfect them. The love of God produced the proposal of the great and precious promises in their favour, upon terms consistent with his justice: Christ as second Adam, out of love to them, accepted of these terms. And when the eternal transaction was, in the gospel, by the demonstration of the Spirit, opened and brought home to their souls; this love shone forth to them, so as they believed it. And that believed love of God in Christ kindled in their souls a superlative love to him again: 1 John iv. 19, "We love him; because he first loved us." And therefore, although that their love is not always alike vigorous, but hath its waxings and warnings according to the increase and decrease of their faith; yet, since their faith never altogether fails, Luke xxii. 32, it never fails altogether neither, from the moment that it is kindled in their hearts. And it is an active principle in them, constraining them to obedience, 2 Cor. v. 14, giving the chief room in their heart and affection to God in Christ, that their soul saith, "Whom have I in heaven but thee? and there is none upon earth that I desire besides thee," Psalm lxxiii. 25. It makes it to be their greatest care to please him, and to be accepted of him, 2 Cor. v. 9; and their greatest fear, to stir him up or offend him, Can. iii. 35. It makes duty agreeable to them, as a matter of choice: 1 John v. 3, "This is the love of God, that we keep his commandments; and his commandments are not grievous." And it renders the remains of sin, the body of this death, a heavy burden which they long to be delievered from, Rom. vii. 24.

V. Jesus Christ the head of the covenant, is their head with their own consent. With heart and good-will they have taken him for their head, for all the purposes of the covenant; and they stand to it, not to alter, if the choice were to make a thousand times. Those to whom the Father from 'eternity choose Christ for a head, do, in the day of their conversion, by faith approve the choice, making it over again personally for themselves; whence they are said to appoint themselves one head, Hos. i. 11. And as often as they reiterate their acts of faith, which they must live by, they do upon the matter reiterate their choice. Being sensible of what they suffered by the miscarriage of Adam their first head, Christ is precious to them as a second Adam. They come into the covenant, and abide also in it, under his wings allenarly; expecting no benefit of it, nor by it, but through him. And they have taken him as their head for government, as well as their head for nourishment and support. They have delivered up themselves unto him, to be ruled by him, as well as to be saved by him; to be governed by his laws, and not by their own lusts, as well as to be saved by his grace, and not by their own works.

VI. The condition of the covenant fulfilled by Jesus Christ, is the alone ground of their confidence before the Lord, as to acceptance with him, or any benefit of the covenant they look to partake of. A crucified Saviour is the foundation laid in Zion, for sinners to build on: and believing on him is the soul's building upon it, 1 Pet. ii. 6. If men build on another foundation, they build on the sand, and their confidence shall be rooted out: if, being driven off from all other foundation, they build not on this neither, they must needs perish as the chaff which the wind driveth away. To believe, or build on Christ's righteousness by him fulfilled, can import no less than one's trusting on it for his salvation. Whether this trust be strong or weak, it must be: else faith is not, building on Christ is not; but the soul is kept in a state of wavering, in opposition to the staying of it by faith on Christ, Jam. i. 6. Now, he that is within the covenant, takes Christ's righteousness as his alone ground of confidence before the Lord: for the covenant shews not, nor allows any other: nothing save Jesus Christ, and him crucified, 1 Cor. ii. 2. He hath some measure of confidence for life and salvation, upon that ground; whereby he is distinguished from the desperate, faithless, and unbelieving: and what confidence he hath for life and salvation, he hath upon that ground alone; whereby he is distinguished from the presumptuous, formalists, and hypocrites. And both these things are joined in the believer's character, Philip. iii. 3, "And rejoice in Christ Jesus, and have no "confidence in the flesh."

VII. The promises of the covenant are a satisfying portion to their hearts. They are indeed sensible they have many wants; but then they see as much in the covenant as would supply them all; that they need not go to another door for supply: they are persuaded there is as much water in that well as would quench all their thirst, if they could but get the art of drawing it. Thus the covenant is all their salvation, and all their desire, 2 Sam. xxiii. 5. This discovery of the covenant is not owing to nature, but to that grace which shews so much worth in the one pearl, as makes a man content to sell all he hath, to gain it, Matth. xiii. 46. But no man will come into the covenant, until once he get it: for who will join himself to one in a marriage-covenant, or contract of service, with whom he cannot see how to live? Faith discerns in the covenant not only a refuge, but a portion, Psalm cxlii. 5, else the man would never come into it. And none who have once got this discovery, will remain out of the covenant, Psalm ix. 10, "They that know thy name, will put their trust in thee." See John iv. 10. If the worth of the treasure hid in the field of the gospel, be perceived, all will go for the obtaining thereof, Matth. xiii. 44, 45; all will be counted loss and dung for the excellency of it, Philip. iii. 8. Certainly the men of the world do not see this in the covenant: it is but an empty hungry thing in their blinded eyes. The covenant is, in the gospel, held out to them in the breadth and length thereof: but it does not take with them: it is far from being all their desire: after all, as-if they had seen nothing that could satisfy, they still cry, "Who will shew us any good?" Psalm iv. 6. The truth is, the heart of man can never see enough in the covenant for to rest satisfied with, till grace give it a new set, and contract its endless desires: for that which the unrenewed heart is most set upon, there is no provision in the covenant for, but against it.

VIII. The Spirit of the covenant is in them: and that is another spirit than what the men of the world are actuated by, Numb. xiv. 24; Ezek. xxxvi. 27, "I will put my Spirit within you." The Spirit of Christ is the Spirit of the covenant, purchased by the blood of the covenant, lodged in the fulness thereof in Christ the head of the covenant, and communicated in some measure to all the covenant-people. And that Spirit may be known by these three characters thereof.

1. The Spirit of the covenant is a Spirit of holiness. The great design of the covenant, next to the glory of God, was the sanctification of sinners, Luke i. 74, 75. All the lines of the covenant, from the first of them unto the last, meet in that as their centre. There is a display of exact justice, in the condition of the covenant; of rich grace and mercy, in the promises of it: of greatest faithfulness and power, in the administration of it: but holiness goes through the whole, and every the least part of it. Wherefore it is called the holy covenant, Dan. xi. 30. Who then can reasonably imagine, that the unholy are within this covenant? that the servants of sin, whether profane, or formalists, strangers to the power of godliness, whom no bands of holiness will hold, can be within the bond of the holy covenant? No, sure they are not; they have not the Spirit of the covenant. The Spirit of the covenant makes the covenanted initially holy; and to press toward the mark, to wrestle, long, groan, and pant for the perfection of holiness, Philip. iii. 14. It makes a vein of holiness run through their whole man; their whole life; their thoughts, their words, their actions; their dealings with God, and their dealings with men. The covenant was erected on purpose to destroy the works of the devil: it was a confederacy entered into by the Father and the Son, for rooting sin out of the hearts and lives of the children of Adam; for restoring the divine image in them; and for bringing them again to a perfect conformity to the moral law of the ten commandments, from which they fell in Adam. For this end was the condition of it performed, the promises of it made,

and the administration thereof committed to the holy Jesus: 1 John iii. 8, "For this purpose the Son of God was manifested, that he might destroy the works of the devil." Wherefore, whosoever partake of the Spirit of the covenant, partake of the Spirit of holiness: Gal. v. 18, "If ye be led by the Spirit, ye are not under the law." Ver. 16, "Walk in the Spirit, and ye shall not fulfil the lust of the flesh."

2. The Spirit of the covenant is an ingenuous free Spirit, Psalm li. 12. It is the spirit of sons, not of slaves; of free men, not of bond-men, Rom. viii. 15. There is some obedience to the holy law given by unbelievers, the men of the first covenant, as well as by believers, the men of the second covenant: and the eyes of the world can perceive no difference between the obedience of some of the former sort, and of those of the latter sort; howbeit there is a vast difference, which is seen by the all-seeing eye. Are these within the covenant, praying persons? So are many, who have no saving part nor lot in it, Isa. lviii. 2. Are they men of temperance and sobriety, justice and honesty, candour and faithfulness, men of blameless lives? So are several others besides them, for all that any man can see, Phil. iii. 6. Thus far they agree. But there is a vast difference of the spirit they are actuated by, which makes a mighty odds in the manner and kind of their obedience. Unbelievers are actuated by a spirit of bondage, suitable to their state of bondage under the covenant of works, Gal. iv. 24, 25. A slavish fear and a servile hope are the weights hung upon them by that covenant, causing them to go: sin is avoided, duty performed, not out of love to God and holiness, but out of love to themselves. Believers are actuated by the Spirit of adoption, suitable to their state of adoption, under the covenant of grace, ver. 26. God is their Father: and they serve him as sons, not as slaves, Mal. iii. 17. Christ is their elder brother, who loved them, and gave himself for them: and his love constrains them, 2 Cor. v. 14. The Holy Spirit dwells in them, hath quickened them, renewed them, making them partakers of the divine nature, 2 Pet. i. 4. So sin is avoided as contrary to their new nature, duty pursued as agreeable to it. Their faith of the love of God in Christ hath begotten in them love to God again, for a new principle of obedience, 1 Tim. i. 5. By faith they trust on Christ, and on him alone for life and salvation: and this at once undermines in them the slavish fear of hell, and the servile hope of heaven; so that these are so far from being their only motives to obedience, that they cannot be their predominant motives; nay they cannot be at all in them, but as enemies to their faith and love, 2 Tim. i. 7; 1 John iv. 18. Yet withal, it is to be remembered,

that it is not slavish for saints to fear God's fatherly anger, and thereby to be stirred up to duty, Psalm cxix. 120; Heb. xi. 7; nor to hold the way of duty, in hope of the enjoyment of God in that way, and the tokens of his favour, John xiv. 21, and in the end perfect happiness in heaven; all through Jesus Christ alone, 1 Cor. xv. 58. Our need of these things for incitements to duty, do indeed argue our childish state, for there will be no need of these fears and hopes in heaven; but by no means a slavish state. Neither is it at all slavish, to have the heart filled with a reverential fear and dread of God, upon the consideration of his tremendous justice, and wrath in hell, against the miserable objects thereof; and to be stirred up to duty thereby, Matt. x. 28; Heb. xii. 28, 29. To look thereunto, and move away towards God in the way of duty, with fear and trembling, is very agreeable to the state of those who have by faith received a kingdom that cannot be moved; but are not yet ascended unto heaven: who are indeed drawn up out of the fearful depth; but are not as yet haled up to the top of the rock, though the strong chain of the covenant is so about them, that they shall never fall down again. For in heaven the awe and reverence of God, on that score, will be perfect, Isa. vi. 1, 2, 3. But it is slavish for saints, to fear their being cast into hell for sin; and servile, to hope their obtaining heaven for their good works. And yet that slavish fear and servile hope, may creep in upon the children of the second covenant, and move them to duty: because their faith is weak, much of the old Adam remains in them, and it is not easy for them, though dead to the law in point of privilege, to be dead to it in point of practice. But these impure mixtures of selfishness in their duties will be humbling unto them: and they will loath themselves, for that they act not, in their obedience, with more of the free spirit and son-like disposition. And their will in that case is accepted through Christ.

3. The Spirit of the covenant is a Spirit of sympathy regulated by the covenant. There is a commonness of interest, and thence a mutual sympathy, among confederates. And this sympathy among the confederates of Heaven, regards both the head and the people of the covenant.

(1.) They have a native and kindly sympathy with the God and head of the covenant. It is true, his essential glory can never be liable to diminution; nor can his eternal rest in himself be in the least disturbed, by whatsoever men or angels may do or suffer: and the man Christ is now beyond the reach of suffering. Nevertheless, his declarative glory in the world hath its times of shining clear, and of being under a cloud. Now, as he hath a sympathy with them, in all their concerns, their distresses and their enlargements, their joys and their griefs, Isa. lxiii. 9; Luke xv. 5; which is a very tender sympathy, insomuch that the touching of them is the touching of the apple of his eye, Zech. ii. 8: so they also have a very tender sympathy with him, in the concerns of his glory. They are glad and rejoice in the prosperity of his kingdom, Acts xi. 23, 24. They pray for it continually, Psalm lxxii. 15: and contribute their endeavours, in their stations to advance it, Phil. i. 21, "For to me to live is Christ." They have a feeling of the indignities done to his Majesty, as done to themselves, Psalm lxix. 9, "The reproaches of them that reproached thee, are fallen upon me." And they are mourners for the sins of others, as well as for their own; on the account of the dishonour they do to God, because they keep not his law, Psalm cxix. 136. The children of the covenant will neither be opposers of the kingdom of Christ, nor will they be neuters; but will put their shoulders to the work of their Lord, to help it forward, according to their vocation: and without such a public spirit, in greater or lesser measure, no man shall be able to prove his saving interest in the covenant: for so hath our Lord himself determined the matter, Matt. xii. 30, "He that is not with me, is against me: and he that gathereth not with me, scattereth abroad."

(2.) They have a native and kindly sympathy with the people of the covenant: for they are members one of another, Eph. iv. 25. The grace of the covenant disposeth men to be loving and beneficial to mankind, but in a peculiar manner to holy men; to "do good unto all men, especially unto them who are of the household of faith," Gal. vi. 10. The common bond of the covenant engageth them in peculiar love one to another; even as in that bond they are the common object of the world's hatred. They bear the same image with Christ their common head; and that image will recommend all who bear it, unto one that is within the covenant himself, so far as he can discern it. Wherefore their love is a love to all the saints, Eph. i. 15. And hence ariseth the sympathy which every true Christian hath with the church of Christ throughout the world, and with the several members thereof known to them; their joint interest in the covenant challengeth it; for by the covenant there is a near relation among them; and from their union under the same head, results their communion, 1 Cor. xii. 12, 26. Therefore a spirit of selfishness, whereby men's concern is all swallowed up in their own things, leaving them no sympathy with the church and people of God, is a shrewd sign of a graceless state. How much more, a spirit of reigning enmity against religion, and the professors thereof: where religion, and what concerns it, make men the special objects of their enmity, spite, and resentment? An habitual course of this is none of the spots of God's people; but it declares men to be of the world, John xv. 19, "I have chosen you out of the world, therefore the world hateth you." The Spirit of the covenant will carry men quite another way; since, taking hold of the covenant, they have embarked in the same bottom with those whose head Christ is, and who have declared war against the devil's kingdom. To them they will say, "We will go with you; for we have heard that God is with you," Zech. viii. 23.

IX. In the last place, The laws of the covenant are in their hearts, namely, the laws of the ten commandments, the eternal rule of righteousness, Heb. viii. 10. That law, in all its parts, is a copy of the divine nature, which in regeneration is transcribed into the heart of every one brought into the covenant: and the whole of it is written there, though every part is not written alike clear, nor any part perfect. As is the image of God restored in us, so is the law written in our hearts: in sanctification there is a new man created; which speaks a perfection of parts, though there is not a perfection of degrees in these parts, Eph. iv. 24; 2 Cor. v. 17; 1 Cor. xiii. 12. This may be taken up in these four things:—

1. They approve of the whole law, so far as it is known to them: Psalm cxix. 128, "I esteem all thy precepts concerning all things to be right." They love God: and every part of the law is a line of his image: wherefore loving the law as expressing the image of his holiness, they must needs love the whole law; since there is nothing in it but what is a transcript of that holiness. And as the head of the covenant is in their eyes altogether lovely, Cant. v. 16, the laws of the covenant being like him, must be so too. Why do not unbelievers love the holy law, but because they do not love a holy God? Rom. viii. 7. But believers loving a holy God in Christ, must love the law also, since in it the image of his holiness is expressed. The holy law condemns many things in them; yea, every thing of theirs, so far as it is morally imperfect: and so they do themselves, consenting unto the law that it is good, chap. vii. 16. It condemns every sin; every one's most beloved sin, the evil he is most easily led aside into; and for that very cause the unrenewed heart hates the law. But the grace of the covenant makes a man to leave his complaint on himself; to approve the law and condemn his own lust contrary thereto: Rom. vii. 12, "The law is holy; and the commandment holy, and just, and good." Ver. 14, "But I am carnal."

2. They have an inclination of heart towards the whole law, so

far as they know it: Psalm cxix. 5, "O that my ways were directed to keep thy statutes!" There is in them a fixed principle, which lies the same way with the holy law; bending away from what the law forbids, and towards what the law directs unto. True, there is a contrary principle in them too, which fights against it; but so do they against that contrary principle, breathing, longing and lusting for the complete victory over it, and for full conformity to the holy law, Gal. v. 17. This is a new set of heart given in the new birth; exerting itself, not in lazy wishes for conformity to the law, but in a resolute struggle for it, enduring to the end. Hence,

3. They will habitually endeavour to conform in their practice to the whole law, so far as they know: Psalm cxix. 6, "Then shall I not be ashamed, when I have respect unto all thy commandments." If the law is written in one's heart, he will write it out again in his conversation: and a sanctified heart will certainly make a holy life; Matt. vi. 22, "If thine eye be single, thy whole body shall be full of light." Where is the efficacy of the holy covenant, if men may be within the covenant, and yet live like those that are without it? Nay, but to whomsoever the grace of God hath effectually appeared, it will have taught them effectually to deny ungodliness, and worldly lusts, and to live soberly, righteously, and godly in this present world, Tit. ii. 11, 12. If the grace of the covenant bring you not to duties of piety towards God, you have no saving part in it. If you are brought unto these, but withal left at liberty from the duties of righteousness toward your neighbour, that you do not loath, but dare to be unjust in smaller or greater matters; you are yet "in the gall of bitterness, and in the bond of iniquity:" Luke xvi. 11, "If ye have not been faithful in the unrighteous mammon, who will commit to your trust the true riches?" If you are brought forward unto both these, and yet not sober, but left slaves to your sensual appetites and fleshly affections, you are no better: for "they that are Christ's, have crucified the flesh, with the affections and lusts," Gal. v. 24. But whoso have fled to the covenant of grace in Christ for life and salvation, and withal are honestly endeavouring conformity to the whole law in their practice, they, howbeit in many things they miss their mark, do shew themselves to be within the bond of the holy covenant, and ought to take the comfort thereof, as the divine allowance to them: 2 Cor. i. 12, "Our rejoicing is this, the testimony of our conscience, that in simplicity and godly sincerity, not with fleshly wisdom, but by the grace of God, we have had our conversation in the world."

4. *Lastly,* Their souls lie open to what of the laws of the covenant they know not. They are content to know them, desirous to be taught them, that they may conform unto them: Psalm cxix. 26, "Teach me thy statutes." There are many sins of ours hid unto us; because there is much of the laws of the covenant we do not discern. And hypocrites do not desire to know the whole law: they are willingly ignorant of some things thereof, because they have no inclination to entertain them. But the sincere, being content to part with every false way, and to take upon them the whole yoke of Christ, hating sin as contrary to God's nature and will, and loving duty as agreeable thereto, do of course lie open to the further discoveries of sin and duty: they come to the light, John iii. 21. They say, "That which I see not, teach thou me," Job xxxiv. 32, "Search me, O God, and know my heart: try me, and know my thoughts. And see if there be any wicked way in me, and lead me in the way everlasting," Psalm cxxxix. 23, 24.

And this much shall suffice to have spoken on the fifth head, namely, The trial of a saving personal inbeing in the covenant of grace.

HEAD VI.

THE WAY OF INSTATING SINNERS PERSONALLY AND SAVINGLY IN THE COVENANT OF GRACE.

By the marks and characters given, it appears, that they are but few who are personally and savingly instated in the covenant of grace, in comparison of those who are strangers to it: but we are allowed to offer it to strangers; to invite and call them who are without the covenant, to come into it, and so to compel them to come in, Luke xiv. 23. Here then are the glad tidings of the gospel: there is a covenant, which was entered into from eternity between God and Christ the second Adam; a covenant of grace, made in favour of sinners of Adam's race, ruined by the breach of the covenant of works. In it there is full provision for your salvation; to relieve you from all the ruining effects of the broken first covenant, and to render you completely happy. The condition of this covenant is indeed high; being screwed up to a pitch by the demands of the law and justice: yet there is nothing on that part to discourage you from the covenant; for your inability being foreseen from eternity, it was laid upon one that is mighty, to perform it; and now it is already performed and fulfilled to your hand by that mighty one, Christ Jesus. Only, the promises remain to be fulfilled. So the burden of the condition is over without you; and ye are called to the benefit of the promises. And that ye may have the more clear access thereto, the administration of the covenant is put into the hand of the same Christ Jesus; and he is intrusted with all the promises, to fulfil them to sinners. He hath begun to fulfil them to all who have taken hold of the covenant; and is ready to fulfil them to all who yet shall take hold thereof. For that end he hath made his testament of these promises, and constituted sinners of mankind his legatees; that whosoever of them will, may come, claim, and take the water of life freely, Rev. xxii. 17. The whole of the covenant is in him. In him is God, the party-contractor on heaven's side, 2 Cor. v. 19. He himself is the party-contractor on man's side: and in him are all believers really, and all the elect legally and representatively. In him is the condition of the covenant, and that as fulfilled: he is the Lord our righteousness, Jer. xxiii. 6. In him are all the promises yea, and amen, 2 Cor. i. 20, all meeting in him, as lines of a circle in their centre; and sure and stedfast, nowise liable to misgive, as did the promise of the covenant of works in the first Adam. And he as a king hath emitted his royal proclamations, bearing, that whosoever will come into him, and unite with him as head of the covenant, shall be taken into it, and have a right to all the privileges thereof in him, and through him.

Thus the covenant is brought to you, and set before you in the gospel; so that ye must needs be either receivers or refusers of it. Refuse it not: that is dangerous beyond expression. Take hold of it; for it is your life. Sinners, ye are under the covenant of works, where there is no life, no salvation for you: but the door of the new covenant is opened unto you: come, enter into it without delay. Flee, and make your escape out of the dominion of the law, the covenant of works, ye were born under, and are living under: and that can in no wise be done, but by your accepting and embracing this covenant offered to you in the gospel; to the instating of you personally in it, to all the purposes of life and salvation.

Sinners instated in the covenant by faith or believing.

To clear your way into the covenant, it is necessary to shew, by what means it is that a sinner embraceth and is instated in it, effectually unto salvation. And this, in one word, is by faith, or believing on Jesus Christ: Acts xvi. 31, "Believe on the Lord Jesus Christ, and thou shalt be saved." The covenant of grace is held forth unto you: God saith to every one of you, "I will make an everlasting covenant with you, even the sure mercies of David :" and to close the bargain with you, and state you personally in it, to all intents and purposes of salvation, all that is required of you is to hear, that is, to believe ; "Hear, and your soul shall live," Isa. lv. 3. He that believeth, is within the covenant of grace personally and savingly : he that believeth not, is still under the covenant of works, where the first Adam left him. Faith is the hand whereby one taketh hold of the covenant, signs it for himself, and closeth the bargain for his own salvation. It is the mouth whereby sinners consent to the covenant, that God becomes their God, and they his people. Although while ye are without the covenant, the working of perfect obedience under the pain of the curse is required of you; and more than that, suffering also, even to the satisfaction of justice; and both these, in virtue of the broken first covenant: and when ye are once brought within the covenant, obedience to all the ten commandments, and suffering of the discipline of the covenant in case of your failures, are required of you, in virtue of the new covenant ye are entered into: yet to enter you into the covenant, and instate you in it unto salvation, nothing is required of you, but that ye believe on Christ. Only believe, Mark v. 36, is the constant doctrine of the gospel in this point. Do what you will, and believe not, you remain in a state of damnation: whatever is done, or not done by you, believe, and you are in a state of salvation. If you should say it with your lips a thousand times over, that you accept of the covenant; if you should come under the most solemn and awful bond and engagement to be the Lord's, expressly taking the same upon you in prayer, or otherwise; if you should write your covenant, and subscribe it with your hand; and should take the sacrament of Christ's body and blood upon it, to confirm all: yet if you do not with the heart believe on Jesus Christ, you embrace not the covenant, you miss the saving hold of it, and remain without the saving bond of it. And if you should this moment with the heart believe on Christ, having no access to speak, pray, write, or communicate: yet the moment you believe, you are personally and savingly instated in the covenant, never to fall out of it through the ages of eternity; God is your God, and all the promises of the covenant are yours: though you had missed the gripe of the covenant ten thousand times before: in that case you have it firm and sure: Mark xvi. 16, "He that believeth and is baptized, shall be saved: he that believeth not, shall be damned."

And that believing on Christ should be the appointed means of entering sinners into the covenant of grace, is very agreeable to the nature and end of that great transaction. The which appears by these two considerations following.

1. Hereby the grace of the covenant is preserved entire in the dispensation of the covenant; and by that means the promise is made sure to all the seed, Rom. iv. 16. Faith is contradistinguished to works, as grace is to debt, chap. iv. 4, 5. If any work or doing of ours were that upon which we were instated in the covenant, and got the right in the promises; then the covenant and benefit thereof would be of debt to us, contrary to the declared end and design of that method of salvation, which is to exalt the free grace of God, and to cut off all boasting from us, Eph. ii. 8, 9. But the nature of faith's efficacy in the business is adapted to that end and design of the covenant; in as much as it is a grace, not giving, but purely receiving; taking all freely from Christ, without money, and without price, laying the stress of the soul's acceptance with God wholly on what Christ hath done and suffered; and entirely renouncing all doings and sufferings of our own in that point. And thus the promise is sure to us: for whereas the plea of any work of ours would be a very uncertain one; faith's plea is ever sure and stedfast, as grounded allenarly on what Christ hath wrought.

2. Hereby the sinner's entering into the covenant is by uniting with Christ the representative, with whom it was made as party-contractor; which is the Scipture-account of the matter, John x. 9, "I am the door: by me if any man enter in, he shall he saved:" and so the unity of the covenant, and the representation in it, are preserved. If men entered into the covenant some other way, as by their accepting properly called terms to them proposed, and promising for themselves the performance of them: in that case the representation in the covenant is marred; and there would be in effect as many covenants of grace as there are persons embracing it at different times; at least, Christ's covenant would be one, and ours another distinct therefrom; the contrary of which is before evinced from the Scripture. But the covenant of grace being made with Christ as second Adam, in the name of all such as should be his; it plainly follows, that the only way of one's entering personally into it, must be by becoming his, standing related to the head of the covenant as our head: and it is by faith, and no work, nor consent of ours differing from faith, that we are united to him, and become members of his body, Eph. iii. 17. How do we all enter personally into the covenant of works, so as to partake of the curse in it? Is it not through our becoming, by natural generation, branches of the first Adam, the representative in that covenant? Hereby every one of us is personally entered, and instated in that covenant, before we are capable to approve or disapprove of the same, to consent to it, or dissent from it. Even so we enter personally into the

covenant of grace, so as to partake of the benefits in it, by our becoming branches of the second Adam the representative therein: and that is through faith, in subjects capable of actual believing. It is by being ingrafted into Christ we come to partake of the covenant and benefits thereof. And hence it is, that infants, not capable of actual believing, nor of knowing what the covenant is, yet having the Spirit of faith, are personally entered into it, and instated in it; forasmuch as that Spirit of faith is effectual in them, to a real uniting them with Christ. Hereunto agrees God's giving Christ for a covenant; that in him people may have the covenant, and all the benefits thereof. As God, in making the covenant, took Christ for all, for the condition, and for the parties to receive the promises; he being the second Adam: so sinners, in accepting and embracing of the covenant, are to take him for all; the whole of the covenant, the parties and parts of it too being in him, forasmuch as he is God as well as man, second Adam.

And thus it appears, that uniting with Christ the head of the covenant, is a sinner's formal entering into the covenant: the which uniting with him being by faith on him, it is evident that it is by believing on Christ a sinner embraceth, enters into, and is instated in the covenant unto salvation. Wherefore reach Christ by faith, and ye reach the covenant: if ye miss him, ye miss the covenant, in point of life and salvation. But here ariseth a weighty question, to wit,

QUEST. What is that believing, by which one unites with Jesus Christ, and so enters into the covenant of grace? ANSW. The clearing of this point being so necessary to direct sinners in their way into the covenant, for their eternal salvation; we shall, for what now remains, address ourselves to the consideration thereof only.

And to begin with the word, by which the Holy Ghost expresseth what we call believing, whether in the Old or New Testament; whosoever shall duly consider the import of it, in the scripture-use thereof, will find, that it is just trusting, trusting a word, person, or thing. And hence the scripture-phrases of believing to, and believing in, that is, trusting to, and trusting in; the former, phrases, however unusual with us in conversation, yet ordinary, both in the Old and New Testament, according to the originals. It is the trusting a word, as to a report, Isa. liii. 1. In his words, Psalm cvi. 12. It is the trusting a person; so, in the style of the Holy Ghost, the Israelites believed in the Lord, and in Moses his servant, Exod. xiv. 31. He believed not in his servants, Job iv. 18, that is, as we read it, he put no trust in them. And it is the trusting a thing too: so, in the same style, Job xxxix. 12, " Wilt thou believe in him," to wit, the unicorn, "that he will bring home thy seed?" *i.e.* Wilt thou trust in him, that he will do it? Deut. xxviii. 66, "Thou shalt not believe in thy life;" that is, as we read it, Thou shalt have none assurance of thy life; no trust in it, because no certainty about it. The phraseology is the same in the New Testament, as being brought into it from the Old, only in a different language. And taking the meaning of the Holy Ghost in this matter, from the words which he teacheth, as we are directed, 1 Cor. ii. 13, we conclude, That faith or believing, so expressed by him in the Scripture, is, in the general, trusting, the trusting of a word, and of a person, and thing, held forth in that word.

Now, there is a twofold word to be believed or trusted of all those who would enter into the covenant of grace in a saving manner; namely, the word of the law, and the word of the gospel. The believing of the former is a faith of the law; the believing of the latter, a faith of the gospel: of which in order.

A faith of the Law preparatory for the covenant.

The faith of the law is not indeed saving faith: for the law is the word and ministration of condemnation, and not of righteousness; as speaking nothing of a Saviour, an atonement, or an imputed righteousness, 2 Cor. iii. 9. Nevertheless, it is a necessary antecedent thereof, according to the stated order of the dispensation of the covenant. The faith of the law is like the hearing of the strong wind, the feeling of the earthquake, and seeing of the fire; in which though the Lord was not, yet they served to prepare for hearkening to "the still small voice," in which he was, 1 Kings xix. 11, 12. Accordingly, the faith of the law is the work of the Spirit of God, as well as the saving faith of the gospel; though wrought in a different manner. The former he works as a Spirit of bondage, convincing of sin and misery, by the law, Rom. viii. 15, with John xvi. 8. The latter he works as a quickening Spirit, enlightening the soul in the knowledge of Christ, by the gospel, 2 Cor. iii. 17, 18.

Whosoever then would enter into the covenant of grace, must in the first place have a faith of the law: for which cause, it is necessary, that the law, as well as the gospel be preached unto sinners. And that faith of the law consists in a belief of these three things.

1. By it a man believes that he is a sinner. The holy law pronounceth him guilty: and he believes the report of the law concerning himself in particular; his heavy and sorrowful heart, by this faith, echoing to the voice of the law, guilty, guilty! Rom. iii. 19. The which faith rests not on the testimony of man, whether spoken or written; but is a divine faith, founded upon the testimony

of God, in his holy law, demonstrated by the Spirit of bondage, to be the voice of the eternal God, and the voice of that God to him in particular. And thus he believes, (1.) That his life and conversation is sinful, displeasing and hateful in the sight of a holy God, according to the divine testimony, Rom. iii. 12, "They are all gone out of the way, they are together become unprofitable, there is none that doth good, no not one." He is convinced, that he is gone out of the way of God, and walking in the way of destruction; that the number of his errors of omission and commission he cannot understand; and that all his righteousness, as well as his unrighteousness, are as filthy rags before the Lord. (2.) That his heart is full of mischief and iniquity, according to the divine testimony, Jer. xvii. 9, "The heart is deceitful above all things, and desperately wicked." The law shining into the heart, discovers divers lusts there, which he little noticed before; and pressing the unholy heart, irritates them: and thus such a mystery of iniquity within his breast opens to his view, as he could never before believe to have been there. Rom. vii. 3, "I was alive without the law once: but when the commandment came, sin revived, and I died." (3.) That his nature is quite corrupted, as one dead in trespasses and sins, according to the divine testimony, Eph. ii. 1. To the verdict of the law, "Who can bring a clean thing out of an unclean?" Job xiv. 4, his soul, by this faith, echoes back, unclean, unclean! "I was shapen in iniquity, and in sin did my mother conceive me." He is convinced his disease is hereditary and natural: and that therefore his nature must be renewed: that otherwise, he not only does no good, but can do no good. In all these respects, he believes himself to be an object loathsome in the sight of God; loathsome in his nature, heart, and life.

2. By it a man believes, that he is a lost and undone sinner, under the curse of the law; liable to vengeance, according to the divine testimony, Gal. iii. 10, "Cursed is every one that continueth not in all things written in the book of the law to do them." He can no more look upon the curse as some strange thing, belonging only to some monsters of wickedness, and not to him: for the Spirit of the Lord, as a Spirit of bondage, applies it closely to him; as if he said, thou art the man. And like one under sentence of death pronounced against him, he groans out his belief of it, under the pressure thereof, Luke xv. 17, I perish.

3 *Lastly*, By it a man believes his utter inability to recover himself. He believes, that he cannot, by any doings or sufferings of his, remove the curse of the law from off him; according to the divine testimony of our being without strength in that point, Rom.

v. 6; nor change his own nature, heart, and life, so as to render them acceptable to God; according to the infallible testimony, Jer. xiii. 23, "Can the Ethiopian change his skin, or the leopard his spots? then may ye also do good, that are accustomed to do evil." He is, in his own eyes, as in the sight of God, a spiritually dead man; legally dead, and morally dead, as the apostle testifies of himself in that case, Rom. vii. 9.

This is the faith of the law. And the effect of it is a legal repentance, whereby a sinner is broken and bruised with fear and terror of the wrath of God; grieves and sorroweth for sin, as a ruining and destructive evil; and therefore really desires to be freed from it; despairs of salvation by himself; and seriously looks out for relief another way, Acts ii. 17, and xvi. 29, 30. Thus the law is our schoolmaster to bring us unto Christ; and the faith of the law, makes way for the faith of the gospel. Not that either this legal faith, or legal repentance, is the condition of our welcome to Christ and the covenant of grace: our access to Christ and the covenant is proclaimed free, without any conditions or qualifications required in us, to warrant us sinners of mankind to believe on Jesus Christ, as was shown before. But they are necessary to move and excite us, to make use of our privilege of free access to Christ and the covenant, insomuch that none will come to Christ, nor embrace the covenant, without them in greater or lesser measure. Even as if a physician should cause proclaim, that he will freely cure all the sick of such a place, that will employ him: in which case, it is plain, none will employ him, but such as are sensible of some malady they labour under; yet that sense of a malady is not the condition of their welcome to that physician; nor is it requisite for his curing them, but for their employing him.

Now, in calling you to embrace the covenant, ye are called indirectly, and by consequence, to this faith of the law, namely, to believe that ye are sinners in life, heart, and nature; lost and undone, under the curse; and utterly unable to recover yourselves. Yet it is not saving faith, nor doth it instate one in the covenant of grace; that is peculiar to another kind of believing: of which in the next place.

The faith of the gospel, instating in the covenant.

Saving faith, which unites to Christ, is the faith of the gospel. For the gospel only is the ministration of righteousness 2 Cor. iii. 9. It is in it that the righteousness, of faith is revealed unto faith, revealed to be believed on, Rom. i. 17. It is the alone word which gives sinners the notice of a Saviour, of the atoning blood, and the new covenant in that blood; and therefore is the only word by which saving faith is begotten in the heart of a lost sinner. In the word of the gospel, the Lord and Saviour Christ, with all his benefits and covenant, is; and that to be believed on, as appears from Rom x. 6, 7, 8, 9. So that, the word of the gospel, being received by believing, we have Christ, and his covenant, with all the benefits thereof: saving faith being indeed the echo of the quickened soul, to the word of grace that bringeth salvation; a trusting of the word of the gospel, and the person, to wit, the Saviour, and the thing, therein held forth to us, to be believed on for salvation. Mark. i. 15, "Believe the gospel." Is. liii. 1, "Who hath believed our report?" Gal. iii. 2, "The hearing of faith." This is that believing, by which we are united to Christ, entered into the covenant of grace, and instated therein unto salvation. The which believing may be explained in four particulars; (1.) The faith of Christ's sufficiency; (2.) The faith of the gospel-offer; (3.) The faith of our right to Christ; and, (4.) The faith of particular trust for salvation. So putting the

QUESTION, What is that believing, by which I, a lost sinner, under the curse of the law, may unite with Jesus Christ, and so enter into, and be instated in the covenant of grace, to my eternal salvation? We ANSWER thereto directly in these four particulars, by way of direction in this momentous point, whereon salvation depends.

1. The faith of Christ's Sufficiency.

In the first place, you are to believe, that there is a fulness of salvation in Christ for poor sinners. This is the constant report of the gospel concerning him, Eph. iii. 8, "That I should preach among the Gentiles the unsearchable riches of Christ." Heb. vii. 25, "He is able to save them to the uttermost, that come unto God by him." In the word of the gospel Christ is held forth as an able Saviour; able to save men from their sins, and from the wrath of God. His merit is a sufficient sconce against the tempest of fiery wrath, which incensed justice is ready to cause to fly forth against transgressors: Isa. xxxii. 2, "A man shall be a covert from the tempest." His Spirit is sufficient to sanctify the most unholy: 1 Cor. vi. 11, "And such were some of you: but ye are washed, but ye are sanctified, but ye are justified in the name of the Lord Jesus, and by the Spirit of our God." The righteousness he fulfilled as the condition of the covenant, is so valuable in itself, and in the eyes of his Father, that it is sufficient to procure justification, sanctification, and all other saving benefits to sinners, who in themselves deserve death and damnation: so that they are happy who are in him; they shall never perish, but have everlasting life, being eternally secure under the covert of his righteousness, as a sufficient defence. Believest thou this?

This is the general faith of the gospel, which being without particular application, doth not unite the sinner to Christ, nor enter him into the covenant; and may be found in reprobates and fallen angels, being only an assent in general to the truth of the doctrine of the gospel, Matth. xiii. 20, 31, and viii. 29. But by the nature of the thing, it is necessarily prerequisite to a faith of particular application: for I must first believe a saying to be true in itself, before I can trust to it for my part: I must first believe a thing to be good in itself, before I can believe that it is good for me.

But where the faith of the gospel is carried forward to uniting with Christ, the effect of this general faith is very valuable, as well as necessary. And that is, an high esteem of Christ and his covenant, an ardent desire of union and communion with him, a longing for his righteousness, as a hungry man longs for meat, or a thirsty man for drink. The man sees indeed, that he has no special interest in Christ and his righteousness; but he would fain have it: all is sapless to him without it; his soul within him cries, give me Christ, or else I die: and he is content to part with all for him, and to take him for all. This is taught us in the parables of the treasure hid in the field, and of the pearl of great price, the finding out of which moves to sell all, and to buy them, Matth. xiii. 44, 45, 46.

Howbeit this esteem and desire of Christ is different from that which follows upon the soul's union with Christ, when once faith hath taken possession of him and his benefits, and hath got a view of his intrinsic supereminent worth and value: the which is mentioned, 1 Pet. ii. 7; Psalm lxxiii. 25. The true spring of all this esteem and desire, is the principle of self-preservation, and the view of Christ as suited to that end. The merchant man is seeking goodly pearls for his own enriching; and seeing that the one pearl will answer that design, he is restless till he have it. The poor sinner is hotly pursued with the law's curse, which is still ringing death and damnation in his ears. In the mean time, he gets a distant view of the city of refuge; and therefore he makes forward to it with all speed: but what makes him run, but life, life, precious life, that he may not perish? Verily, he cannot be expected to act from a generous principle, before he is united to Christ: John xv. 5, "Without me ye can do nothing." But let him not fear: he is welcome to Christ, even coming to him from no higher principle. The truth is, the Lord Jesus, by his Spirit, sets the principle of self-preservation astir, being a thing in itself good; and useth it as a mean to hasten sinners unto him. This is evident from the complaint, John

v. 40, "And ye will not come to me, that ye might have life." Can one imagine our Lord will reject a sinner coming to him for life. when he complains that sinners will not come to him for that end?

II. The faith of the gospel-offer.

In the next place, you must believe, that Jesus Christ, with his righteousness, and all his salvation, is by himself offered to sinners, and to you in particular. This is the plain voice of the gospel to all unto whom it comes, Isa. lv. 1, "Ho, every one that thirsteth, come ye to the waters, and he that hath no money; come ye, buy and eat, yea, come, buy wine and milk without money, and without price." Rev. xxii. 17, "Whosoever will, let him take the water of life freely." Prov. viii. 4, "Unto you, O men, I call, and my voice is to the sons of man." But alas! few believe it: yea, none will believe it to purpose till the Spirit of the Lord make it plain to them, and persuade them by an inward illumination. Many secure sinners hear the gospel, and are glad of the offer: but they discern not Christ's voice in it. They hear it not, as the word of the Lord Christ himself to them; but as the word of men: hence it hath no due authority upon their consciences; so they pass it over lightly. Thus were his offers of himself entertained, when made by his own mouth, but he not discerned as the eternal Son of God, and Saviour of the world. So, in the congregation of Nazareth, all bare him witness, and wondered at the gracious words which proceeded out of his mouth. But they said, is not this Joseph's son? Luke iv. 22. And in a little they rose up, and thrust him out of the city, ver. 29. Again, when the voice of Christ is discerned in the offer by the convinced sinner; then the sinner is ready to conclude, that it is to others, but not to him. Unbelief saith, but our bones are dried, and our hope is lost, we are cut off for our parts, Ezek. xxxvii. 11. They cannot believe, that so good news from heaven concerns them, or that such a word is directed unto them. And thus men not believing God in the record given of his Son, that he is, with all his salvation, offered to them, do make him a liar, 1 John v. 10.

But where saving faith is a-working, the word of the gospel-offer is, by the Holy Spirit, applied to the soul in particular with power, as the word of the Lord himself, and not of men; whereby the man is assured, that it is the voice of Christ, and to him in particular: whereupon he applies it to himself by believing: 1 Thess. i. 5, "For our gospel came not unto you in word only, but also in power, and in the Holy Ghost, and in much assurance." Chap. ii. 13, "The word of God, which ye heard of us, ye received it not as the word of men, but (as it is in truth) the word of God, which effectually worketh also in you that believe." This is altogether necessary; insomuch that without it there can be no receiving of Christ, forasmuch as otherwise the soul can see no solid ground and foundation of faith, for it is evident there can be no receiving aright, where the sinner doth not believe the offer to be to him in particular. And here begins the application of faith, an application tending to union with Christ.

Wherefore, if you would unite with Christ, and so enter into the covenant of grace, sist yourselves before the Lord as condemned sinners, under the curse of his law; and hear and believe the word of his gospel, as directed to you condemned and cursed sinners in particular. So will it come unto you, as the rising sun, to one sitting in darkness, and in the shadow of death; or as the offer of a pardon, to one under sentence of death. And let not your heart misgive you by unbelief; but firmly believe the offer to be made by Christ himself unto you, as it is in very deed, Isa. lv. 3, "Hear, and your soul shall live, and I will make an everlasting covenant with you."

But here it is necessary to remove the following objections.

OBJECTION 1. But Christ is now in heaven, and I hear no voice from thence: how then can I believe that he himself is offering himself to me? ANSWER. Though Christ is in heaven, yet he is speaking from heaven to us; howbeit not by a voice sounding through the clouds, yet by a voice sounding in the gospel: Heb. xii. 25, "See that ye refuse not him that speaketh—that speaketh from heaven." And not only is his voice in the word of the gospel, but he himself by his Spirit is in it, as the apostle teacheth, Rom. 6, 7, 8. Thence it is, that it is a quickening word to dead souls: John vi. 63, "The words that I speak unto you, they are spirit, and they are life." It is the lively seed, whereof the new creature is formed, 1 Pet. i. 23. Jesus Christ did once, by a voice sounding through the clouds, speak a word of conviction, Acts ix. 4, 5. But even in that case, the word of the offer of himself was remitted to the preaching of the gospel by a messenger thereto appointed, ver. 6. And the voice of Christ sounding in his written word, is more sure than a voice sounding through the clouds, 2 Pet. i. 18, 19. This voice in the word is the stated ground of faith, with which faith must close for salvation: Rom. i. 16, "The gospel of Christ: it is the power of God unto salvation, to every one that believeth." Ver. 17, "For therein is the righteousness of God revealed from faith to faith." And there is no true saving faith, where it is not received as the very voice of the Lord himself, 1 Thess. ii. 13.

Therefore you must receive the word of the gospel, as the word of Christ himself, as in very deed it is.

Objection 2. But Christ in the word of the gospel doth not name me: how then can I believe that he offereth himself, his righteousness and salvation, to me in particular? Answer. Neither doth he name you in the word of the law, whether in the commands thereof, or in the curse thereof. How do you come to believe that you are a sinner? Is it not, that, the commands of the law being directed to all men, you conclude and believe, that, you being of the number of mankind, they are therefore directed to you in particular, as well as to others? And how come you to believe that you in particular are under the curse of the broken law? Is it not, that, since the law denounceth its curse against every one that, being under it, breaks it, Gal. iii. 10; Rom. iii. 19, you do conclude and believe, that it curseth you, forasmuch as you are one of these breakers thereof? Now, you have as sufficient ground to believe that the offer of the gospel is to you in particular; forasmuch as it is made to all, without exception, unto whom the gospel comes, Rev. xxii. 17; Isa. lv. 1. It is ordered to be made to every creature under heaven, Mark xvi. 15: and how sinful soever you are, you are one of these creatures. Christ's voice is unto men, sons of men: and be what you will, you are one of mankind-sinners: and therefore the offer is to you in particular, Prov. viii. 4. Accordingly, we are warranted to apply the general offer to every one in particular; and every one is warranted to apply it to himself: Acts xvi. 31, "Believe on the Lord Jesus Christ, and thou shalt be saved."

Objection 3. But alas! I fear I want the qualifications determinative of those to whom the gospel offer is particularly directed. I dread that I have not as yet got a due sense of sin: and our Lord says expressly, "They that be whole need not a physician, but they that are sick. I am not come to call the righteous, but sinners to repentance," Matth. ix. 12, 13. The gospel-offer runs in these terms, "Ho, every one that thirsteth, come," Isa. lv. 1, "Come unto me, all ye that labour and are heavy laden," Matth. xi. 28, "Whosoever will, let him take the water of life freely," Rev. xxii. 17. But when I view my own condition, I very much fear I have not as yet reached that thirst after Christ, and that willingness to take him, which these texts speak of; and that I cannot be accounted one truly labouring and heavy laden: how then can I believe that Christ offers himself to me in particular? Answer. It is most certain truth, that, unless you have a due sense of sin, unless you thirst after Christ and his righteousness, unless you be heavy laden with the felt burden of sin, and willing to take Christ on any terms, you will never take him by a true faith. Nevertheless, whatever qualifications you have, or have not; yet if you are a sinner of Adam's race, (and I hope you doubt not that), Christ is offered to you, together with his righteousness, and all his salvation, Prov. viii. 4; John iii. 16; Mark xvi. 15. For howbeit there are indeed certain qualifications necessary to move you to take Christ; yet there are none at all to hamper the gospel-offer: but Christ is really offered to you, be in what case you will; so really, that if you do not believe it, and thereupon receive an offered Saviour, you will be damned for not believing, Mark xvi. 16.

It is undeniable, the less that sinners are sensible of their sins, they are the farther from righteousness; they do the more need Christ, and are the more to be called to repentance. This is evident from the whole tenor of the holy Scripture, and from the very nature of the thing. And therefore it is sinners in the general, and not sensible sinners only, who are meant, Matth. ix. 12, 13. Even as it is sick people in general, comprehending even those of them who are so delirious, as to think nothing ails them, that need a physician; and not those sick only, who are sensible of their state and hazard. This is the plain literal sense of that passage, from which there is no necessity to depart: and the departing from it is attended with a manifest inconvenience.

Neither is the thirst mentioned, Isa. lv. 1, to be restricted to a gracious thirst, a thirst after Christ and his righteousness. For some at least of the thirsting ones, to whom the offer is there made, are "spending money for that which is not bread, and their labour for that which satisfieth not," vers. 1, 2. But it is evident, that sinners duly sensible, who are thirsting after Christ and his righteousness, are not spending their money and labour at that rate; but, on the contrary, for that which alone is bread, and satisfieth, namely, Jesus Christ the true bread which came down from heaven. Wherefore the thirst there meant, must needs comprehend, yea, and principally aim at, that thirst after happiness and satisfaction, which being natural, is common to all mankind. Men pained with this thirst do naturally run, for quenching thereof, to the empty creation, and their fulsome lusts: and so they "spend money for that which is not bread, and their labour for that which satisfieth not;" finding nothing there that can satisfy that their appetite or thirst. Now, to men in this wretched case is the gospel-offer of the waters of life made: Christ is offered to them, as bread, fatness, what is good, and will satisfy that their painful thirst, which otherwise will never be quenched, *ibid.*

And as little is the solemn gospel-offer, Matth. xi. 28, restricted to a certain set of men endowed with some laudable qualifications, going under the name of labouring, and being heavy laden; the which do indeed denote the restlessness natural to the sinful soul of man, spending its labour for that which satisfieth not, Isa. lv. 2. Our father Adam left his whole family with a conscience full of guilt, and a heart full of unsatisfied desires. Thus we naturally having a restless conscience, and a restless heart, the soul as naturally falls a labouring for rest to them. And it labours in the barren region of the fiery law, for a rest to the conscience; and in the empty creation, for a rest to the heart. But after all, the conscience is still heavy laden with guilt, whether it has any lively feeling thereof, or not; and the heart is still under a load of unsatisfied desires. So neither the one, nor the other, can find rest indeed. This is the natural case of all men. And to souls thus labouring and laden, Jesus Christ calls, that they may come to him, and he will give them rest; namely, a rest for their consciences, under the covert of his blood; and a rest to their hearts, in the enjoyment of God through him. To this interpretation we are led by the style of the Scripture, the phraseology of the Holy Ghost, both in the Old and New Testament; the which may be viewed in the following texts compared, to wit, Eccl. x. 15; Hab. ii. 13; Isa. lv. 2, and i. 3, 4; 2 Tim. iii. 6, 7.

Finally, as for the willingness which you are afraid you are defective in, surely, in all other cases, he that saith, Whosoever will, let him take such a thing, will, according to the common sense and understanding of such words amongst mankind, be reckoned to offer that thing unto all, and to exclude none from it; however it may bear an intimation, that it is not to be forced on any. Why then should this manner of speech, Rev. xxii. 17, be thought to limit the gospel-offer to a certain set of men?

Wherefore we conclude, that Christ lays no bar in the way of any of you: do not ye put bars in your own way, and then complain ye cannot get over them. For, according to the holy Scripture, it is infallible truth, that Christ is offered to you, and every one of you, in particular: believe it, else ye make God a liar, 1 John v. 10.

III. The faith of our right to Christ.

Furthermore, you must believe that Jesus Christ is the Saviour of the world, and your Saviour in particular, by his Father's appointment, and his own offer: and that, by the same appointment and offer, his righteousness, the condition of the covenant, and eternal life, the promise of the covenant are yours; yours, I mean not, in possession, but, in right thereto; so far as that you may lawfully and warrantably take possession of the same, and use them as your own to all intents and purposes of salvation, John iv. 42, "We know that this is indeed the Christ, the Saviour of the world." 2 Sam. xxii. 3; and Luke i. 47, "my Saviour." Do not think this too much for you: it is no more than what is necessary to saving faith in Christ. If you believe only, in the general, that Christ is the Saviour of the world, but believe not that he is your Saviour in particular; what do you believe more than devils do? They believe him to be Jesus a Saviour, Mark i. 24. If you would go beyond them, you must believe he is your Saviour; and consequently, that his righteousness and salvation are yours, in the sense before opened: for where Christ is given, with him are freely given all things. And pray consider, how can ye take him or receive him as your Saviour, if he is not yours indeed? A man may fraudulently take possession of what he doth not believe to be his by right: but no man can fairly and honestly claim and take possession of what he doth not believe to be his own. Certainly, God must first give Christ us, before we can receive him: for "a man can receive nothing, except it be given him from heaven," John iii. 27. Giving on God's part, and receiving on ours, here, are corelates: and the former is the foundation of the latter. Now, God's gift is sufficient to make a thing ours. Therefore believe firmly, that Christ is your Saviour in particular; that his righteousness is yours, and eternal life yours.

Question. But how can I, a poor sinner, by nature under the curse, believe that Christ is my Saviour, that his righteousness, and eternal life, are mine? Answer. You may firmly believe it, because you have the word and testimony of the eternal God upon it, in his holy Gospel. What is the gospel, which the apostles were sent, in the name of God, to *testify*? The apostle John declares it, 1 John iv. 14, "We *testify*, that the Father sent the Son to be the Saviour of the world." Is not Jesus Christ then, by office, whatever he is in the event, Saviour of the world? and if he is so, and you are one of that world of mankind, is he not therefore your Saviour? Why then will ye not believe it? God set the sun in the heavens to be a light to the world: and do not you therefore judge, that you have a right to the light of that sun, as well as the rest of mankind; and accordingly use it freely, to work or read by it, as your own by God's free gift? Jesus Christ also is the light of the world, John viii. 12; given for a light to the Gentiles, Is. xlix. 6.: and faith appropriates him, saying, The Lord is my light, and my salvation, Psalm xxvii. 1. Now, you are a member of these societies, to wit, the world, and the Gentiles: therefore he is your light, that is, given for a light to you. Will you take Christ's own word upon it? You have it John vi. 32, "My Father giveth you the true bread from heaven." If your neighbour give you bread, you will reckon his gift thereof sufficient to make it yours; and so eat of it freely as your own. If your prince shall give you a house or land, which he hath an unquestionable right to dispose of, you would reckon them truly yours by his gift; and would freely go and dwell in that house. and possess that land, as your own. How is it then, that when the Father gives you his Christ, yet you will not believe that he is yours, nor take possession of him as your own? Why, the truth of the matter lies here: you believe your neighbour, you believe your prince; but you believe not your God, in his holy gospel, but make him a liar, not believing the record that God gave of his Son, 1 John v. 10. But, whether you will believe it or not, it is a truth, that Christ is your Saviour: and if you will not believe it now, to your salvation, you will undoubtedly see your mistake hereafter; when perishing, you will be convinced that you perish, not because you had not a Saviour, but because you neglected to make use of him.

In like manner, the righteousness of Christ is yours, namely, that which he fulfilled as the condition of the covenant. It is yours by Heaven's gift, being given you with himself: and therefore it is called the gift of righteousness, Rom. v. 17. It is a testamentary gift, made over to you in Christ's testament, wherein sinners of mankind, without exception, are the legatees, as hath been already cleared. Eternal life is another such gift or legacy: so it is yours too. And you have the record, testimony or witness, of God himself upon it, that it is given you, 1 John v. 11, "And this is the record, that God hath given to us eternal life: and this life is in his Son." Is not God's own record a sufficient ground for believing? will you venture to disbelieve it on any pretence whatsoever? Here you have that record, namely, that God hath given to us eternal life. It may be you will imagine that it relates only to actual believers in Christ, or at most to the elect; and use that for a defence of your unbelief. But, I pray you, consider it is the ground and warrant for all to believe on Christ, and to lay hold on eternal life in him; being the witness of God, which he hath testified of his Son, to be received by all to whom the gospel comes, ver. 9: but that God hath given eternal life to a certain select set of men, can never, in reason, be deemed to be a warrant for all men to believe. Moreover, the great sin of unbelief lies in not believing this record: but it doth not lie in not believing that God hath given eternal life to actual believers, or to the elect; for the most desperate unbelievers believe that, insomuch that their belief of it adds to their torment; but it lies in their not believing, that to mankind sinners, and to themselves in particular, God hath given eternal life. This is what flies in the face of the gospel of God, which is the proclaimed deed of the gift and grant of Christ and all his benefits, to sinners of mankind, declaring the grant thereof to be made them, and calling them to take possession of the same as their own, Isa. ix. 6, "Unto us a child is born," (the word signifies presented born, as to his relations having a particular interest in him; as Machir's children were presented to Joseph, and laid on his knees, Gen. l. 23, and Ruth's son to Naomi, Ruth. iv. 17.), "unto us a son is given." John iii. 16, "God so loved the world, that he gave his only begotten Son, that whosoever believeth in him, should not perish, but have everlasting life." 1 Cor. i. 30. Christ Jesus, who of God is made unto us (namely, by legal destination) wisdom, righteousness, sanctification, and redemption.

And thus you see you have an infallible ground for this act of faith, namely, the testimony of God that cannot lie. Wherefore, as ever you would be united to Christ, and so instated in the covenant, believe firmly that Christ is yours, and his righteousness yours, and eternal life in him yours.

This is a more close application of faith than the former, and ariseth from it; for thus one believeth the efficacy of the divine appointment, and of the gospel-offer. If God appoints Christ a Saviour to you, with his righteousness and eternal life, and Christ offers himself to you accordingly; surely the effect of that appointment and offer must be, that they are indeed yours, to be used by you, as your own, for your salvation. If you believe that appointment of the Father, and the Son's offer, you must needs believe this: for if they be real, and not ludicrous deeds, they certainly convey to you a right to Christ, his righteousness and salvation: so that, in virtue of them, these must be yours, to be warrantably claimed and used by you as your own, for the purposes of salvation. It is not doubted, but men's deeds of gift, and their offers, real and not ludicrous, do convey such a right to the parties in favour of whom they are made. If a friend of yours, having a sum of money lying in a neighbour's hand, should, especially by a deed in writing under his own hand, appoint and ordain that sum a gift to you, to relieve you out of a certain strait; you would make no question but you might go and claim it, and take it up: if, having the sum in his own hand, he should offer it to you, as a gift, you would make no question but you might take it to you; and, in both cases, use it as your own by your friend's appointment or offer. And shall not the Father's ordinances and appointment, and Christ's offer, be as efficacious? Why then will you not believe this its efficacy? why will ye not believe, that Christ with his righteousness and eternal life are yours?

Truly, the believing hereof is the very next step to the soul's uniting with Christ: and therefore it is proposed to the sinner, as the nearest means to bring him close unto God in Christ, Hos. xiv. 1, "Return unto the Lord thy God," he is thy God, thou hast a right to him, return, come even to him, take possession of him as thine own God: Accordingly, the sinner coming unto him by faith, comes on this very ground, Jer. iii. 22, "Behold, we come unto thee, for thou art the Lord our God." Ver. 23, "Truly in the Lord our God is the salvation of Israel." As Hagar's eyes were seasonably opened to see she had a well by her, when she had given up her son for dead; so when the sinner lies in his death's wounds from the law, in a work of conviction, the spirit of faith opens his eyes, by means of the glorious gospel, in a work of saving illumination, so that he sees he hath a Saviour, a righteousness, and salvation. And then he presently apprehends or grips the same as his own. Thus the prodigal first believed that he had yet a father, and a father's house, where there is enough and to spare; and then ariseth and goeth to him, Luke xv. 17, 18.

Objection 1. If it be true, that Christ is my Saviour, that his righteousness, and eternal life in him, are mine; then I may be easy, I will certainly be saved without any more ado. Answ. That is but a cavil, best suiting those who, being indifferent about Christ and salvation, think it not worth their pains seriously to consider such things. One truly impressed with the matter, and duly considering, being once brought to believe this, would rather say, "Then, since Christ is really my Saviour, his righteousness and eternal life mine; I will take him to me, I will receive and rest on him as my Saviour, I will rely on his righteousness, and look for eternal life in him: why should I be lost for ever, since I have a full Saviour? why should I go naked, since I have a complete righteousness made over to me by heaven's gift? why should I die, when I have eternal life in Christ?" Put the case, you did see a man at the point of starving for want of bread; and, out of kindness and pity to him, you should appoint and ordain meat for him, out of your own store, for preservation of his life; and withal should carry it to him, and set it before him, saying, Ha, there is meat I and my father have ordained for you, eat, and welcome. If that man should say, Oh! I may not take it, for it is not mine own; would you not tell him, that your gift, appointment, and offer of it to him, makes it his, so that, with a good conscience, he may freely eat it as his own bread? But should he then reply, and say, Why then, if it is mine, without any more ado I am secured from starving; I need not at all be at pains to take and eat it; would you not reckon him either mad, or but jesting with you, not sensible of his hazard of starving? The application is obvious. It is not meat being one's own, so that he may use it freely as such, that will keep him from starving: he must take and eat it, and so use it as his own, if he would have that benefit by it. Even so it is not Christ being yours, with his righteousness and salvation, that will save you: you must take possession of him, and make use of him as your own, for salvation, if you would be actually saved by him. There is a wide difference betwixt a thing being ours in simple right thereto, and its being ours in possession. It is in the former way only that Christ is yours before uniting with him: and if you do not improve that, by receiving him, and taking possession, you will perish eternally for all it: Heb. iv. 1, "Let us therefore fear, lest a promise being left us of entering into his rest, any of you should seem to come short of it." Luke xvi. 12, "If ye have not been faithful in that which is another man's, who shall give you that which is your own?"

Objection 2. But Christ a Saviour, his perfect righteousness, and eternal life, are things so exceeding great and precious, and I am so very sinful and unworthy, that it is mighty hard for me to believe they are mine. Answ. Yea, here indeed lies a great difficulty of believing; when once a sinner's eyes are opened, to see the transcendent excellency of Christ, the exceeding sinfulness of sin, and his own utter unworthiness: a difficulty not to be surmounted, but by the effectual operation of the Spirit of faith, causing one to believe, according to the working of his mighty power, Eph. i. 19. But for your help consider they are yours by mere free gift; which is so far from requiring any work in the creature, that it excludes all respect thereto. Christ himself is the Father's gift to you, John iv. 10, and vi. 32. His righteousness is a gift too, Rom. v. 17. And so is eternal life in him, 1 John v. 11. Now, what is freer than a gift? And then, howbeit they are indeed a gift far beyond whatever you could have expected, yet they are not too great for an infinite God to give. In making this gift, he acted not according to the dignity of the party in whose favour it was made; but according to himself, his own greatness and majesty. Meanwhile, though the gift is quite above your dignity, yet it is no more than what your need required. If less could have answered your necessity, there is no ground to think, a crucified Christ, the Son of God, would have been prepared for you. If you do but suppose it, you mar that expression of matchless love, John iii. 16, "God so loved the world that he gave his only begotten Son." Wherefore, argue with yourself in this manner: "The gift is indeed unspeakable, but no less can serve my need; if Christ be not mine, I must perish: since therefore God hath said it, that he hath given me Christ; and the gift is not above him to give, and no less can serve my turn; I must and will believe that he is mine, with his righteousness and salvation."

IV. The faith of particular trust for salvation.

Finally, You must wholly trust on him as your Saviour, and in his righteousness as made over to you; and that for his whole salvation to you in particular, upon the ground of God's faithfulness in his word. And this is that saving faith, or believing on Christ Jesus, by which a sinner is united to him, and personally entered within the covenant of grace unto salvation: Acts xvi. 31, "Believe on the Lord Jesus Christ, and thou shalt be saved." Psalm ii. 12, "Kiss the Son lest he be angry, and ye perish:—blessed are all they that put their trust in him." And Psalm xxxvii. 40, "He shall save them, because they trust in him." Rom. xv. 12, "In him shall the Gentiles trust." Compare Isa. xi. 10; Rom. i. 17, "Therein is the righteousness of God revealed from faith to faith;" or, "Therein is the righteousness of God by faith, revealed unto faith," to wit, to be believed or trusted on. See Philip. iii. 9: Gal. ii. 16, "We have believed in Jesus Christ, that we might be justified." Acts xv. 11, "We believe, that, through the grace of the Lord Jesus Christ, we shall be saved." 1 Thess. ii. 13, "Ye received it not as the word of men, but (as it is in truth) the word of God." 1 Cor. ii. 5, "That your faith should not stand in the wisdom of men, but in the power of God." This, according to the scripture, is a sinner's receiving and resting upon Christ for salvation, as saving faith is defined in our Catechism: and this is indeed believing, and nothing but believing, according to the scriptural use of that word.

1. I say, this is the scriptural receiving and resting on Christ. It is the receiving of him in sense of the holy Scripture: John i. 12, "As many as received him, to them gave he power to become the sons of God, even to them that believe on his name;" where the receiving of Christ is explained by believing on his name. God hath appointed Christ Saviour of the world, and your Saviour. You hear the same published in the gospel; and you accordingly believe that he is your Saviour by his Father's appointment, and his own

offer; hereupon you trust on him, and on him alone, for salvation, and all that you need for your salvation. Is not this a receiving of him for your part in the character of a Saviour, wherein his Father sent him forth to you? Is it not a taking of him to yourself, as offered to you? Our Lord complains of the Jews, John v. 43, that whereas he came in his Father's name, they received him not, to wit, in the character wherein he was sent, namely, as the Messias, the Saviour of the world, and their Saviour, trusting in him that he would save them. This plainly appears to be the meaning, if one compares herewith the words there immediately following: "If another shall come in his own name, him will ye receive:" *q. d.* Ye will believe him to be the Messias, and your Saviour, and trust on him accordingly, that he will save you; the which has been often verified in that unbelieving people. Moreover, this is resting on Christ in the scripture-sense of that manner of expression: Isa. xxvi. 3, "Thou wilt keep him in perfect peace, whose mind is stayed on thee: because he trusteth in thee." And indeed one cannot devise what way a person can rest on a word, or a soul or spirit can rest upon a person, but by trusting them, or trusting in or on them. It is said, 2 Chron xxxii. 8, "The people rested themselves upon the words of Hezekiah." What way can one imagine they did so, but by trusting them? Chap. xiv. 11, "Help us, O Lord our God; for we rest on thee." How could they do so, but by trusting on him for their help?

2. This is believing, in the scriptural use of that word, which, in our entry on the question under consideration, we established from the scripture itself. For it is a trusting of, or trusting in a person, namely, Jesus Christ, and God in him, the personal object of saving faith, Acts xvi. 31; a trusting in a thing, namely, the righteousness of Christ, the ultimate real object of faith, Rom. i. 17; and a trusting in a word, namely, the record and testimony of God, the word of the promise of the gospel, the proximate or nearest real object of faith, *ibid.;* and all this for the great purpose of salvation. And then it is nothing but such believing: for thus faith is not explained away into, but is a thing quite distinct from the nature of a work, as the scripture contradistinguisheth works to faith.

Wherefore we conclude, that this trust is that believing on Christ, by which the soul is united to him, and savingly instated in the covenant. And for opening of it, we shall take notice of these five things plainly imported in it.

1. This trust imports, not only a willingness, but a sincere and honest desire to be delivered from sin and wrath; a desire to be sanctified, as well as to be justified; to be delivered from the reign-

ing power, pollution, practice, and inbeing of sin, as well as from the guilt of it; according to that of the apostle, Rom. vii. 24, 25, "Who shall deliver me from the body of this death; I thank God, through Jesus Christ our Lord." For it is a trusting on Christ, not for the half of his salvation, to wit, salvation from wrath only, which is all the trust of many, being by no means desirous to part with sin; but for the whole of it, namely, salvation from wrath, and salvation from sin too, which is the principal part thereof, Matth. i. 21. Now, a man may indeed fear that from one, which he doth not desire: but no body trusts in one for what he desires not. Faith is a believing with the heart, Rom. x. 10. The whole salvation of Christ is the believer's choice; it is the end he desires to compass: and the trust of faith is exerted as the means to compass that end.

2. A renouncing of all confidence in all that is not Christ, or in Christ, as to the matter of salvation particularly. In this trust is overturned self-confidence, law-confidence, creature-confidence; and the soul builds on a quite new ground: Phil. iii. 3, "We rejoice in Christ Jesus, and have no confidence in the flesh." Jer. xvi. 19, "The Gentiles shall come unto thee, and shall say, surely our fathers have inherited lies, vanity, and things wherein there is no profit." For it is a trusting wholly on Christ and his righteousness, a trusting, or a believing with all the heart, Prov. iii. 5; Acts viii. 37. At this rate the believer is carried off from the works of the law, to the blood of Jesus, for his justification; and carried out of himself too, unto the Spirit of holiness in Christ, for his sanctification: being persuaded, that no doing nor suffering of his own, can procure him the pardon of, or atone for the least of his guilt; and that he is not able truly to mortify one lust, more so as to purge away the guilt of one sin, Matth. v. 3; Isa. xlv. 24.

3. A hearty approbation of the plan or device of salvation according to the covenant, manifested in the gospel, as suited to the divine perfections, and to the case of sinners, and their own in particular: 1 Cor. i. 23, "We preach Christ crucified, unto the Jews a stumbling-block, and unto the Greeks foolishness;" ver. 24, "But unto them which are called, both Jews and Greeks, Christ the power of God, and the wisdom of God." Without this, no man knowing what God is, what sin is, and what is the worth of his own soul, will ever venture his salvation upon it; but one's trusting his salvation and his righteousness, speaks him to be well pleased therewith, as what one may safely trust to, even in the sight of a holy God. And this is that rejoicing in Christ Jesus, which makes an illustrious mark in the believer's character, Phil. iii. 3.

Withal it bears three things. (1.) An eying of Christ in this matter, as a crucified Saviour, who hath fulfilled all righteousness, according to the stated condition of the covenant, 1 Cor. ii. 2. It is not Christ in the eternal glory he had with his Father before the world was; that faith fixeth its view on, while the soul in this case stands trembling before a holy God; but Christ the Son of God made man, come in the flesh, being born holy, leading a life perfectly righteous, and at last dying on the cross, to satisfy the demands which the law had on poor sinners. It looks unto him lifted up on the cross, as those who were bitten by the serpents in the wilderness looked unto the brazen serpent lifted up on the pole, Isa. xlv. 22; Numb. xxi. 8; John iii. 14, 15. Therefore it is called faith in his blood, Rom. iii. 25, his righteousness, whereof the shedding of his blood was the completing part, being the spring of the believer's hope. (2.) A real persuasion of the sufficiency of Christ's righteousness to save sinners, and us in particular, from sin and wrath; to answer for us before a holy just God, in the eye of his holy law; and to procure for us eternal holiness and happiness. There is no saving faith without this: Christ's ability to save must be believed, and that with application to your own case in particular, Matth. ix. 28, "Believe ye that I am able to do this?" And in order hereunto, faith eyes Christ's righteousness as the righteousness of God, and therefore of infinite value and efficacy, Phil. iii. 9; 1 John i. 7. The reason why the gospel, and no other doctrine whatsoever, is the power of God unto salvation of sinners, is, because therein is revealed the righteousness of God unto faith, Rom. i. 16, 17, and that is the only righteousness, suited at once to the divine perfections and our case. (3.) An acquiescing in that way of salvation, for ourselves in particular. The believer hath a cordial liking of it, for the way of his salvation, as perfectly safe, being the power of God, and the wisdom of God, 1 Cor. i. 24. His soul pronounceth them safe and happy, that are in it, he desires for his own part to be found in it; and is persuaded he would be saved if he were in it. Thus faith acted in the woman diseased with an issue of blood, Matth. ix. 21, "She said within herself, if I may but touch his garment, I shall be whole." And thus it acteth in all believers, determining them to that way, and to that way alone, for their case in particular. And here unbelievers are always unsettled.

4. A betaking one's self unto Christ and his righteousness alone for salvation from sin and wrath. This is done by this trusting. For the sinner believing that Christ is his Saviour, and that his righteousness is made over to him by free gift; and withal, that this his Saviour, with his righteousness, is sufficient to save him from sin and wrath; doth accordingly trust on Christ and his righteousness

for his own salvation, and so betake himself thereto: even as a beggar once having, and withal believing himself to have riches and wealth made over to him by a friend, leaves off to beg, and for his maintenance trusts to that wealth allenarly; and thereupon betakes himself to it. It is true, that wealth being a corporal thing, to which there is a bodily motion, the betaking one's self thereto is not the same thing with the trusting to it; howbeit the former is a native consequent of the latter: but Christ and his righteousness, as revealed unto faith, being things purely spiritual, to which there is no bodily motion requisite, that we may betake ourselves to them; the trusting and betaking one's self thereto, are one and the same. So by this trust, the soul takes possession of Christ and his righteousness; and useth the same as its own, to the purpose of salvation. By it the sinner betakes himself as a condemned man, unto Jesus Christ as the propitiatory mercy-seat through his blood, affording safety to the guilty before a holy God: and by it the sinner betakes himself as a sick man, unto the same Jesus as the physician of souls having the fulness of the Spirit of sanctification in him, to be communicated. Accordingly faith is called a coming to Christ, John vi. 35; a fleeing for refuge, as one in hazard of his life by a pursuer, Heb. vi. 18; and is often expressed, as Psalm ii. 12, by a word which properly signifies, to retire as into a shadow, Judg. ix. 15, or as the chickens do under the wings of the hen, Ruth ii. 12, "The Lord God of Israel, under whose wings thou art come to trust;" properly to retire. Compare Matth. xxiii. 37, "How often would I have gathered thy children together, even as a hen gathereth her chickens under her wings!"

5. *Lastly*, This trust of faith imports an affiance, confidence, or trust on Christ and his righteousness, that he will save us from sin and wrath, according to his promise set before us in the gospel; "Whosoever believeth in him, shall not perish, but have everlasting life." Isa. xxv. 9, "We have waited for him, and he will save us." Heb. iii. 6, "Whose house are we, if we hold fast the confidence." Isa. l. 10, "Let him trust in the name of the Lord, and stay upon his God." And that this trust of faith is thus particular, is evident also from the nature of the thing. For whosoever trusts in a person for any thing, hath a persuasion of the same degree of firmness with the trust, that that person will do that thing for him. And for a sure token of this, where the party trusted fails, the party trusting is ashamed and confounded; as being disappointed in that which he trusted he would do for him. Wherefore, since the trust of faith is never disappointed, the scripture doth therefore assure us, that he that believeth on him shall

not be confounded, 1 Pet. ii. 6. nor ashamed, Rom. x. 11. The which doth sufficiently intimate, that he that believeth on Jesus Christ for salvation, doth trust that he will save him: otherwise there could be no place for his being confounded or ashamed whatever should be the event of his trust. Accordingly the trust of faith doth, in proportion to the firmness thereof, establish and fix the heart, Psalm cxii. 7, "His heart is fixed, trusting in the Lord:" and hereof we have a plain instance in Paul's case, 2 Tim. i. 12, "I am not ashamed, for I know whom I have believed," marg. or trusted. Agreeable hereunto, faith is called in effect a building on Christ, as upon a foundation that will bear our weight, Isa. xxviii. 16, with 1 Pet. ii. 6. It is called a leaning upon him, Cant. viii. 5; a staying on him, Isa. xxvi. 3; a resting or relying on him, 2 Chron. xiv. 11, and xvi. 8. as upon one that will bear us up; a looking unto him, Isa. xlv. 22, having our eyes upon him, 2 Chron. xx. 12, as one from whom we look for life and salvation; and finally, believing on him, 1 Pet. ii. 6, as one by whom we shall be saved, Acts xv. 11.

The sinner being shaken out of all confidence for life and salvation in other things, stays himself by faith on Jesus Christ and his righteousness; trusting on him, that he shall have life and salvation through his righteousness. It is true, indeed, this particular trust and confidence may be assaulted with many doubts and fears: but these are things that faith hath to conflict with, as its opposites; and the stronger that faith is, the less they prevail; the weaker it is, they prevail the more: Matt. xiv. 31, "O thou of little faith, wherefore didst thou doubt?" It is indeed of very different degrees in different persons, and in one and the same person at different times: but if you remove all trust and confidence in Christ for one's own salvation, from faith, the very nature and essence of it is destroyed. For at that rate, the sinner, whose confidence in the flesh for his salvation is razed, having no confidence for it in Christ neither, is left quite unsettled and wavering, like a wave of the sea, or a reed in the water: and where then is faith's building, leaning, staying, relying and resting the soul on Christ? James i. 6, "Let him ask in faith, nothing wavering: for he that wavereth is like a wave of the sea, driven with the wind, and tossed." Ver. 7, "For let not that man think that he shall receive any thing of the Lord." But the believing sinner, finding his confidence in the flesh razed, doth, by believing, cast the anchor of his trust and confidence on Christ Jesus and his righteousness, confiding and trusting that he will save him. And however he may indeed waver in that matter; being tossed with doubts and fears about his salvation, weakening the actings of that his confidence; and sometimes prevailing so far, as to cause an intermitting of the exercise thereof: yet, even in that case, under all that tossing, he doth not waver like a wave of the sea, that hath nothing to fix it; but only like a ship at anchor. His confidence is never quite rooted out, as to the habit thereof; but will again exert itself: and in that respect every believer, as a real "partaker of Christ, holds the beginning of his confidence stedfast unto the end," Heb. iii. 14. And this trust and confidence is what our reformers called assurance, and described faith by.

Objection 1. Since it is not true of all who hear the gospel, that they shall be saved; there cannot be, in the case of every one of them, a ground on which this particular trust may be warrantably founded. Answer. All and every one of them, notwithstanding that, have a solid ground for it, even for trusting on Christ and his righteousness for their own salvation in particular. And that is the record and testimony of God in his gospel, that "whosoever believeth in him shall not perish, but have everlasting life," John iii. 16. The true sense of which, as appears from what is said, is, that whosoever shall have this trust and confidence in Christ, shall not be disappointed, but shall certainly be saved. Here then is the faithfulness of God in his word, for the foundation of this faith of particular trust: and true faith is always built on that foundation. It is certain indeed, that, in the event, many to whom the gospel comes will not be saved: but then, it is as certain, that those who will not be saved, will not believe neither; that is, they will not come up to this particular trust and confidence, we have described from the word, Isa. liii. 1, "Who hath believed our report? and to whom is the arm of the Lord revealed?" Howbeit, at this rate they have a firm ground of particular confidence. If they will not believe for all this, their ruin is of themselves, they will perish without excuse: and their unbelief will be the great ground of their condemnation. Jesus Christ, with his righteousness and salvation, is so far made theirs, by the Father's appointment, and his own offer, that they may lawfully and warrantably trust on him as their Saviour, each one for his own salvation. If they will not believe it, or not trust on him accordingly; they do, by their unbelief and distrust, dishonour the Father and his Son, and most justly perish.

Objection 2. Many trust in Christ as their Saviour, with a particular confidence that he will save them; and yet are grossly ignorant, profane, or formal hypocrites; and therefore not true believers, nor united to Christ. Answer. The apostle speaking of faith unfeigned, 1 Tim. i. 5, doth suppose that there is a feigned faith.

And indeed such trusters in Christ have it: but as for this trust which we have described from the word, it is as certain they have it not, as it is certain that true faith purifies the heart, Acts xv. 9, and truly sanctifies, chap. xxvi. 18. As such trusters say, that they receive Christ, and rest on him alone for salvation, embrace, accept, and consent to him in the gospel-offer: even so they say, that they trust on him. But this trust on him they really have not. For, first, They trust not on him for his whole salvation; nay, as for the chief part thereof, to wit, salvation from sin, they are by no means reconciled thereto: wherefore it may well be an object of their fears and aversion; but it cannot be an object of their trust. *Secondly*, They trust not on him alone for the salvation they really desire: they do not trust on him with all their heart; but partly to him, and partly to their own doings and sufferings, betwixt which and the Saviour their heart is divided. This is clear from Matth. v. 3, "Blessed are the poor in spirit: for theirs is the kingdom of heaven." *Lastly*, Their trust is not grounded on the faithfulness of God in the free promise of the gospel; but reared up on some one or other sandy foundation: Isa. liii. 1, "Who hath believed our report?" Matth. vii. 26, "Every one that heareth these sayings of mine, and doth them not, shall be likened unto a foolish man which built his house upon the sand."

And thus have we shown, what is that faith or believing by which a sinner unites with Jesus Christ, and so enters savingly into the covenant of grace. Why God hath appointed it to be the means of union with Christ, may be learned from Rom. iv. 16, "Therefore it is of faith, that it might be by grace;" of which before. Here I shall only observe, that this trusting wholly on Christ and his righteousness for his whole salvation, is an apt means or instrument of union, betwixt Christ the party trusted, and the soul trusting on him; forasmuch as the soul is therein so carried forth unto him, that from that moment it is thereby, as it were, wholly to stand or fall with him; as the superstructure with the foundation; the leaner with the leaning-stock; the thing relying, resting, staying upon another thing, with the stay or base on which it is laid. Wherefore, the object of faith being infallible, they that thus trust in the Lord, shall be as mount Zion, which cannot be removed, but abideth for ever, Psalm cxxv. 1. Thereby they are united to Christ, and being united to him, are personally instated in the covenant to their eternal salvation.